Lecture Notes in Computer Science 12611

More information about this subseries at http://www.springer.com/series/7408

Juliana Bowles · Giovanna Broccia ·
Mirco Nanni (Eds.)

From Data
to Models and Back

9th International Symposium, DataMod 2020
Virtual Event, October 20, 2020
Revised Selected Papers

 Springer

Editors
Juliana Bowles (iD)
University of St Andrews
St Andrews, UK

Giovanna Broccia (iD)
ISTI-CNR
Pisa, Italy

Mirco Nanni (iD)
ISTI-CNR
Pisa, Italy

ISSN 0302-9743   ISSN 1611-3349   (electronic)
Lecture Notes in Computer Science
ISBN 978-3-030-70649-4   ISBN 978-3-030-70650-0   (eBook)
https://doi.org/10.1007/978-3-030-70650-0

LNCS Sublibrary: SL2 – Programming and Software Engineering

This Springer imprint is published by the registered company Springer Nature Switzerland AG
The registered company address is: Gewerbestrasse 11, 6330 Cham, Switzerland

Preface

DataMod is an annual, international symposium which aims to bring together practitioners and researchers from academia, industry and research institutions interested in the combined application of computational modelling methods with data-driven techniques from the areas of knowledge management, data mining and machine learning.

DataMod has a wide range of themes and topics. Considered modelling and analysis methodologies include: *Agent-based Methodologies, Automata-based Methodologies, Big Data Analytics, Cellular Automata, Classification, Clustering, Segmentation and Profiling, Conformance Analysis, Constraint Programming, Data Mining, Differential Equations, Game Theory, Machine Learning, Membrane Systems, Network Theory and Analysis, Ontologies, Optimization Modelling, Petri Nets, Process Calculi, Process Mining, Rewriting Systems, Spatio-temporal Data Analysis/Mining, Statistical Model Checking, Text Mining and Topological Data Analysis.*

There is a particular interest in submissions from various application domains such as: *Biology, Brain Data and Simulation, Business Process Management, Climate Change, Cybersecurity, Ecology, Education, Environmental Risk Assessment and Management, Enterprise Architectures, Epidemiology, Genetics and Genomics, Governance, HCI and Human Behaviour, Open-Source Software Development and Communities, Pharmacology, Resilience Engineering, Safety and Security Risk Assessment, Social Good, Social Software Engineering, Social Systems, Sustainable Development, Threat Modelling and Analysis, Urban Ecology, and Smart Cities and Smart Lands.*

Synergistic approaches may include:

1. the use of modelling methods and notations in a knowledge management and discovery context,
2. the development and use of common modelling and knowledge management/discovery frameworks to explore and understand complex systems from the application domains of interest.

This year, for its 9th edition, DataMod was held as a satellite event of the International Conference on Information and Knowledge Management (CIKM 2020). The symposium was held as a one-day fully virtual workshop, due to Covid-19. This enabled, however, the participation of a wider audience across several different time zones. All presentations and discussions were done online using the conference facilities provided and Zoom.

All contributions in the form of either regular papers (up to 18 pages) or short papers (up to 10 pages) were reviewed by three Program Committee members using single-blind peer review, and were evaluated on the basis of originality, contribution to the field, technical and presentation quality, and relevance to the symposium. On average, each Program Committee member reviewed three papers and no external reviewers were involved in the review process. EasyChair was used as an online system for both the submissions and the reviews bidding and assignment. Before notifications were sent to authors, a few days were left for a discussion amongst Program Committee members to finalise the acceptance/rejection decisions.

All accepted presentations at the workshop were invited to submit a paper to be reviewed after the workshop and to be considered for the post-proceedings. From all submissions, this resulted in 11 long papers and 3 short papers being accepted for publication in the post-proceedings.

Michael Vinov, IBM Research Laboratory in Haifa, gave an invited keynote at the symposium, and presented two complementary methods for data modelling and synthetic data fabrication, as well as ongoing developments on IBM's Data Fabrication Platform. The abstract of the talk is included in this volume.

January 2021

Juliana Bowles
Giovanna Broccia
Mirco Nanni

Organization

Program Committee Chairs

Juliana Bowles	University of St Andrews, UK
Giovanna Broccia	ISTI-CNR, Italy
Mirco Nanni	ISTI-CNR, Italy

Steering Committee

Oana Andrei	University of Glasgow, UK
Antonio Cerone	Nazarbayev University, Kazakhstan
Vashti Galpin	University of Edinburgh, UK
Riccardo Guidotti	University of Pisa, Italy
Marijn Janssen	Delft University of Technology, The Netherlands
Stan Matwin	University of Ottawa, Canada
Paolo Milazzo	University of Pisa, Italy
Anna Monreale	University of Pisa, Italy
Mirco Nanni	ISTI-CNR, Italy

Program Committee

Oana Andrei	University of Glasgow, UK
Davide Basile	ISTI-CNR, Italy
Mario Boley	Monash University, Australia
Juliana Bowles (Co-chair)	University of St Andrews, UK
Giovanna Broccia (Co-chair)	ISTI-CNR, Italy
Marco Caminati	University of St Andrews, UK
Antonio Cerone	Nazarbayev University, Kazakhstan
Ricardo Czekster	Newcastle University, UK
Flavio Ferrarotti	SCCH, Austria
Lars Kotthoff	University of Wyoming, USA
Giulio Masetti	ISTI-CNR, Italy
Sotiris Moschoyiannis	University of Surrey, UK
Paolo Milazzo	University of Pisa, Italy
Anna Monreale	University of Pisa, Italy
Reshma Munbodh	Brown University, USA
Mirco Nanni (Co-chair)	ISTI-CNR, Italy
Lucia Nasti	University of Pisa, Italy
Céline Robardet	INSA Lyon, France

Towards AI-driven Data Analysis and Fabrication (Abstract of Invited Talk)

Michael Vinov

IBM Research Laboratory, Haifa, Israel
vinov@il.ibm.com

Abstract. IBM plays a significant role in the domain of Data Management and Data Analysis tools. IBM research team in Haifa explores and develops two complementary methods for data modelling and synthetic data fabrication. The first one is a rule-based approach that provides declarative language to model data logic and data rules. The second approach is based on machine-learning methods both for analysis of existing data and for creation of synthetic data.

The IBM Optim Test Data Fabrication (TDF) is a tool aimed to fabricate synthetic but realistic structural data, required for the development and testing of data-driven tools, where data availability and privacy is a major concern. Insurance and banking applications are just two of many other business domains of such a kind. Synthetic data is fabricated based on a solution found by a powerful Constraint Satisfaction Programming (CSP) solver that finds data values satisfying all the defined rules/constraints. While being proven as very effective, the TDF tool has a couple of inherent weaknesses:

- Manual modeling of fabrication rules/constraints
- Data fabrication performance (especially for big-data use cases)

A set of human-defined rules must be provided to the tool as an input. Rule definition is a laborious, time and resource-consuming process, involving data analysis as a prerequisite. Dealing with real-world data might be even more challenging in presence of data irregularities and anomalies, or in cases when intrinsic data dependencies and constraints are difficult to comprehend.

We propose a Machine Learning (ML) based method and an algorithm for automatic data analysis and constraint definition which, in presence of original (presumably production) data, will significantly simplify and speed up the fabrication rules definition process, improve the tool's efficiency and shorten time-to-market for our customers. We propose to combine the analytic capabilities of ML methods with a solving power and precision of a CSP solver.

ML based fabrication of synthetic data with the ability to add human-defined constraints can be used for the following major use cases:

- ML training data sets enrichment (for insufficient or imbalanced data)
- Synthetic data for testing of ML models and data driven applications.

Contents

Data Mining and Processing Related Approaches

Machine Learning

Synthesis and Pruning as a Dynamic Compression Strategy for Efficient Deep Neural Networks

Alastair Finlinson$^{(\boxtimes)}$ ⓘ and Sotiris Moschoyiannis

Department of Computer Science, University of Surrey, Guildford, UK
{a.finlinson, s.moschoyiannis}@surrey.ac.uk

Abstract. The brain is a highly reconfigurable machine capable of task-specific adaptations. The brain continually rewires itself for a more optimal configuration to solve problems. We propose a novel strategic synthesis algorithm for feedforward networks that draws directly from the brain's behaviours when learning. The proposed approach analyses the network and ranks weights based on their magnitude. Unlike existing approaches that advocate random selection, we select highly performing nodes as starting points for new edges and exploit the Gaussian distribution over the weights to select corresponding endpoints. The strategy aims only to produce useful connections and result in a smaller residual network structure. The approach is complemented with pruning to further the compression. We demonstrate the techniques to deep feedforward networks. The residual sub-networks that are formed from the synthesis approaches in this work form common sub-networks with similarities up to ∼ 90%. Using pruning as a complement to the strategic synthesis approach, we observe improvements in compression.

Keywords: Sub-network · Optimisation · Compression · Pruning · Synthesis

1 Introduction

Modern Artificial Neural Networks are increasingly used in a wide range of domains. One emerging issue, however, is that they can often become large and take considerable time to compute results. Despite recent approaches to real-time, on-demand AI deployments [1] practical examples of deployed systems often are simply not feasible in edge and IoT use cases [2]. There are approaches to increase the compression of a deep neural network (DNN) by reducing the size of the model's parameter space and therefore, memory and storage requirements. The compression also has improvements on compute time for the device where the model is deployed.

This work explores the notion of synthesising neural networks [3–7]. The proposal is for a network to generate weights that are beneficial to the outcome from a very sparse network. Sparse networks are networks that have most of the connections in the network disabled for training and in deployment. Synthesis would begin with a random sub-network of a substantial architecture, that is unlikely to be optimal for the problem.

© Springer Nature Switzerland AG 2021
J. Bowles et al. (Eds.): DataMod 2020, LNCS 12611, pp. 3–17, 2021.
https://doi.org/10.1007/978-3-030-70650-0_1

These sub-networks are viable and trainable networks, but by design are random and unlikely to be optimal in structure and weights for solving the problem.

The synthesis algorithms start generating connections, randomly or strategically, to increase the complexity of the network until the capacity threshold for generation is met. The threshold is a hyperparameter that is fixed during training.

The strategic approach to the generation of connections focuses on the high performing areas of the network (targets). These high performing connections are used to determine an origin and termination neuron for the new connections. The areas are defined as having the highest impact on the output of the network. The impact is positive when the network makes an overall improvement over a range of statistics, for example, AUC and validation accuracy [8].

Primarily, the widely used example of compression is magnitude-based pruning [9]. The compression does come at the cost of accuracy, and this is more so at higher compression ratios. The decay of accuracy is minimal until reaching a nearly completely sparse, highly compressed, network [3, 10–15]. This is clearly seen in [11], where compression at $\sim 104\times$ with a drop in accuracy of less than 4% on CIFAR-10.

The main objective is to be able to use the pruning and synthesis approaches as complementary techniques to train a model. The combination of the techniques is expected to lead to higher compression in the same models.

The key contribution of the paper is a strategic approach to reconfiguring a network, while training, so that its structure is optimal for the problem set. More specifically, we describe a synthesis approach which complements current pruning techniques and is targeted at deep neural network models. We show that our proposed approach results in a smaller residual network structure which is a more optimal configuration for the dataset, in terms of compression, while maintaining accuracy.

The remainder of this paper is structured as follows. Section 2 outlines related work. Section 3 presents the different approaches and variants we worked with. Section 4 describes the application of these approaches to a dataset and layered network. We present results in Sect. 5 and provide insights from these in Sect. 6. Section 7 concludes the paper and outlines ideas for future work.

2   Related Work

The works of [3–7] make direct use of synthesis and pruning networks to achieve compressed and accurate architectures. A direct comparison of the improvements made when using the combination of grow-prune techniques is given in [3] where the use of the techniques provide an improvement of 40% over the original accuracy and compression of eight times smaller over the prune only model of 5.7 times smaller. This is achieved using a combination of synthesis and pruning the long short-term memory cells (LSTMs) [16] during training. The synthesis and pruning processes are attributed to decreasing the inference time of the models by $\sim 16\%$ and error rates by 10% on average.

Xiaoliang Dai et al. [4] show that their implementation has reduced the learning costs of training the model by over 65% from scratch. They also claim that the results of the algorithm attain a higher accuracy over the baseline network. The implementation seen in [6] uses a random approach to select the next artifact to be added to the network labelled "Random Growth" and is hence closely related to our work. Shayan Hassantabar et al. also refers to a "gradient-based growth" [3] proposed initially by Dai et al. [4] and "full growth".

Neuron pruning and synthesis are techniques used in this work. The techniques for pruning and synthesis of neurons is similar to that used by Shayan Hassantabar et al. [6], Hengyuan Hu et al. [15] and Timur Ash [17], whereby, the neurons are selected at random but also by their activation values. The activation-based generation uses the fact that an active neuron is highly active; this neuron can be duplicated in the network. It is claimed that the aggressive network reduction can sustain the accuracy of the network. Our proposed approach draws from these techniques and extends them towards a strategic approach to the growth phase of the training.

In [18], a random synthesis approach on a fully connected network is proposed, where neurons are enabled until the accuracy of the network is achieved. The random generation involves a fully connected neuron being added to the network. The weights of the neuron are also fully initialised randomly. The technique described is close to the random approach to synthesis in our work.

Currently, a significant component of the compression and reduction of networks is the use of pruning. Pruning is widely used when trying to reduce complexity and maintain accuracy in the model. Pruning has been used to achieve high compression on large architectures such as with 60 times less dense on ResNet [19] and 36 times less dense MobileNet [20], while also achieving 13 times smaller with ShuffleNet [21].

Pruning is used to remove weights from a network that are contributing small value to the network. Pruning is most used to remove weights that centre around zero in their magnitude. Some of the earliest works on pruning [22, 23] show that this method of network compression can coarsely be applied and still achieve high levels of compression.

In the TensorFlow library, there are built-in pruning methods which are referred to as schedules. The available schedules are the ConstantSparsity [9] and PolynomialDecay [24]. The ConstantSparsity refers to the use of a pruning schedule that tries to prune a constant number of weights for each time it is applied to the network. This allows the user to specify a sparsity that the algorithm prunes throughout the training. The parallel drawn from TensorFlow's implementations in our work is constant sparsity. The constant sparsity model is closely replicated, in this work, to achieve similar effects as in the TensorFlow library. Constant sparsity was implemented as this is the simple case and has a lower complexity for implementation.

It transpires that the current state of the art and foundational approaches provide high levels of compression using pruning [12–14, 19]. There are also generative techniques [3–7] that show advances in the growing, referred to as synthesis in this work. The limitations in the synthesis in the above techniques show that only random techniques are directly explored. The review also shows that some explore the combination of pruning and synthesis, but this is limited. Where this work builds on compression is the use of a strategic method of synthesising networks but also then to explore the feasibility of the combination of the pruning with different approaches to synthesis. There is also a gap in the literature reviewed when looking at comparing the generated networks from different approaches. This work also touches on the network structures that form because of the different approaches. These structures may show similarity if the networks can find similar optimal solutions to the same problem and initial state.

3   Method

3.1   Approaches

There are five developed methods for compression of the models.

Random Synthesis
Random synthesis makes use of the initialised minimum network. From this starting point, the network is augmented with random new connections and weights until the end of the training period.

Strategic Synthesis
Strategic synthesis makes use of the initialised minimum network. From this starting point, the network is then augmented with new connections and weights which are selected and generated based on a ranking of current network weights. This continues until the end of the training period.

The weights are ranked according to the absolute magnitude of the tensor weights in all layers (L) of the network (γ). The set Φ is the top ranked magnitudes and is bound by the parameter N which is defined as the number of focal junctures.

$$X = \{\Phi : \text{MAX}(||\gamma_L \setminus \Phi||), |\Phi| < N\} \tag{1}$$

With the top N focal junctures selected, the process of generating a Gaussian distribution curve to then select the terminus of the new synthesis connection is formed.

$$f(x) = \frac{1}{\sigma\sqrt{2\pi}} * e^{\left(-\frac{(|x-\beta|-\mu)^2}{2\sigma^2}\right)} \tag{2}$$

The function uses the standard Gaussian distribution but uses the absolute distance in the potential terminus (x) relative the the orgin of the connection (β). The values of μ and σ are set to 0 and 1, respectively.

Pruning
Pruning begins with a fully dense network with all connections and weights enabled and initialised. In this work, the pruning algorithm used is the constant pruning style. Constant pruning assumes that a fixed number of connections are removed during each step that pruning is applied.

Random Synthesis with Pruning
This approach begins with the minimum network. From here, the combination of random synthesis and pruning is applied on a fixed schedule.

Strategic Synthesis with Pruning
This approach begins with the minimum network. From here, the combination of strategic synthesis and pruning is applied on a fixed schedule.

3.2 Procedure

The proposed strategic approach is the first step in steering the network towards its goal of equalling or improving upon the same network. The improvement is the network's ability to solve the problem presented – measured using validation accuracy and AUC.

Validation accuracy is defined as the networks ability to correctly classify data samples as a percentage of the total number of validation samples (test samples) during training.

AUC is defined as the area in 2D space the is occupied underneath an Receiver Operating Characteristic (ROC). The ROC itself is defined as the performance of the model over varying classification thresholds.

When the combination of synthesis and pruning algorithms are applied, they are applied with the pruning first taking place then the synthesis. The ordering is used to stop newly generated connection instantly being removed from the network as there is potential for a new connection to be initialised with a low magnitude.

The steering is achieved by dynamically defining *focal junctures* (targets) in the network. These focal junctures are defined as connections in the network that are the most influential on the output (large magnitudes). The algorithm targets the highest contributing junctures, given absolute magnitudes. The aim is to reinforce the strong connections and propagate the critical features and information through the network.

The junctures have an origin (neuron) and are aware of the number of neurons in the subsequent layer. The size of the subsequent layer is used to generate a Gaussian distribution vector of the same dimensions. The vector is used to select the terminus of the new connection using the origin of the target in the subsequent layer.

The Gaussian distribution for the vector is an assumption that adjacent neurons have more relevance to one another. A neuron on the graph that exists further from the origin of the new connection is considered less likely to develop an effective pathway through the graph, and this is the initiation the vector attempts to emulate (Figs. 1, 2 and 3).

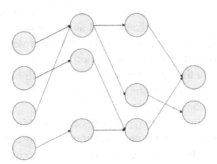

Fig. 1. An instance of a neural network architecture (sub-network) at a point in time during the training of the network.

Before the network can begin training the networks require initialisation. The initialisation enables the networks from an empty architecture to be trainable, even in the infantile state. The initialisation of the network begins at each input neuron. From

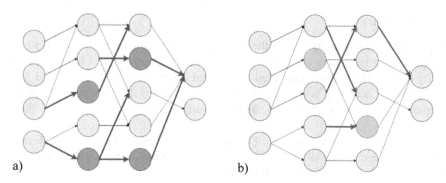

Fig. 2. a) Application of a synthesis algorithm; green connections and neurons are representing synthesised connections. b) Application of magnitude-based pruning; red connections and neurons are representing pruned connections. (Color figure online)

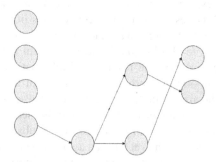

Fig. 3. Resulting sub-network structure after pruning and synthesis is applied

each neuron at most, one random path is generated through to the output. The pathways of neurons can intersect and overlap. This guarantees a connection to the output and that all inputs, at the beginning, are considered at the output.

The sub-network initialisation describes the state of a network when the synthesising processes are involved. The network is initialised to a state whereby the inputs are connected to the output through a random walk. The sub-network is initialised with this procedure such that the information about the training samples is not lost, as it could be integral to the models learning.

The connections from the initial layer to the subsequent layer are defined as having a single connection from each input neuron. From the subsequent layer, where there has been a connection made to the previous layer, a new connection can be formed. The process is a random walk from all inputs to the output along a single path. The paths can overlap or be entirely separate from the rest of the pathways. If the pathways overlap, the network only maintains a single connection at this juncture.

4 Problem Dataset

The dataset [25], has been selected to test the compression algorithm and is a simple binary classification problem. The data set is comprised of 303 samples, each having 13 fields, which after applying techniques such as one-hot or Boolean encoding the networks input parameters such as age, sex, chest pain type become 27 in number. The task of the neural network is to classify if the patient has heart disease or not correctly. For testing, the dataset is split into 80% for training, and the remaining 20% is used for validation. A network architecture has been selected and fixed for each of the different training methods. The architecture is shown in Fig. 4, the architecture has been selected as it is a small and simple architecture, but still contains a large enough set of parameters to tune and modify. The 50 models initialised for testing were generated through TensorFlow and are the same models for all different approaches (Sect. 3.1).

The network used for testing is composed of an input space of 27 neurons. The subsequent layers are 16 and 8 neurons wide – Fig. 4.

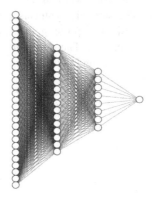

Fig. 4. Network architecture diagram for problem dataset.

5 Results

Table 1 presents the highest performing models across different pruning and synthesis thresholds. The thresholds are defined as an upper and lower limit for the algorithms to apply pruning and synthesis, respectively. The results indicate that the performance of the strategic synthesis with pruning algorithm, as averaged over the 50 test networks, has the highest performance, by $\sim 1.5\%$. The AUC of the strategic synthesis with pruning varies below the dense network between 3–11%. Whereas pruning alone varies below the dense network by 10–12% - Table 3.

The networks using strategic synthesis are within 0.5% of the sub-networks sparsity. This means the synthesis approach can add a minimal set of connections to the network, and this achieved an improved accuracy over the sub-networks of $\sim 6\%$. With the $\sim 3\%$ drop in accuracy, the strategic approach alone, with the current set of

Table 1. Mean performance results for all algorithms with sparsity threshold 99%

Model type	Accuracy	AUC
Dense	84.83%	78.19%
Pruning	**86.21%**	72.52%
Sub-Network	77.31%	72.04%
Random Synthesis	77.31%	72.04%
Strategic Synthesis	83.28%	**78.70%**
Random Synthesis with Pruning	80.79%	76.46%
Strategic Synthesis with Pruning	83.62%	75.80%

parameters, is a competitive process and provides functional improvements for compression. The strategic synthesis also has the highest AUC from all results.

Figure 5 shows that pruning is highly influential over the varying values for sparsity thresholding. With pruning as the benchmark, the strategic with pruning synthesis algorithm shows improvement towards the performance of the pruning as the compression ratio is increased. The strategic synthesis with pruning, as with the random synthesis and random synthesis with pruning, at lower thresholds are generating too many new connections in the network. The over synthesising of connections could be the inhibitor in early training cycles and contributing to false starts.

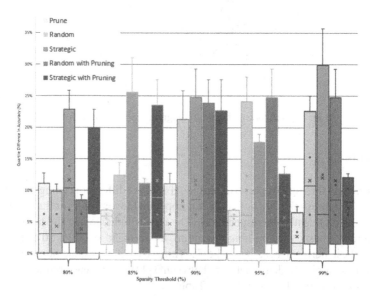

Fig. 5. Model validation accuracy with varying sparsity threshold. Typical values for the validation accuracy of the 50 models generated. Mean value of the samples is represented by 'x'. The 'o' represents outliers for the data. All plot plotted values are calculated using an exclusive median.

When analysing the hybrid approaches, the random synthesis approach can achieve higher compression. The higher compression, compared to the strategic synthesis, is likely to be the random weight initialisation and the instant pruning that can happen to these connections. Where the strategic is a copy of the large weight, the random can have small values approaching zero as new connection weights.

With marginally lower compression, the strategic synthesis approach can improve the performance over the random synthesis with pruning by ~3%. The performance improvement can be further enhanced, as in Table 2, where the strategic and strategic with pruning can find a solution(s) that achieves the 93.1% accuracy.

The results show that the strategic with pruning is the most capable model, achieving optimal solutions at 93.1% overall accuracy thresholds. The high performance of finding these optimal solutions shows that the problem space is better explored with this guided approach to finding a consistently optimal solution in the population of tested networks.

Table 2. Maximum achieved validation accuracy for each algorithm over varying sparsity thresholds from 80% to 99%

Model type	Sparsity threshold				
	80%	85%	90%	95%	99%
Dense	87.93%	87.93%	87.93%	87.93%	87.93%
Sub-Network	89.66%	89.66%	89.66%	89.66%	89.66%
Pruning	90.43%	89.66%	91.38%	89.66%	91.38%
Random Synthesis	89.66%	91.38%	93.10%	89.66%	93.10%
Strategic Synthesis	87.93%	91.38%	**96.55%**	91.38%	91.38%
Random Synthesis with Pruning	89.66%	**93.10%**	93.10%	89.66%	91.38%
Strategic Synthesis with Pruning	**93.10%**	**93.10%**	93.10%	**93.10%**	**93.10%**

The sub-network models can perform, in the case of the maximum accuracy, better than that of the dense case. The high performance implies that one or more the randomly generated subnetworks had a structure that is more optimal than a fully dense network. The sub-network models perform within ~1% inaccuracy to the pruning networks.

With strategic synthesis with pruning performing well in searching for an optimal network, the strategic synthesis approach without pruning was able to find the most optimal sub-network for all approaches reaching an accuracy of 96.55% at a threshold of 90%.

The sub-networks are also able to achieve stability, as with the dense networks. The lower performance at a sparsity averaging 92.1% the small performance loss over the dense is marginal and when optimising for compression much more desirable.

Pruning has a lower AUC for all thresholds. Once the models set at a threshold of 85% or above, the networks exceed the performance of the pruning networks. The improvement could suggest that the other approaches better handle the changing structure of the network in training and that they are better able to persist information more effectively than pruning alone. The behaviour is particularly evident in the strategic synthesis with pruning where the algorithm is managing to outperform pruning at all thresholds.

Table 3. Maximum achieved validation AUC for each algorithm over varying sparsity thresholds

Model type	Sparsity threshold				
	80%	85%	90%	95%	99%
Dense	**87.04%**	**87.04%**	**87.04%**	**87.04%**	**87.04%**
Sub-Network	81.56%	81.56%	81.56%	81.56%	81.56%
Pruning	76.78%	76.19%	75.13%	74.61%	75.67%
Random Synthesis	72.04%	75.93%	78.26%	77.06%	76.93%
Strategic Synthesis	76.65%	79.04%	78.70%	80.91%	81.85%
Random Synthesis with Pruning	70.65%	76.46%	77.19%	76.46%	75.20%
Strategic Synthesis with Pruning	76.91%	83.62%	75.80%	77.70%	81.07%

6 Further Considerations

6.1 Residual Networks

The networks generated using all the compression approaches form residual networks. These networks are all solving the same problem, with the same architecture and same perceived learning time, these networks converge to follow a typical core structure. The typical core structure would suggest that the optimal solution to the problem for this network can be deduced from overlaying and finding commonality in these structures.

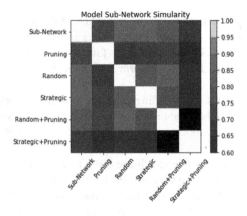

Fig. 6. Sub-network similarity matrix

The results visualised in Fig. 6 are taken from a representative network for each compression approach; therefore, the networks selected may not fully represent and average the structure. Networks for different initialisations of the graph by TensorFlow may show that on average, the graphs share more characteristics (connections) and that a shared core network can be extracted. The extracted network would have an exceedingly high sparsity.

If a common network could be extracted, this could then be used to initialise the sub-networks. With the sub-network structure known to be performant, the network training may be reduced as well. The subnetwork could also be trained and tuned in isolation to explore its capability in the highly sparse configuration.

6.2   Sub-networks

When evaluating the sub-networks used to initialise the networks for the synthesis, testing showed that there are many cases where the network can initialise and learn the problem with high accuracy. The learning of the sub-network is beneficial and has enabled the synthesis approaches to perform well.

6.3   False Starts

The sub-networks perform competently, on average $\sim 77\%$ accurate, but in the case of a false start, the accuracy can be as low as $\sim 45\%$. When the algorithm does not manage to connect new useful pathways and introduces redundant connections, these networks are ineffective and useless.

The false start is propagated to the strategic synthesis as this network, in the case of the lowest-performing networks, is as low as 53.45%. This means that the strategic process was able to generate connections that would improve the network in all cases when compared to the sub-networks.

The strategic synthesis with pruning can eliminate the false starts with a minimum accuracy of 67.24%. The accuracy improvement over the sub-network at the start of training shows that the network can be improved, and that combination improves the accuracy.

6.4   Strategic Targets

The success rate of the networks, under synthesis, can be improved using many targets and allowing for a more significant threshold for synthesis per cycle. Increasing the number of targets does, however, have the potential to satisfy the network synthesising capacity very quickly. The earlier the network generates connections and reaches capacity, the higher the risk that the connections could stem from a connection that eventually has a weight near zero. This would make the new connections propagate low-quality information.

The increase in the number of targets should also be coupled with pruning to manage the unnecessary and rapid growth of the network and to reduce the velocity of convergence for a better-generalised model.

6.5   Redundancy

As the algorithms for synthesis are designed to start generating connections, randomly or strategically, there are bound to be connections generated that make no meaningful connection – suggesting that the connection either has no input or no output. With all the synthesised models, there are redundant connections. These connections, when removed post-training, would further reduce the size of the models.

6.6   Hybrid Scheduling

With the hybrid approaches using two sub-approaches, the scheduling and execution of these sub-processes may impact on the network. Where the approaches work synchronously, the network is managed at an approximate fixed size from the start of the processing. The network remains at the desired compression throughout training with variations in the structure. When considering an offset of different schedules for the pruning of the networks, the network can synthesise more artefacts and training them before removal. The change in the periodicity of the pruning schedule may also enable more complex pathways through the layers of the network before removing and breaking these, in-progress, pathways.

7   Conclusions and Future Work

Modern Artificial Neural Networks are increasingly used in a wide range of domains, from intrusion detection in cybersecurity [26], to robotics [27], image processing, or even controlling complex networks [28, 29] with applications to transport [30], business networks [31, 32] and web transactions [33, 34] among others.

In this paper we have shown that synthesising network connections has shown that it can, in some cases, perform as well as a dense or pruned network. The initialised minimum network has also shown that an optimal sub-network can be generated at random to solve this binary classification problem. The use of the sub-network generation at the start of the algorithm, before and during synthesis or pruning, provided the algorithms with a good baseline from which they successfully managed to improve upon the baseline.

The strategic synthesis with no pruning was able to improve upon the sub-network and random synthesis. The strategic algorithm in its current state is not able to improve the accuracy of the dense or pruned networks. This mismatch suggests that more parameter tuning is required. The strategic synthesis falls short of matching the dense networks by only 1.5% and the pruned networks by 3%.

When combining the strategic synthesis approach with pruning, many of the redundant connections were removed, and this resulted in improved performance, by 0.5%.

In the context of the small model used for this work, the small difference in sparsity equates to a small number of parameters. If the architecture were scaled to many thousands or millions of connections, then it would be reasonable to expect that the compression to accuracy comparison that the strategic with pruning achieves would exhibit a much more significant reduction in density.

With more rigorous tuning and improvements to the algorithm, the strategic with pruning has the potential to match the performance of the pruning process in terms of accuracy and surpass the process in terms of network sparsity (compression) and AUC.

The consistency of the strategic synthesis with pruning over varying thresholds, concerning compression and accuracy, shows that this is a stable form of generating networks. Our results show that we have produced a viable alternative and complementary technique to pruning. It manages to reproduce the same accuracy, within $\sim 3\%$ to 6% of the pruning approach.

There are several pathways to take this work forward. We note the following.

Parameter Tuning
The most interesting parameters to explore would be the initialisation strategy for artifact synthesis. The results are based on the use of the 'copy' method. This initialisation strategy has performed well and shows that the method has scope to improve. However, it would be worth exploring the 'Gaussian decay' method. This premise is because the new connections generated at the extreme of a large distribution function would be near zero and therefore, immediately pruned. This is also true for the random initialisation strategy.

Post Training Pruning
For this work, pruning was used as an in-process approach. However, pruning can also be used post-training to remove redundant connections. The application of this post-training pruning could further yield compression on connections that are trained out after the stop delay has occurred.

Directed Acyclic Graph Pruning
Directed Acyclic Graph (DAG) pruning could be devised and implemented as a post-training pruning method, that will look for pathways in the DAG that terminate before reaching the output of the network – disconnected pathways. Any path through the network that is connected from input to output is a connected pathway. The theoretical method would find all connections at the leaf of each disconnected pathway and recursively remove these connections until the pathway is no longer disconnected. It is expected that many connections are redundant, and this method of DAG pruning could remove redundant connections.

Convolutional Neural Networks
The future work of the strategic approaches is testing its application to the CNNs. These are classically complex and parameter dense architectures. This testing could yield results that concur with that of this work. With the much larger architectures the compression, if it follows the results of this work, could be significant. The strategic artifact selection strategies would require minimal modification to be applied to the CNN architectures.

References

1. Christidis, A., Moschoyiannis, S., Hsu, C.H., Davies, R.: Enabling serverless deployment of large-scale AI workloads. IEEE Access **8**, 70150–70161 (2020). https://doi.org/10.1109/ACCESS.2020.2985282
2. Mohammadi, M., Al-Fuqaha, A., Sorour, S., Guizani, M.: Deep learning for IoT big data and streaming analytics: a survey. IEEE Commun. Surv. Tutor. **20**(4), 2923–2960 (2018). https://doi.org/10.1109/COMST.2018.2844341
3. Dai, X., Yin, H., Jha, N.K.: Grow and prune compact, fast, and accurate LSTMs. IEEE Trans. Comput. **69**(3), 441–452 (2020). https://doi.org/10.1109/TC.2019.2954495
4. Dai, X., Yin, H., Jha, N.K.: Incremental Learning Using a Grow-and-Prune Paradigm with Efficient Neural Networks, p. 10 (2019). https://arxiv.org/abs/1905.10952
5. Dai, X., Yin, H., Jha, N.K.: NeST: a neural network synthesis tool based on a grow-and-prune paradigm. IEEE Trans. Comput. **68**(10), 1487–1497 (2019). https://doi.org/10.1109/tc.2019.2914438
6. Hassantabar, S., Wang, Z., Jha, N.K.: SCANN: Synthesis of Compact and Accurate Neural Networks, p. 11 (2019). https://arxiv.org/abs/1904.09090
7. Dai, X.: Synthesis of Efficient Neural Networks, no. September (2019)
8. Mitchell, T.M.: Machine Learning. McGraw-Hill Inc. (1997)
9. T. (Google). tfmot.sparsity.keras.ConstantSparsity. https://www.tensorflow.org/model_optimization/api_docs/python/tfmot/sparsity/keras/ConstantSparsity. Accessed 10 Jan 2020
10. Han, S., Mao, H., Dally, W.J.: Deep compression: compressing deep neural networks with pruning, trained quantization and Huffman coding. In: 4th International Conference Learning Representation, ICLR 2016 - Conference Track Proceedings, p. 14 (2016)
11. He, Y., Zhang, X., Sun, J.: Channel pruning for accelerating very deep neural networks. In: Proceedings IEEE International Conference on Computer Vision, vol. 2017-October, pp. 1398–1406 (2017). https://doi.org/10.1109/ICCV.2017.155
12. Li, H., Samet, H., Kadav, A., Durdanovic, I., Graf, H.P.: Pruning filters for efficient convnets. In: 5th International Conference on Learning Representation, ICLR 2017 - Conference Track Proceedings, no. 2016, p. 13 (2019)
13. Zhu, M.H., Gupta, S.: To prune, or not to prune: exploring the efficacy of pruning for model compression. In: 6th International Conference on Learning Representation, ICLR 2018 - Workshop Track Proceedings (2018)
14. Anwar, S., Sung, W.: Compact Deep Convolutional Neural Networks with Coarse Pruning, vol. 1, no. 2015, p. 10 (2016). https://arxiv.org/abs/1610.09639
15. Hu, H., Peng, R., Tai, Y.-W., Tang, C.-K.: Network Trimming: A Data-Driven Neuron Pruning Approach towards Efficient Deep Architectures (2016). https://arxiv.org/abs/1607.03250
16. Hochreiter, S., Schmidhuber, J.: Long short-term memory. Neural Comput. **9**(8), 1735–1780 (1997). https://doi.org/10.1162/neco.1997.9.8.1735
17. Courbariaux, M., Hubara, I., Soudry, D., El-Yaniv, R., Bengio, Y.: Binarized Neural Networks: Training Deep Neural Networks with Weights and Activations Constrained to +1 or −1 (2016). https://arxiv.org/abs/1602.02830
18. Ash, T.: Dynamic node creation in backpropagation networks. In: International 1989 Joint Conference on Neural Networks, vol. 2, p. 623 (1989). https://doi.org/10.1109/IJCNN.1989.118509
19. Ma, X., Yuan, G., Lin, S., Li, Z., Sun, H., Wang, Y.: ResNet Can Be Pruned 60x: Introducing Network Purification and Unused Path Removal (P-RM) after Weight Pruning (2019). https://arxiv.org/abs/1905.00136

20. Howard, A.G., et al.: MobileNets: Efficient Convolutional Neural Networks for Mobile Vision Applications (2017). https://arxiv.org/abs/1704.04861

21. Zhang, X., Zhou, X., Lin, M., Sun, J.: ShuffleNet: an extremely efficient convolutional neural network for mobile devices. In: Proceedings of the IEEE Computer Society Conference on Computer Vision and Pattern Recognition, pp. 6848–6856 (2018). https://doi.org/10.1109/CVPR.2018.00716.

22. LeCun, Y., Denker, J.S., Solla, S.A.: Optimal brain damage (pruning). In: Advance Neural Information Processing Systems, pp. 598–605 (1990)

23. Hassibi, B., Stork, D.: Second order derivaties for network prunning: optimal brain surgeon. In: Advance NIPS5, pp. 164–171 (1993)

24. T. (Google). tfmot.sparsity.keras.PolynomialDecay. https://www.tensorflow.org/model_optimization/api_docs/python/tfmot/sparsity/keras/PolynomialDecay. Accessed 10 Jan 2020

25. Janosi, A., Steinbrunn, W., Pfisterer, M., Detrano, R.: Heart Disease UCI (2019). www.Kaggle.com. https://www.kaggle.com/ronitf/heart-disease-uci. Accessed 10 Jan 2020)

26. Ferrag, M.A., Maglaras, L., Moschoyiannis, S., Janicke, H.: Deep learning for cyber security intrusion detection: approaches, datasets, and comparative study. J. Inf. Secur. Appl. **50**, 102419 (2020). https://doi.org/10.1016/j.jisa.2019.102419

27. Goodfellow, I.J., Koenig, N., Muja, M., Pantofaru, C., Sorokin, A., Takayama, L.: Help me help you: interfaces for personal robots. In: 5th ACM/IEEE International Conference on Human-Robot Interaction HRI 2010, no. March, pp. 187–188 (2010). https://doi.org/10.1145/1734454.1734536

28. Liu, Y.Y., Slotine, J.J., Barabási, A.L.: Controllability of complex networks. Nature **473** (7346), 167–173 (2011). https://doi.org/10.1038/nature10011

29. Karlsen, M.R., Moschoyiannis, S.: Evolution of control with learning classifier systems. Appl. Netw. Sci. **3**(1), 1–36 (2018). https://doi.org/10.1007/s41109-018-0088-x

30. Karlsen, M.R., Moschoyiannis, S.: Learning condition–action rules for personalised journey recommendations. In: Benzmüller, C., Ricca, F., Parent, X., Roman, D. (eds.) RuleML+RR 2018. LNCS, vol. 11092, pp. 293–301. Springer, Cham (2018). https://doi.org/10.1007/978-3-319-99906-7_21

31. Razavi, A., Moschoyiannis, S., Krause, P.: A scale-free business network for digital ecosystems. In: Proceedings of the IEEE Digiial EcoSystems and Technologies (IEEE DEST), pp. 241–246 (2008)

32. Schoenenberger, L., Tanase, R.: Controlling complex policy problems: a multimethodological approach using system dynamics and network controllability. J. Simul. **12** (2017). https://doi.org/10.1080/17477778.2017.1387335

33. Moschoyiannis, S., Krause, P.: True concurrency in long-running transactions for digital ecosystems. Fundam. Informaticae **138**(4), 483–514 (2015). https://doi.org/10.3233/FI-2015-1222

34. Razavi, A., Marinos, A., Moschoyiannis, S., Krause, P.: RESTful transactions supported by the isolation theorems. In: Gaedke, M., Grossniklaus, M., Díaz, O. (eds.) ICWE 2009. LNCS, vol. 5648, pp. 394–409. Springer, Heidelberg (2009). https://doi.org/10.1007/978-3-642-02818-2_32

Exploring Graph-Based Neural Networks for Automatic Brain Tumor Segmentation

Camillo Saueressig[1,2] (iD), Adam Berkley[1], Elliot Kang[1],
Reshma Munbodh[3(✉)] (iD), and Ritambhara Singh[1,2(✉)] (iD)

[1] Department of Computer Science, Brown University, Providence, USA
ritambhara@brown.edu
[2] Center for Computational Molecular Biology, Brown University, Providence, USA
[3] Department of Radiation Oncology, Brown Alpert Medical School,
Providence, USA
reshma_munbodh@brown.edu

Abstract. Manual evaluation of medical images, such as MRI scans of brain tumors, requires years of training, is time-consuming, and is often subject to inter-annotator variation. The automatic segmentation of medical images is a long-standing challenge that seeks to alleviate these issues, with great potential benefits for physicians and patients. In the past few years, variations of Convolutional Neural Networks (CNNs) have established themselves as the state-of-the-art methodology for this task. Recently, Graph-based Neural Networks (GNNs) have gained considerable attention in the deep learning community. GNNs exploit the structural information present in graphical data by aggregating information over connected nodes, allowing them to effectively capture relation information between data elements. In this project, we propose a GNN-based approach to brain tumor segmentation. We represent 3D MRI scans of the brain as a graph, where different regions in the images are represented by nodes and edges connect adjacent regions. We apply several variations of GNNs for the automatic segmentation of brain tumors from MRI scans. Our results show GNNs give reasonable performance on the task and allow for realistic modeling of the data. Furthermore, they are far less computationally expensive and time-consuming to train than state-of-the-art segmentation models. Lastly, we assign Shapley value-based contribution scores to input MRI features to learn what features are relevant for a particular segmentation, generating interesting insights into explaining the predictions of the proposed model.

Keywords: Graph neural networks · Brain tumor segmentation · Deep learning

1 Introduction

Over 87,000 people are expected to be diagnosed with brain tumors in 2020 [19]. With a low survival rate for malignant tumors, timely detection and diagnosis of brain tumors are crucial for developing effective treatment plans for the

J. Bowles et al. (Eds.): DataMod 2020, LNCS 12611, pp. 18–37, 2021.
https://doi.org/10.1007/978-3-030-70650-0_2

patients. Neuroimaging using multimodal magnetic resonance imaging (MRI) is integral in the diagnosis and management of brain tumors, including for surgical and radiation treatment planning, longitudinal tumor monitoring, treatment response evaluation, and predictive analysis. These require accurate delineation of the tumor boundary on the MRI images to characterize the tumors.

Automatic tumor segmentation methods seek to address the time and inter-observer variability limitations posed by manual segmentation. Furthermore, they underlie advances in quantitative tumor analysis and clinical workflow automation. The development of such automatic segmentation methods is challenging due to several intrinsic and extrinsic factors, such as the heterogeneity in appearance and shape of different tumor types on MRI, a lack of standardized imaging protocols, variability in equipment, and the presence of imaging noise and artifacts. Furthermore, advances in neuroimaging and the clinical management of brain tumors have increased the desired complexity of the segmentation, with an emphasis on a compartmentalized segmentation of the tumor into subregions describing necrosis, enhancing and non-enhancing tumor and vasogenic edema.

The use of deep learning methods for brain tumor segmentation has progressed rapidly in the past few years [4,16]. As opposed to conventional segmentation models that rely on the extraction of pre-defined features from the images [10,14,20], deep learning models automatically learn relevant features to perform accurate segmentation. However, current deep learning segmentation methods [8,9,18,34] are computationally intensive, require the division of the images into local patches, and do not explicitly account for brain connectivity information. They fail to capture adequately both the global structure of the 3D images and the relational dependencies between different regions in the tumor. We hypothesize that these properties are important for accurate and robust brain tumor segmentation.

We propose using Graph-based Neural Networks (GNNs) to segment brain tumors from multimodal 3D MRI. Unlike previous methods, GNNs allow for the processing of the entire brain simultaneously, while explicitly incorporating both local and global connectivity into their predictions by aggregating information across neighboring nodes in the graph. As such, GNNs effectively capture relational information between the data elements. Our framework, summarized in Fig. 1, first represents the 3D MRI scans of the entire brain as a graph, where nodes represent different regions in the images and edges connect adjacent regions. Next, a GNN classifies each node of the graph into healthy tissue, enhancing tumor, necrotic tissue and non-enhancing tumor, or edema. The node predictions are subsequently mapped back to their respective supervoxels on the MRI. We explore different GNN models for brain tumor segmentation from MRI scans on the BraTS 2019 challenge [3,4,16]. The best performing model achieves good performance that is comparable to other recent work. We also show that our approach is between 5 and 15 times faster than such computationally intensive methods. Finally, we provide explanations for the predictions of the deep learning GNN models in terms of the relative contributions of the inputted MRI

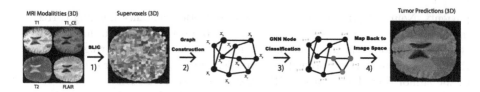

Fig. 1. Model Overview. MRI Modalities are first stacked to create one 3D Image with 4 channels. 1) Combined modalities are clustered into supervoxels. 2) Supervoxels are converted to a graph structure such that each supervoxel becomes one graph node. 3) Graph is fed through a Graph Neural Network, which predicts a label for each node. 4) Node predictions are overlaid back onto the supervoxels.

modalities. We generate these explanations via Shapley values, a game-theoretic approach for fairly attributing contributions to an overall outcome among the game participants. Such interpretations are vital for applications of these models in the health domain.

2   Related Work

2.1   Convolutional Neural Networks

Convolutional Neural Networks (CNN) have, so far, been the most successful models for fully automatic brain tumor segmentation. They excel at object classification and segmentation tasks by classifying pixels based on surrounding image content through 2D or 3D convolutional filters. These convolutional filters are translation invariant and can detect image edges and combine them into higher-level image features, making them well suited for image processing. The three best performing models of the recent 2018 BraTS Challenge [3,4,16] all consisted of CNN-based architectures. The BraTS challenge is a brain tumor segmentation competition where teams submit their models for testing on a multi-institutional database of MRI scans. The best performing model by Myronenko et al. [18] used an autoencoder-based regularization with a 3D-CNN to achieve state-of-the-art segmentation results. The next best-performing work by Isensee et al. [9] proposed that a well trained baseline 3D U-net could outperform other models with various architectural modifications. Finally, McKinley et al. [15] used a CNN with contextual and attentive information and tied for third place with Zhou et al. [34] who used a U-net with a novel loss function that modeled noise and uncertainty.

These CNN-based architectures take an extended amount of time to train, and many have harsh GPU-requirements. The best performing model requires 34 GB of VRAM [18] and most require anywhere from 8 to 12 GB of VRAM. Combined with the training times greater than a week, this constitutes a resource bottleneck on training and evaluating models on new datasets. Furthermore, these models generally require the division of the images into local patches for training and segmentation and, hence, fail to capture the global information of the entire MRI scan.

2.2   Graph Neural Networks

The computational burden of segmentation with CNNs can be circumvented by summarizing the MRI images as a graph representation. This approximation reduces image complexity by two orders of magnitude, from millions of voxels down to several thousand nodes, while preserving most image information. A recently popularized form of deep learning, Graph Neural Networks, is specifically designed to learn over such graph structures. The theoretic underpinnings of learning on graphs have been established for close to a decade [7,22], but GNNs have only recently seen widespread use following, among others, Kipf and Wellings's [5,12,35] introduction of the graph convolutional network (GCN). Their work refined the convolution operation on graph-structured data and established a layerwise approach to learning over graphs, thus aligning it more closely to existing deep learning paradigms.

Subsequently, Hamilton *et al.* [6] developed GraphSAGE, which extends GCN [12] by generalizing graph learning as a series of alternating sampling and aggregation steps to share information across a graph. In a GraphSAGE layer, for each node, a predefined number of neighbors are sampled. Their information is aggregated by combining their features and applying a learnable transformation, the output of which becomes the node's features in the next layer. Notably, GraphSAGE allows GNNs to be extended to the inductive setting, i.e. to generalize to previously unseen graphs.

The Graph Attention Network (GAT) developed by Velickovic *et al.* [29] introduced the self-attention mechanism to graph learning. Self-attention is an operation which allows each input feature to assign weights, or "attend", differently to the other input features, and has shown the state-of-the-art performance on natural language processing (NLP) and other tasks (Vaswani *et al.* 2017) [28]. In the GAT formulation, attention is instead computed between each graph node and its neighbors. Like GraphSAGE, GAT readily allows for inductive learning and achieves the state-of-the-art performance on an inductive protein-protein interaction (PPI) task.

GNNs have previously been applied to medical image segmentation tasks. Yan *et al.* 2019 [32] successfully applied a GCN variant, ChebNet, to segment brain tissue (gray matter, white matter, cerebro-spinal-fluid). They first used the SLIC algorithm [1] to cluster MRIs into supervoxels, and then predicted the tissue type of each supervoxel. The present work is partially inspired by their approach and follows a similar workflow. Juarez *et al.* [11] proposed a joint U-Net-GNN model for airway segmentation from CT scans and matched state-of-the-art performance. They replaced the last two layers of a U-Net with a sequence of graph convolution layers, which allowed the model to aggregate information globally across the entire CT scan while maintaining the pattern-recognition capabilities of the early convolutional layers. However, GNN-based methods have not previously been attempted for brain tumor segmentation, and thus, we here explore the applicability and performance of several GNN variants on the same.

2.3   Explanation of Deep Learning Models

Many interpretation methods for deep learning fall under the umbrella of *saliency maps* [23,26,27]. These methods utilize the gradients computed by a model with respect to the input to highlight regions of interest, i.e., those where the output changes greatly in response to small input changes. Saliency maps are especially useful in image processing, as they allow for easy visualization of pixel saliency and visual interpretation of results. However, one shortcoming of saliency maps is that they are often driven by the input image and largely agnostic to the model. In particular, it has been shown that the saliency outputs for a model trained on random labels can closely resemble those of a legitimate model, indicating that the saliency map is less a reflection of the model than of the input [2].

An interpretability method explicitly developed for GNNs is GNNExplainer [33]. GNNExplainer learns a mask on both the edges and features of an input graph to build a subgraph that seeks to summarize the connections and features that lead to the prediction on a node of interest. Unlike more general methods, GNNExplainer allows for interpreting how graph connectivity factors into a GNN prediction. A drawback of GNNExplainer is that it is difficult to optimize for larger subgraphs. We find that information from nodes far away from the target node often contributes to a prediction for tumor segmentation. Consequently, GNNExplainer was unable to identify meaningful subgraphs for our models.

In this work, we interpret our results using the SHAP (SHapley Additive exPlanations) library [13]. SHAP values are a computational approximation of Shapley values, a method for assigning payouts to players in a cooperative game, or in this case, contribution values to input features in a prediction task. SHAP values maintain many of the theoretical properties of Shapley values, such as additivity and consistency, which make them attractive as a interpretative tool. Section 3.7 presents the details of the SHAP values.

3   Methods

In this section, we first introduce the dataset we use and associated pre-processing followed by a description of transforming patient images into a graph structure. Subsequently, we present in greater detail our experimental setup. Finally, we describe our use of SHAP values to help interpret the results of the proposed model.

3.1   Imaging Data

The imaging data used in this study, including ground truth annotations, were obtained from the training data of the BraTS 2019 challenge [3,4,16]. The dataset consists of 76 low-grade glioma and 259 high-grade glioma MRIs from 19 contributing institutions. Each sample is composed of four imaging modalities obtained from the same patient: T2-weighted fluid attenuated inversion recovery (Flair), T1-weighted (T1), T1-weighted contrast-enhanced (T1CE), and T2-weighted (T2), which provide complementary information about the tumor. All provided imaging data has been skull-stripped, normalized to a resolution of 1 mm^3, and spatially aligned to the other modalities for the same patient [4]. Domain experts manually segmented the provided ground truth annotations following a standardized annotation protocol, and they were further reviewed for consistency and accuracy by additional neuro-radiologists. The ground truth annotation labels were as follows:

Label 0. Normal brain tissue
Label 1. Volume comprising necrotic core and non-enhancing gross tumor abnormality
Label 2. Vasogenic edema
Label 4. Active core or enhancing region within the gross tumor abnormality

Label 3 (non-enhancing tumor) was removed from the competition as a distinct region. Instead, it was combined with Label 1 (necrotic tumor) because the BraTS organizers found that it can be subject to significant inter-annotator variation and therefore bias the ground truth segmentation based on the annotating institution [4].

For this paper's purposes, one set of MRIs (all four modalities) from the same patient is referred to as a patient sample.

3.2   Data Preprocessing

Before segmentation, each MRI is cropped to the tightest possible bounding box of the brain tissue. This step is accomplished by excluding all image planes where all voxels have zero intensity. Next, we standardize each modality separately to a mean of zero and a standard deviation of one. Bias correction of the MRIs did not improve performance, so we report our final results without bias correction (two-sided t-test, $p \approx 1$).

3.3   Graph Construction

In order for the patient samples to be used as training examples for a GNN, they must first be converted to graph representations (Fig. 1 Step 2). To create the graph nodes, all four MRI modalities are concatenated to create one 3D image with four channels. The combined image is then fed through the Simple Linear Iterative Clustering (SLIC) algorithm [1] to generate a set of k supervoxels, where k is a tunable parameter of the SLIC algorithm. SLIC uses a K-means approach to cluster voxels that are similar in both intensity values and physical location in the brain (Eq. 1). In the concatenated MRI images, the spatial distance between two voxels is simply the 3D Euclidean distance between their coordinates. The intensity distance is the Euclidean distance calculated across all four intensity channels. A compactness parameter, m, controls the trade-off between intensity and spatial information.

The distance, D, calculation between two voxels i and j used for the supervoxel clustering thus becomes

$$D = \sqrt{d_I^2 + \left(\frac{d_s}{S}\right)^2 m^2} \tag{1}$$

$$d_I = \sqrt{(I_{T1,i} - I_{T1,j})^2 + (I_{T1CE,i} - I_{T1CE,j})^2 + (I_{T2,i} - I_{T2,j})^2 + (I_{FLAIR,i} - I_{FLAIR,j})^2}$$

$$d_s = \sqrt{(x_i - x_j)^2 + (y_i - y_j)^2 + (z_i - z_j)^2}$$

where x,y,z are the spatial position of a voxel in image coordinates, I is the intensity value of a modality at that pixel, and S is the expected spacing between supervoxels.

After clustering, supervoxels outside of the brain mass, that is, those with zero intensity, are filtered out, typically reducing the number of supervoxels by a factor of 2. Each remaining supervoxel is then assigned a feature vector consisting of the 10th, 25th, 50th, 75th, 90th percentiles of its constituent voxels' intensity values across all four modalities. This formulation results in a feature vector of length 20 for each supervoxel. We chose to use quantiles as it empirically performed better than only the mean intensity. Each supervoxel is also assigned a label, which is determined by finding the most common label (mode) of all of its constituent voxels in the ground truth labeling.

To determine the appropriate values of k and m used in constructing the graphs, we calculated the achievable segmentation accuracy (ASA) of several different combinations of values on a subset of the patient samples. The ASA quantifies how well the SLIC supervoxels recover the ground truth segmentation. This metric is equivalent to our model's accuracy at the voxel level when it predicts every supervoxel correctly. Because of the class imbalance skewing towards healthy tissue, we only consider the tumorous region when computing ASA. These results are presented in Sect. 4.1.

Once the supervoxels are generated for a patient sample, they are used to construct a regular graph. The graph takes the form $\{N, E\}$, where N is the set of vertices (referred to here as nodes), and E is the set of edges between them. Each node in the graph corresponds to exactly one generated supervoxel and is represented by its feature vector and its label (during training). The edge set E captures proximity information between nodes and is composed of undirected and unweighted edges constructed between each supervoxel and the r supervoxels spatially closest to it in the patient sample, where r represents the desired degree of the graph. We define the distance between two supervoxels as the Euclidean distance between the centroids of their constituent voxels' x-y-z coordinates.

3.4 GNN Details

We evaluated several standard GNN models on their ability to segment the tumors: GCN [12], GAT [29], and the gcn, mean, and pool variants of Graph-SAGE [6]. In broad terms, each model is composed of individual layers that share information across adjacent nodes. That is, each layer updates each node's feature vector as a transformed combination of its own features and those of its neighbors. As in a standard neural network, an arbitrary number of these layers can then be stacked sequentially. As the number of layers increases, the nodes indirectly receive information from nodes further and further from their immediate neighborhood. The mathematical formulations of each of these graph learning layers are shown in Eqs. 2 through 5.

In each case, $h_u^{(l)}$ is the features of node u at layer l, σ is a differentiable, non-linear activation function, $W^{(l)}$ is a layer specific trainable weight matrix, $\|$ is the concatenation operator, and $V(u)$ is the subset of nodes which are connected to u via the edge set E, also known as the neighborhood of u.

GCN/GS-gcn:

$$h_u^{(l+1)} = \sigma(\frac{1}{q}W^{(l)} \cdot (h_u^{(l)} + \sum_{v}^{V(u)} h_v^{(l)})) \tag{2}$$

where q is a normalization constant that differs between formulations from Kipf et al. [12] and Hamilton et al. [6]. In the case of a regular graph as considered here, however, q is equal to r, the graph degree, for both.

GS-mean:

$$h_u^{(l+1)} = \sigma(W^{(l)} \cdot (h_u^{(l)} \| mean(h_v^{(l)} \forall v \in V)) \tag{3}$$

GS-pool:

$$h_u^{(l+1)} = \sigma(W^{(l)} \cdot (h_u^{(l)} \| max(\sigma(W_{pool} \cdot h_v^{(l)}) \forall v \in V(u))) \tag{4}$$

where W_{pool} is a global trainable weight matrix.

GAT:

$$h_u^{(l+1)} = \|_{b}^{B} \sigma(\sum_{v \in V(u)} a_{uv}^b W_b^{(l)} h_u) \tag{5}$$

where B are multiple attention heads per layer, which each compute their own pairwise self-attention (a_{uv}^b) between each pair of neighboring nodes u and v. Here, we use ReLU as the non-linear activation function for all models.

3.5 Training and Evaluation Metrics

Prior to training, each patient sample is converted to a graph as described in Sect. 3.3. We split the dataset into training (60%), validation (20%), and test sets (20%).

The input to the GNN is defined formally as a graph of the form $\{N, E\}$, and a feature matrix $H \in \mathbb{R}^{n \times f}$, where n is the number of nodes, and f is the number of features per node. $f = 20$ for all experiments, as described in Sect. 3.3. The output is of size $n \times c$, where for each graph node, the model returns the probability of that node belonging to each of the four classes (c) defined in Sect. 3.1.

To determine the best hyperparameters for each of the GNN variants, we perform a random hyperparameter search on the validation set. We sweep over regularly spaced intervals of learning rate from 0.00001 to 0.001, feature dropout between 0 and 0.5, model depth from 3 to 9, and hidden layer size between 64 and 256. For GAT models, we additionally examine attention dropout between 0 and 0.5 and attention heads between 3 and 10 for each layer.

Each model is trained to minimize node-wise multi-label cross-entropy loss (Eq. 6) on the validation set using the Adam optimizer. The class weights are adjusted to be inversely proportional to their prevalence in the test set to address the class imbalance.

$$\text{Loss} = \sum_{c=0}^{C} (\mathbf{1}_{c=y}) w_c log(\hat{p}_y) \tag{6}$$

where C are the possible classes, w_c is the class weight, y is the true label, $\mathbf{1}_{c=y}$ is an indicator function, and $\hat{p}_y$ is the predicted probability of that label.

Upon convergence, each model is evaluated on the average Dice scores of its predictions, as defined in Eq. 7.

$$\text{Dice} = \frac{2TP}{2TP + FP + FN}. \tag{7}$$

where TP, FP, and FN are the number of true positives, false positives, and false negatives, respectively. True positive voxels are defined as those correctly assigned as belonging to a specific tumor compartment.

Specifically, we calculate the Dice score for the following tumor subregions: Whole Tumor (WT: union of labels 1,2,4), Core Tumor (CT: 1,4), and Active Tumor (AT: 4). These metrics provide insight into the ability of the model to assess tumor shape correctly as well as to differentiate between the different tumor subregions. To allow for direct comparison to published models in the literature, we report voxelwise Dice scores, rather than the Dice score on node (supervoxel) classification.

After the best hyperparameters have been selected for each GNN model, we train a final model on the combined training and validation sets and evaluate it on the test set. All models were implemented in PyTorch using Deep Graph Library (DGL) [31].

3.6   Baseline Method

We use the popular U-net model as a baseline to which to compare the results obtained with the GNN models. The top-performing 3D-CNN model [18] of the BraTS2018 [3,4,16] competition uses state-of-the-art GPUs with 34GB of VRAM that were not easily accessible. Therefore, we selected the second-best model, nnU-net [9], which requires only 11GB VRAM and is easily trainable through an included Python module and available code. GNN and CNN models were trained using the same train and test data sets.

3.7 Model Interpretation

In addition to accurately segmenting brain tumors, it is vital that we understand how and why our models make their predictions. Model interpretation allows us to 1) ensure that a model learned robust and generalizable features by cross-referencing important features with known predictive ones, and 2) identify novel features that aid in tumor segmentation. One method for assigning the contribution scores of the input features for a model is to compute Shapley values. The concept of Shapley values is borrowed from Game Theory. It corresponds to a fair payout to all the players in a cooperative game, given the outcome of the game. In the case of a predictive model, Shapley values can be interpreted as the contribution of each input feature towards the prediction of the model. Formally, they are defined as the average marginal contribution of a feature to a given prediction when added to a subset of other features, over all possible subsets [17]. Since the complexity of computing exact Shapley values is combinatorial in the number of features, we instead use the DeepSHAP model [13] to approximate them. This method takes in a background feature distribution and a query prediction it seeks to explain, and assigns each feature a score representing its contribution to the model output. First, it calculates the difference in model output when given the true features versus background features. Next, it backpropagates this difference back to each of the input features in a way that satisfies the properties of additivity, consistency, and local accuracy [25]. The backpropagated value at each feature can then be considered the part of the difference it is 'responsible' for.

The background feature distribution is obtained by randomly sampling 500 nodes across the entire dataset of input graphs such that the relative proportions of node labels remain consistent. Since predictions on nodes cannot be made in isolation (i.e., they rely on the graph structure and surrounding nodes), SHAP values are computed for each node in a graph simultaneously.

4   Results

4.1 Supervoxel Generation Affects Achievable Accuracy

The graph construction step involves two parameters, the choice of the number, k, and compactness, m, for the supervoxel generation via SLIC. We find that $k = 15000, 20000$ and $m = 0.1$ led to the highest ASA (Appendix, Fig. 4). We choose $k = 15000$ for all subsequent experiments as $k = 20000$ required longer to train with no noticeable improvement in performance.

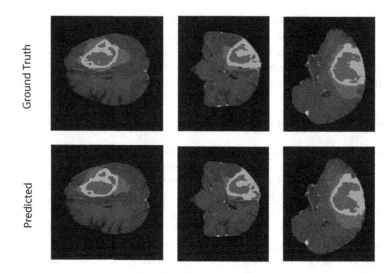

Fig. 2. An example segmentation produced by the best-performing GNN model vs. the ground truth segmentation. Shown are an example horizontal, coronal, and sagittal slice of the same MRI. The colors correspond to the different tumor subtypes: blue = NET/necrosis, yellow = ET, red = Edema. Tumor predictions are overlaid onto the T1-Contrast Enhanced Image. There is a close correspondence between the predicted tumor and the ground truth. (Color figure online)

Of note, even the best SLIC parameters result in an ASA of only 0.9, on average (Appendix, Fig. 4). The diminished accuracy is caused by SLIC-generated supervoxels, which encompass voxels of multiple different labels. A drawback of clustering into supervoxels is that it approximates the brain as a collection of homogeneous regions, while each supervoxel may be somewhat heterogeneous. This effect is especially pronounced along the borders between tumor subtypes and regions with low contrast. Here, the transition in intensity across the different modalities and the ground truth labels may not be well aligned, or the intensity differences are gradual while the shift in labels is abrupt. In these cases, supervoxels are created with a mixture of labels, yet can only be labeled as one of them.

The partial volume effects introduced by supervoxel creation adversely affect the performance of our model. As shown in Fig. 5 (Appendix), the voxel-wise Dice score achieved by our model are significantly lower than the supervoxel-wise Dice score across all tumor regions for both the training and testing data.

4.2   Brain Tumor Segmentation Performance of Different GNN Models

We summarize the segmentation results of the different GNN models on the test set in Table 1. The best performing GNN is a GraphSAGE-pool network with 5

Table 1. Average Dice coefficients across different GNN models for whole tumor (WT), enhancing tumor (ET), and tumor core (TC) trained and evaluated on same train-test split from the training set of the BraTS 2019 data set [16].

Model	WT Dice	TC Dice	ET Dice
GraphSAGE-pool	0.841	0.737	0.671
GraphSAGE-mean	0.804	0.720	0.70
GraphSAGE-gcn	0.536	0.483	0.302
GCN	0.564	0.455	0.341
GAT	0.742	0.687	0.588

Table 2. Average Whole Tumor Dice on training and test sets, along with training time in hours, for GraphSAGE pool models trained and evaluated on graphs of varying degrees.

Model	Train WT Dice	Test WT Dice	Time to Train (hours)
GSpool-10	0.917	0.819	8.7
GSpool-20	0.912	0.832	10.2
GSpool-30	0.915	0.841	15.5

hidden layers of 256 units each, which is trained until convergence at a learning rate of 0.0001. The mean aggregator function performs slightly worse than the pooling operator. The worst performing models by a substantial margin are the GCN models. We hypothesize that this is because they lack the implicit skip connection built into the mean and pooling aggregators via the concatenation step. These results are consistent with those reported by both Velickovic *et al.* [29] and Hamilton *et al.* [6] for the performance trend on protein-protein interaction (PPI) dataset. Surprisingly, GAT performs much worse on this task than GraphSAGE-pool, despite demonstrating improved performance on other inductive tasks. Several factors could account for this discrepancy, including a larger average graph size, less expressive node feature vectors, the different label classification scheme, or simply because attention may be less suited for brain segmentation.

We note that our best performing model is deeper than those reported in previous works [6,12,29], with 5 hidden layers, rather than 2 or 3. We hypothesize that aggregating information from further away is more important for tumor segmentation than other graph learning applications, such as social networks or PPI.

4.3   Performance and Runtime Results for Varying Neighborhood Sizes

For the best performing model, GraphSAGE-pool, we compare model performance on datasets with varying graph degrees. We create three different sets of graphs from the raw MRIs, with identical node features but either 10, 20, or 30 neighbors. These results are reported in Table 2. While increasing graph degree has no noticeable effect on model performance on the training set, a higher degree does seem to allow the model to generalize better to the unseen data in the test set. However, this comes at the cost of increased training time, with the degree 30 dataset requiring about twice as long to finish training as the degree 10 dataset.

4.4   Comparison of GNN Model with Other Recent Models

Next, we compare the GraphSAGE pool model trained on graphs of degree 30 to nnU-Net, the second place model in the BraTS 2018 competition [9]. Both models are trained and evaluated on the same train and test splits. These results are presented in Table 3. While our GNN model fails to match the state of the art performance of the nnU-Net, the results nonetheless show that GNNs can successfully perform the segmentation task, despite the approximations made in graph construction and the relative novelty of inductive graph-learning techniques. In particular, for the segmentation of the whole tumor, our model achieves a median Dice score that is quite close to nnU-Net. This result indicates that 1) our model is better at outlining the gross tumor than at identifying tumor subregions, and 2) while on most patient samples, GNN models are quite effective, it fails to generalize for some, adversely affecting the mean more than the median.

Our GNN-based approach compares favorably to many other experimental techniques submitted to the BraTS challenge in recent years. Serrano-Rubio *et al.* [24] also attempt a supervoxel-based technique, coupled with Extremely Randomized Trees, to achieve Dice scores of 0.80, 0.63, and 0.57 on the official 2018 validation dataset [4] for whole tumor, core tumor, and enhancing tumor, respectively. Another group, Rezaei *et al.* [21], presents a novel Generative Adversarial Network (GAN) termed voxel-GAN, which seeks to address the label imbalance present in tumor segmentation. This model achieves mean Dice scores of 0.84, 0.79, and 0.63 on the BraTS 2018 validation set. Like ours, these models may not achieve state-of-the-art performance, but identify an important issue in tumor segmentation and attempt to solve it using a novel approach.

Moreover, GNNs' running requirements are relatively modest. Each GNN model was trained on 6 GB of GPU memory with a batch size of 4 brains within hours (Table 2). By contrast, [18] and [9] require 32 GB and 12 GB of RAM, take days to weeks to train to completion, and are limited to a batch size of maximally one image, and typically only image *patches*. The eased computational burden could be an important consideration when developing online segmentation models that are regularly updated with new MRIs.

Table 3. Results on our test set (a partition of the BraTS2019 training set). We report both mean and median Dice scores for the whole tumor, tumor core, and enhancing tumor.

Test Set Results						
Statistic	Median			Mean		
Tumor Compartment	WT	TC	ET	WT	TC	ET
nnU-Net [9]	0.929	0.919	0.857	0.906	0.827	0.745
GSpool-30	0.892	0.841	0.783	0.841	0.737	0.672

4.5 Explaining GNN Predictions Using SHAP

Finally, we compute the SHAP values for a subset of representative patient samples. We stratify the computed SHAP values by modality, label, and whether the corresponding feature value was high intensity (bright) or low intensity (dark) (Fig. 3). Bright intensities are defined as the top 15% of intensity values within a given modality, while dark intensities are those in the bottom 15%.

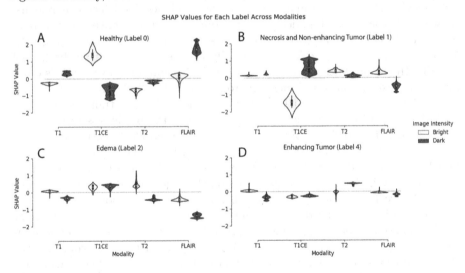

Fig. 3. SHAP values distribution grouped by label and stratified by modality. Dark Violin plots correspond to dark image regions in a particular modality, while lighter plots correspond to bright regions in the corresponding modality. Positive SHAP values indicate that the modality contributes to the prediction of a particular label, while negative SHAP values indicate that a modality contributes negatively to predicting that label. Panels A-D represent the SHAP values computed for different tissue labels.

We identify several trends for each modality's contribution to different labels in Fig. 3. Bright T1CE regions and dark FLAIR regions drive the prediction of healthy tissue (Fig. 3A), while the inverse is predictive of the necrotic and non-enhancing tumor core (Fig. 3B). Edematous tissue is defined by bright T2 regions and the lack of dark FLAIR regions (Fig. 3C). Lastly, in the tissue predicted to be enhancing tumor, dark T2 and dark T1 regions are assigned the highest and lowest SHAP values, respectively (Fig. 3D). For the enhancing tumor, we also observe that the absolute magnitudes of the SHAP values are substantially lower than those of the other 3 possible classifications. This observation indicates that predicting a node as an enhancing tumor is driven by a "process of elimination", not by intrinsic characteristics of the enhancing tumor. Rather than learning which features uniquely identify the enhancing tumor, the model instead relies on recognizing feature combinations that make the other labels unlikely.

Overall, the T1CE and FLAIR modalities are consistently assigned the most variable SHAP values, while the T1 modality remains relatively constant. The relative utility of each modality is consistent with that determined by the BraTS organizers, who state that the T1CE and FLAIR modalities are also the most useful for manual segmentation [4].

Many of our findings for individual tumor regions also conform to radiation oncology practices for manual segmentation of brain tumors. For example, both non-enhancing tumor and necrosis are typically delineated by dark T1-CE, bright T2, and bright FLAIR regions of the MRI. Our model's SHAP value analysis recovers all three of these trends for the combined NET/necrosis regions. Interestingly, however, it indicates that T1CE and FLAIR have a much more pronounced effect on the prediction of these regions than T2 does. (Fig. 3B). Vasogenic edema (Label 2) may be visually assessed by contrasting bright T2 and FLAIR regions with moderate intensity T1CE and T1. However, it is often difficult to distinguish from other tumorous labels (1 and 4), since these can all appear bright on the T2 and FLAIR images, depending on tumor grade. Our analysis shows that the model correctly recognizes the brightness trend in the T2 and FLAIR modalities, but learns a more nuanced classification scheme to circumvent this issue. Rather than using bright FLAIR intensities as a marker for edema, it instead learns that a brain region that *lacks* dark FLAIR intensities are unlikely to be healthy, and then relies on the other modalities to distinguish further between the tumor subregions. Lastly, enhancing tumor is traditionally defined as bright (enhanced) regions in the T1CE modality. Surprisingly, bright T1CE regions are not assigned high SHAP values for the enhancing tumor, indicating that they play little to no role in the model's predictions thereof (Fig. 3D). When coupled with the relative scarcity of enhancing tumor labels, this observation could explain the inferior performance of the model in predicting the enhancing tumor (Label 4).

The above analysis indicates agreement between the feature combinations used by the model and clinical practice. Furthermore, the analysis provides insight into how the model distinguishes between regions that are known to be difficult to differentiate on MRI. Insight into why the results might not be optimal for enhancing tumor will allow us to address this issue. Such interpretability analysis is key to ensuring the adoption of deep learning models in healthcare [30].

5   Discussion

The development of effective automatic segmentation techniques can improve timely treatment for thousands of brain tumor patients annually. Furthermore, integrating automatic segmentation into routine clinical workflows could save physicians thousands of hours of painstaking manual annotation and standardize segmentations otherwise subject to inter-annotator variation. Here, we have presented the application of Graph Neural Networks to brain tumor segmentation from MRIs. With this work, we provide several important contributions to the field. Firstly, we compare several common GNN variants and determine that GraphSAGE with the pooling aggregator performs the best. Secondly, we show that, compared to CNNs designed for the same task, GNN is less resource expensive and time-consuming to train. Lastly, we provide an interpretation of our model's predictions using Shapley value-based contribution scores.

A logical extension to this work is to combine the graph construction (involving supervoxel generation) and graph prediction in an end-to-end model, similarly to [11]. While the use of supervoxels to represent the images improves computational efficiency, our current model performance is heavily gated by the discrepancy between the SLIC output and the true segmentation labels. The treatment of supervoxels which contain voxels with different labels is poorly defined and consequently results in misclassified voxels. Even a model that classifies every graph node correctly achieves a voxel-wise Dice Whole Tumor score of only about 0.93 (Appendix, Fig. 5). A task-specific, end-to-end approach has the potential to alleviate this concern and increase performance substantially. End-to-end training would allow graph nodes to be delineated in greater accordance with the underlying tumor subregions, limiting the number of supervoxels spanning multiple labels. Furthermore, it would allow the model to *learn* node descriptors, which would likely be more informative than hand-engineered summary statistics for each modality. Another direction for future improvement is training the model hierarchically, that is, first determining the outline of the tumorous region(s) as a whole, and then segmenting each tumor subtype within the tumorous region. Many brain tumor segmentation models are effective at outlining the gross tumor, but struggle to delineate tumor compartments [4]. Such a training scheme should allow for a more nuanced capacity to distinguish the regions.

Appendix

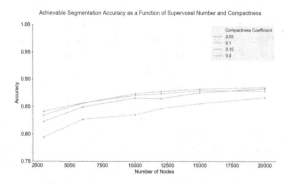

Fig. 4. The achievable segmentation accuracy as a function of supervoxel number and compactness. More supervoxels increase the achievable accuracy.

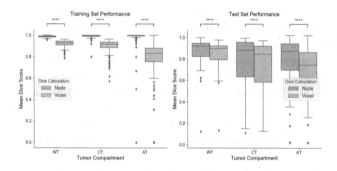

Fig. 5. Boxplot of Dice scores for the same brains computed by voxel vs. by supervoxel (node). Results shown for both test and train set. **** shows $p < 0.0001$ in paired t-test. Across every comparison, Dice scores calculated on voxels are significantly lower than when calculated by node. This effect is especially pronounced on the test set.

Table 4. Hausdorff Distances (95 percentile) calculated on test set for our model and nnUnet. Both median and mean scores are reported.

Test Set Results						
Statistic	Median			Mean		
Tumor Compartment	WT	TC	ET	WT	TC	ET
nnU-Net [9]	2.828	2.27	1.414	4.645	6.17	5.011
GSpool-30	4.359	5.10	3.317	7.60	10.30	5.45

References

1. Achanta, R., Shaji, A., Smith, K., Lucchi, A., Fua, P., Süsstrunk, S.: SLIC super-pixels compared to state-of-the-art superpixel methods. IEEE Trans. Pattern Anal. Mach. Intell. **34**(11), 2274–2282 (2012)

2. Adebayo, J., Gilmer, J., Muelly, M., Goodfellow, I., Hardt, M., Kim, B.: Sanity checks for saliency maps. In: Advances in Neural Information Processing Systems, pp. 9505–9515 (2018)

3. Bakas, S., et al.: Advancing the cancer genome atlas glioma MRI collections with expert segmentation labels and radiomic features. Sci. Data **4**, 170117 (2017)

4. Bakas, S., et al.: Identifying the best machine learning algorithms for brain tumor segmentation, progression assessment, and overall survival prediction in the brats challenge. arXiv preprint arXiv:1811.02629 (2018)

5. Defferrard, M., Bresson, X., Vandergheynst, P.: Convolutional neural networks on graphs with fast localized spectral filtering. In: Advances in Neural Information Processing Systems, pp. 3844–3852 (2016)

6. Hamilton, W., Ying, Z., Leskovec, J.: Inductive representation learning on large graphs. In: Advances in Neural Information Processing Systems, pp. 1024–1034 (2017)

7. Hammond, D.K., Vandergheynst, P., Gribonval, R.: Wavelets on graphs via spectral graph theory. Appl. Computat. Harmonic Anal. **30**(2), 129–150 (2011)

8. Havaei, M., et al.: Brain tumor segmentation with deep neural networks. Med. Image Anal. **35**, 18–31 (2017)

9. Isensee, F., Kickingereder, P., Wick, W., Bendszus, M., Maier-Hein, K.H.: Brain tumor segmentation and radiomics survival prediction: contribution to the BRATS 2017 challenge. In: Crimi, A., Bakas, S., Kuijf, H., Menze, B., Reyes, M. (eds.) BrainLes 2017. LNCS, vol. 10670, pp. 287–297. Springer, Cham (2018). https://doi.org/10.1007/978-3-319-75238-9_25

10. Islam, A., Reza, S.M.S., Iftekharuddin, K.M.: Multifractal texture estimation for detection and segmentation of brain tumors. IEEE Trans. Biomed. Eng. **60**(11), 3204–3215 (2013). https://doi.org/10.1109/TBME.2013.2271383

11. Garcia-Uceda Juarez, A., Selvan, R., Saghir, Z., de Bruijne, M.: A joint 3D UNet-graph neural network-based method for airway segmentation from chest CTs. In: Suk, H.-I., Liu, M., Yan, P., Lian, C. (eds.) MLMI 2019. LNCS, vol. 11861, pp. 583–591. Springer, Cham (2019). https://doi.org/10.1007/978-3-030-32692-0_67

12. Kipf, T.N., Welling, M.: Semi-supervised classification with graph convolutional networks. arXiv preprint arXiv:1609.02907 (2016)

13. Lundberg, S.M., Lee, S.I.: A unified approach to interpreting model predictions. In: Guyon, I., et al. (eds.) Advances in Neural Information Processing Systems 30, pp. 4765–4774. Curran Associates, Inc. (2017). http://papers.nips.cc/paper/7062-a-unified-approach-to-interpreting-model-predictions.pdf

14. Ma, C., Luo, G., Wang, K.: Concatenated and connected random forests with multiscale patch driven active contour model for automated brain tumor segmentation of MR images. IEEE Trans. Med. Imaging **37**(8), 1943–1954 (2018). https://doi.org/10.1109/TMI.2018.2805821

15. McKinley, R., Meier, R., Wiest, R.: Ensembles of densely-connected CNNs with label-uncertainty for brain tumor segmentation. In: Crimi, A., Bakas, S., Kuijf, H., Keyvan, F., Reyes, M., van Walsum, T. (eds.) BrainLes 2018. LNCS, vol. 11384, pp. 456–465. Springer, Cham (2019). https://doi.org/10.1007/978-3-030-11726-9_40

16. Menze, B.H., et al.: The multimodal brain tumor image segmentation benchmark (brats). IEEE Trans. Med. Imaging **34**(10), 1993–2024 (2014)
17. Molnar, C.: Interpretable Machine Learning (2019). https://christophm.github.io/interpretable-ml-book/
18. Myronenko, A.: 3D MRI brain tumor segmentation using autoencoder regularization. In: Crimi, A., Bakas, S., Kuijf, H., Keyvan, F., Reyes, M., van Walsum, T. (eds.) BrainLes 2018. LNCS, vol. 11384, pp. 311–320. Springer, Cham (2019). https://doi.org/10.1007/978-3-030-11726-9_28
19. Ostrom, Q.T., et al.: CBTRUS statistical report: primary brain and other central nervous system tumors diagnosed in the United States in 2012–2016. Neuro-Oncol. **21** (2019)
20. Pei, L., Bakas, S., Vossough, A., Reza, S.M., Davatzikos, C., Iftekharuddin, K.M.: Longitudinal brain tumor segmentation prediction in MRI using feature and label fusion. Biomed. Signal Process. Control **55**, 101648 (2020). https://doi.org/10.1016/j.bspc.2019.101648
21. Rezaei, M., Yang, H., Meinel, C.: voxel-GAN: adversarial framework for learning imbalanced brain tumor segmentation. In: Crimi, A., Bakas, S., Kuijf, H., Keyvan, F., Reyes, M., van Walsum, T. (eds.) BrainLes 2018. LNCS, vol. 11384, pp. 321–333. Springer, Cham (2019). https://doi.org/10.1007/978-3-030-11726-9_29
22. Scarselli, F., Gori, M., Tsoi, A.C., Hagenbuchner, M., Monfardini, G.: The graph neural network model. IEEE Trans. Neural Netw. **20**(1), 61–80 (2009)
23. Selvaraju, R.R., Cogswell, M., Das, A., Vedantam, R., Parikh, D., Batra, D.: Grad-CAM: visual explanations from deep networks via gradient-based localization. In: Proceedings of the IEEE International Conference on Computer Vision, pp. 618–626 (2017)
24. Serrano-Rubio, J.P., Everson, R.: Brain tumour segmentation method based on supervoxels and sparse dictionaries. In: Crimi, A., Bakas, S., Kuijf, H., Keyvan, F., Reyes, M., van Walsum, T. (eds.) BrainLes 2018. LNCS, vol. 11384, pp. 210–221. Springer, Cham (2019). https://doi.org/10.1007/978-3-030-11726-9_19
25. Shrikumar, A., Greenside, P., Kundaje, A.: Learning important features through propagating activation differences. arXiv preprint arXiv:1704.02685 (2017)
26. Smilkov, D., Thorat, N., Kim, B., Viégas, F., Wattenberg, M.: SmoothGrad: removing noise by adding noise. arXiv preprint arXiv:1706.03825 (2017)
27. Sundararajan, M., Taly, A., Yan, Q.: Axiomatic attribution for deep networks. arXiv preprint arXiv:1703.01365 (2017)
28. Vaswani, A., et al.: Attention is all you need. In: Advances in Neural Information Processing Systems, pp. 5998–6008 (2017)
29. Veličković, P., Cucurull, G., Casanova, A., Romero, A., Lio, P., Bengio, Y.: Graph attention networks. arXiv preprint arXiv:1710.10903 (2017)
30. Vellido, A.: The importance of interpretability and visualization in machine learning for applications in medicine and health care. Neural Comput. Appl. (2019). https://doi.org/10.1007/s00521-019-04051-w
31. Wang, M., et al.: Deep graph library: towards efficient and scalable deep learning on graphs. arXiv preprint arXiv:1909.01315 (2019)
32. Yan, Z., Youyong, K., Jiasong, W., Coatrieux, G., Huazhong, S.: Brain tissue segmentation based on graph convolutional networks. In: 2019 IEEE International Conference on Image Processing (ICIP), pp. 1470–1474. IEEE (2019)
33. Ying, Z., Bourgeois, D., You, J., Zitnik, M., Leskovec, J.: GNNExplainer: generating explanations for graph neural networks. In: Advances in Neural Information Processing Systems, pp. 9244–9255 (2019)

34. Zhou, C., Chen, S., Ding, C., Tao, D.: Learning contextual and attentive information for brain tumor segmentation. In: Crimi, A., Bakas, S., Kuijf, H., Keyvan, F., Reyes, M., van Walsum, T. (eds.) BrainLes 2018. LNCS, vol. 11384, pp. 497–507. Springer, Cham (2019). https://doi.org/10.1007/978-3-030-11726-9_44
35. Zhou, J., et al.: Graph neural networks: a review of methods and applications. arXiv preprint arXiv:1812.08434 (2018)

STDI-Net: Spatial-Temporal Network with Dynamic Interval Mapping for Bike Sharing Demand Prediction

Weiguo Pian[1], Yingbo Wu[1(✉)], and Ziyi Kou[2]

[1] Chongqing University, Chongqing, China
{pwg,wyb}@cqu.edu.cn
[2] University of Notre Dame, Notre Dame, USA
zkou@nd.edu

Abstract. As an economical and healthy mode of shared transportation, Bike Sharing System (BSS) develops quickly in many big cities. An accurate prediction method can help BSS schedule resources in advance to meet the demands of users, and definitely improve operating efficiencies of it. However, most of the existing methods for similar tasks just utilize spatial or temporal information independently. Though there are some methods consider both, they only focus on demand prediction in a single location or between location pairs. In this paper, we propose a novel deep learning method called Spatial-Temporal Dynamic Interval Network (STDI-Net). The method predicts the number of renting and returning orders of multiple connected stations in the near future by modeling joint spatial-temporal information. Furthermore, we embed an additional module that generates dynamical learnable mappings for different time intervals, to include the factor that different time intervals have a strong influence on demand prediction in BSS. Extensive experiments are conducted on the NYC Bike dataset, the results demonstrate the superiority of our method over existing methods.

Keywords: Bike sharing system · Demand prediction · Deep learning

1 Introduction

With the rapid development of sharing economy around the world, Bike Sharing System (BSS) has become more and more popular in recent years [4,18]. It provides people with a convenient and environment-friendly way of traveling. Users can rent a bike from a BSS station by some apps on their mobile phones and then return the bike to a station after completing their travels.

However, efficiently maintaining these systems is still challenging since the schedule and allocation of these transportation resources vary a lot depending on specific user requirements. For example, the number of rental orders on the morning of a day has an extremely imbalanced distribution between residential areas and commercial places. Therefore, a demand prediction method for adjustments of bikes in advance can improve the efficiency of BSS greatly.

J. Bowles et al. (Eds.): DataMod 2020, LNCS 12611, pp. 38–53, 2021.
https://doi.org/10.1007/978-3-030-70650-0_3

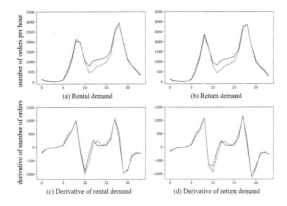

Fig. 1. Number of orders and the rates of their changes during one day for both *rent* and *return* mode. The two lines with blue and orange color represent two single days in April 2014. (Color figure online)

To tackle this problem, there have been several methods proposed in recent years focusing on different prediction tasks. Besides some methods applying hand-crafted features [3,13,19], one of the first deep learning methods was introduced by Wang et al. [21] who concatenated several related factors as inputs to predict the gap between taxi supply and demand via a non-linear MLP network. After that, Zhang et al. [26] proposed a deep convolutional network named ST-ResNet to predict in-out traffic flow among different areas. However, both of them did not consider the temporal information hidden in the sequential data which is an important factor in transportation issues. Based on that, Yao et al. [24] constructed a spatial-temporal model to predict various taxi demands. Moreover, they further created a graph embedding module to pass information among different areas. But their networks only consider a single area with its neighbors as inputs, thus obtains predicted results for different locations separately, which resulted in a serious lack of correlated spatial information on the global level.

Therefore, in our method, we construct a joint spatial-temporal network on a large scale area that contains hundreds of connected BSS stations in a long day hours. The network takes the number of both rental and returning orders of all stations in the past few hours as integrated inputs and predicts all of them in the near future together for once. By this way, the spatial correlation shared by all stations can be captured at the same level and same time, with global transportation information passing through each of them. Besides, the joint consideration of both operations for bikes, renting and returning, helps to maintain the sequential relation at each time interval. For the convolutional part, instead of applying the same filters for all features in different temporal indexes, we assign features in each index with one independent convolutional group. That is, we consider that indexes serve different roles in sequential data, which is far from enough to be captured by the same convolutional kernels. Compared

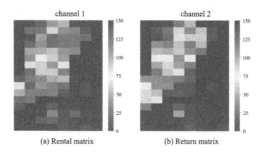

(a) Rental matrix   (b) Return matrix

Fig. 2. *rental* and *return* matrices as inputs for our joint spatial-temporal network. The sidebars for both matrices denote the relationship between colors and the number of orders. (Color figure online)

with previous methods, our network can achieve much better performance with measurements of both accuracy and efficiency in demand prediction tasks.

Although all the previous methods have explored temporal information in a wide range, they all ignore an important factor that different time periods influence a lot on the change of demands. Based on that, we analyze the number of orders in BSS for each day and found in some periods, the orders increase or drop dramatically while for other times, no apparent fluctuation can be observed. As shown in Fig. 1, two colored lines are representing the change of orders in two single days and also their corresponding derivatives that further demonstrate the variety of demand changes in a continuous way. Therefore, we propose the dynamic interval module that takes different time intervals as inputs to improve the predictions of the main spatial-temporal network. Instead of applying a regular feature fusion for the outputs of the module, we are inspired by some few-shot learning methods [2,22] and directly assign the generated features as learnable parameters for the top layer that is responsible for final predictions in the main network. In such a learning framework, time intervals participate in the formulation of learning weights in a more straightforward way, which helps the whole model to learn a mapping that is adapted based on different time periods from the extracted spatial-temporal feature to the predicted demands.

In summary, we collect our contribution into the following three folds:

- We propose a joint spatial-temporal network with time-specific convolution layers to predict both renting and returning demand for all the stations in the BSS.
- We further propose a Dynamic Interval module that builds the relationship between different time intervals in a day to the learning representation that is assigned as learnable weights in the top regression layer.
- We conducted large scale experiments on the NYC Bike dataset. The result shows that our approach outperforms all other previous methods and several competitive baselines.

2   Related Work

Traffic prediction problems include many tasks, such as traffic flow prediction, destination prediction, demand prediction (our task), etc. The methods applied to these tasks are kind of similar. Essentially, they predict the data on future timestamps based on the historical one [21,24,26,27]. Some traditional methods only rely on information in time series and regress final predictions. For instance, one of the most representative methods is Autoregressive Integrated Moving Average (ARIMA) which is widely used in traffic prediction problems [13,19]. It takes continuous temporal information as inputs and regresses desired results. Besides, some other works included external context data, such as weather conditions and event information, to further improve the model's performance [14,23].

Deep learning has been successfully used in a large number of problems, such as computer vision [6,11], which also widely used in traffic prediction. Zhang et al. [27] proposed a DNN-based model for predicting crowd flow. After that, they further introduced the residual connection originated from CNN-based networks [6] for the same task [26]. To utilize context data, Wang et al. [21] used a large number of multiple sources as inputs of their network to predict the gap between the supply and demand of taxi in different sub-areas. Besides, some other methods [25,28] proposed to use the recurrent neural network, like LSTM and BiLSM, to encode temporal information. With the popularity of a convolutional neural network (CNN), Yao et al. [24] jointly modeled spatial-temporal information in a single network, and generated graph embedding additionally to extract the constant feature for each region. Though they achieved a great success in some traffic prediction fields, they neglect the discriminative temporal information hidden in time intervals and encoded sequential data without special consideration, which will both be tackled in our proposed method.

Though deep learning methods have been successful in many areas, most of them require a large amount of annotated data to be optimized. Meta Learning methods [1,2,5,22], however, exist to help relieve such a strict requirement by proposing more general training models that can be adjusted well to new tasks with a few new samples. Especially, Bertinetto et al. proposed a siamese-like network to receive image pairs and enforce one sub-network to generate learning weights directly for another one [2]. Similarly, the TAFE-Net proposed by Wang et al. [22] successfully generates weights for both convolutional and fully connected layers to another network. Inspired by such a weight generating strategy, in our work, we also explore the possibility to apply it to the demand prediction tasks, hoping to adjust our model with more adapted parameters captured by external knowledge hidden in our specific sequential data.

3   Preliminaries

In this section, we first introduce some basic conceptions in BSS and then formulate our demand prediction problem mathematically.

Following the definition of [24] and [26], we denote $S = \{s_1, s_2, \ldots, s_N\}$ as the set of all stations in which the number of orders needs to be predicted, where N is the total number of stations used in our dataset. These stations are further converted into a matrix $M \in \{s_n\}^{i \times j}$ where $N = i \times j$, according to the geographical distribution of these stations. For temporal information, suppose each day can be segmented into H time intervals and there are D days in a dataset, we define $T = \{t_{0,0}, t_{1,0}, \ldots, t_{H-1,D-1}\}$ as the set of whole time intervals. Given the above definitions, we further formulate the following conceptions.

Rental Order: A rental order A can be defined as $\langle A.s, A.t \rangle$ that contains the station where people rent their bikes and the corresponding start time interval. We represent it as $\langle A.s, A.t \rangle$ with a *tuple* structure where s is the station and t denotes the interval.

Return Order: Similarly, a return order R can be also defined as $\langle R.s, R.t \rangle$ in which s and t correspond to the same meaning in A.

Rental/Return Demand: The rental and return demand in one station n and time interval $t_{h,d}$ are both defined as the total number of rental/return orders during that time and location, which can be denoted as m_A/m_R. Therefore, when dealing with all BSS stations, we set $M_A^t/M_R^t \in \mathbb{N}^{i \times j}$ as matrices with each element representing the demand of each station. Furtherly, demand matrices for all time intervals can be defined as M_A and M_R respectively.

Demand: With all definitions above, we finally concatenate two demand matrices, M_A^t and M_R^t, together as joints input $M^t \in \mathbb{N}^{2 \times i \times j}$ for our proposed network in time interval t. As shown in Fig. 2, our demand matrix has two channels representing rental and return demands respectively. Each grid is one station and the corresponding color describes the number of orders.

Demand Prediction: Given the sequential data from the beginning time to the current, demand prediction aims to predict the data in the future one time step or several steps. Especially, for the BSS demand prediction, we denote it as

$$M^t = \mathcal{F}(\{M^{t-L}, \ldots, M^{t-2}, M^{t-1}\} \mid \mathbb{P}) \tag{1}$$

where L is the length of the input sequence, $\mathbb{P}$ represents some additional information that can help for prediction tasks as prior knowledge, like the spatial connection among stations [24] and different time intervals in a day in our method.

4 Proposed Spatial-Temporal Dynamic Interval Network

In this section, we provide the details of our proposed Spatial-Temporal Dynamic Interval Network (STDI-Net) for the demand prediction task of BSS. We first talk about our spatial-temporal module separately and then introduce the dynamic interval module which generates different parameters for the network based on time intervals in a day. Figure 3 shows the overview architecture of our model.

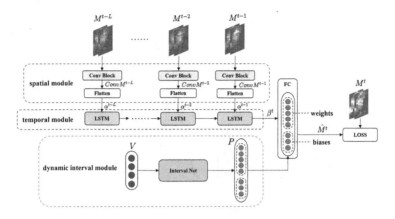

Fig. 3. The Architecture of STDI-Net. The spatial module uses Conv Blocks to capture the spatial feature among stations. The Conv Block consisted of a convolutional layer and residual units. Flatten layers are used to transform the output of Conv Blocks to vectors. The temporal module uses an LSTM model to extract temporal information. The dynamic interval module takes different time intervals as inputs to generate the learnable parameters (weights and biases) for the fully connected layer.

4.1 Spatial Module

The spatial module of the network aims to extract the joint features of all stations in each demand matrix. For each data node in one sequential input, we apply a residual convolutional block to operate on it. Inspired by [6] that proposed the residual link to solve problems brought by very deep networks, like the vanishing gradient problem, we utilize a similar idea in our spatial module. With a concatenation between different levels of layers, the block can not only extract more abstracted representations of the demand matrix in a deep layer but also consider context information connected through different layers from the sparse input as the number of orders to the compact spatial relationships among different stations. More details are shown in Fig. 4 and the process $\mathcal{F}_s$ can be denoted as

$$
\begin{aligned}
X_1 &= X_0 * W_1 + b_1 \\
X_2 &= X_1 * W_2 + b_2 \\
X_3 &= f(X_1 + X_2)
\end{aligned}
\tag{2}
$$

where $X_0 \in \mathbb{R}^{c_0 \times i \times j}$ denotes the input of a ResUnit. $X_1 \in \mathbb{R}^{c_1 \times i \times j}$ and $X_2 \in \mathbb{R}^{c_2 \times i \times j}$ are the outputs of the first and second convolutional layers in the ResUnit respectively. $X_3 \in \mathbb{R}^{c_3 \times i \times j}$ represents the output of the ResUnit. The $f(\cdot)$ denotes the non-linear activation function like $ReLU$. W_1, b_1, W_2, and b_2 represent the weights and biases of the first and second convolutional layers in the ResUnit separately.

To further consider that matrices in each sequential data serves different roles based on their indexes, we create multiple independent Conv Blocks with

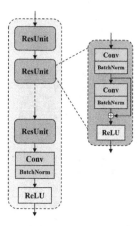

Fig. 4. Internal structure of Conv Block

the same structure and each of the block is responsible for one corresponding demand matrix. We denote the process as

$$ConvM^l = \mathcal{F}_s^l(M^l), \, l \in t - L, ..., t - 2, t - 1 \tag{3}$$

where $M^l \in \mathbb{R}^{2 \times i \times j}$ is the two-channel demand matrix as original input on time interval l and $ConvM^l \in \mathbb{R}^{c \times i \times j}$ is the output from M^l operated by the Conv Block $\mathcal{F}_s^l$. l represents the index of both sequential inputs and Conv Blocks, and L denotes the length of the input sequence. Therefore, the number of different convolutional blocks is equal to the number of intervals in a sequential input. Each block captures the discriminative information hidden in the indexes of the data.

After the convolutional operation, we apply flatten layers to transform $ConvM^l$ that outputs from Conv Block $\mathcal{F}_s^l$ to a feature vector $\alpha_l \in \mathbb{R}^{cij}$, where c is the number of channels of the output matrix. The whole output $S_t \in \mathbb{R}^{l \times cij}$ represents all features extracted from temporal demand matrices separately, which can be denoted as:

$$S_t = [\alpha_l | l = t - L, ..., t - 2, t - 1] \tag{4}$$

4.2   Temporal Module

Since the transportation data is a type of time series, we apply the temporal module to capture the temporal dependence of the sequential demand matrices. In the task of sequence learning, Recurrent Neural Networks (RNN) have achieved good results [20]. The incorporation of Long Short-Term Memory (LSTM) overcomes the shortage of traditional recurrent networks that learning long-term dependencies is difficult [7,8]. Some previous works [17,24] have proved the great performance of LSTM in processing traffic sequential data. To follow them, we apply the LSTM network for the BSS sequential data in our temporal module.

Briefly speaking, LSTM maintains a memory cell c_t to accumulate the previous sequence information. Specifically, at time t, given an input x_t, the LSTM uses an input gate i_t and a forget gate f_t to update its memory cell c_t, and uses an output gate o_t to control the hidden state h_t.

In our model, the LSTM net takes S_t as input, which is the output of the spatial module. We use $\beta^t \in \mathbb{R}^d$ to represent the output of the LSTM net in our temporal module.

4.3   Dynamic Interval Module

Though the sequential demand data of BSS holds a kind of trend during the day, their changes will vary according to different time intervals. Therefore, we propose a dynamic interval module that extracts temporal information from each hour and then apply them to influence the learning strategies of the main spatial-temporal network directly.

To encourage such a learning mode, some meta-learning methods [2, 22] have been proposed to create a siamese-like network in which one network is responsible for generating learning weights for another. Inspired by these advanced works, we also apply a similar network structure to map (time) to be directly the learning weights of the top fully connected layer in the main network.

In our module, for the input number of hours ranging from 0 to 23, we first use $GloVe$ [16] to embed the numbers into feature vectors $V_t \in \mathbb{R}^h$. After that, our Interval Net in the module transforms embedding vectors to features whose dimension is the same as the learnable parameters in the fully connected layer of the main network, including weights and biases. The generated vectors are then directly assigned to be the values in the fully connected layer, and the Dynamic Interval Module participates in the back-propagation process in an end-to-end manner.

However, it is too difficult and too large for parameters in Interval Net to learn, since the parameters space of the Interval Net grows quadratically with the number of the output units. Following [2], we construct a factorized representation of the output weights that is decomposed of 2 operating matrices and a diagonal matrix as Fig. 5 shows, which is analogous to the Singular Value Decomposition. By this way, the parameters in the Interval Net needed to be learned only grow linearly with the number of output units. The whole process can be formulated as

$$W_{FC} = O' \, diag(W(V)) \, O \qquad (5)$$

where $W_{FC} \in \mathbb{R}^{k \times d}$ is the generated weights for the fully connected layer. $W(V) \in \mathbb{R}^a$ represents the output vector of the Linear layer W in Interval Net while $diag(\cdot)$ is the diagonal operating to transform the vector $W(V)$ to a diagonal matrix. As a consequence, the net only needs to generate low-dimensional parameters for each time interval. In addition, two matrices $O \in \mathbb{R}^{a \times d}$ and

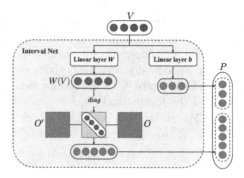

Fig. 5. Internal structure of Interval Net

$O' \in \mathbb{R}^{k \times a}$, where $k = 2 \times i \times j$, project $diag(W(V))$ again to keep the same dimension with the fully connected layer.

Similarly, biases of the fully connected layer are also generated as following:

$$b_{FC} = b(V) \tag{6}$$

where b_{FC} represents the generated biases for the fully connected layer. $b(V) \in \mathbb{R}^k$ denotes the output vector of the linear layer b in Interval Net. After the above operation, we obtain $\langle W_{FC}, b_{FC} \rangle$ as the parameters P in Fig. 3 of the fully connected layer (FC).

To get the final results, the fully connected layer takes the output of temporal module $\beta^t \in \mathbb{R}^d$ as input for the time interval t. As we mentioned, P consists of the weights $W_{FC} \in \mathbb{R}^{k \times d}$ and biases $b_{FC} \in \mathbb{R}^k$ where $k = 2 \times i \times j$. Therefore, the formulation of the layer can be expressed as follows:

$$\hat{M}_t = f(W_{FC}\beta^t + b_{FC}) \tag{7}$$

where the $f(\cdot)$ denotes the non-linear activation function of prediction layer. $\hat{M}_t \in \mathbb{R}^k$ represents the predicted demand matrix of the ground truth M_t.

4.4   Implementation Details

In the experiments, we set the length of the input sequence L to 3. In the spatial module, each Conv Block has 2 ResUnits with the same structure. That is, it contains 2 convolutional layers with each layer followed by a batch normalization (BN) [9] and a residual link. All the convolutional layers in the Conv Block have 32 filters. The size of each filter is set to 3×3 with $stride = 1$. In the temporal module, the LSTM net has 1 hidden layer with 1024 neurons. The activation functions used in the fully connected layer and Conv Blocks are *ReLU* while *LeakyReLU* is used as the activation function at the linear layers in the dynamic interval module. We optimize our model via Adam [10] optimization by minimizing the Mean Squared Error (MSE) loss between the predicted result and the ground truth. The learning rate and the weight decay are set to 10^{-3}

and 5e−5 respectively. For the training data, 90% of it is for training and the remaining 10% is chosen as a validation set for early-stop. We implement our network with Pytorch [15] and train it for 200 epochs on 2 NVIDIA 1080Ti GPUs.

5 Experiment

5.1 Dataset

In the paper, we use the NYC Bike dataset in 2014, from Apr. 1st to Sept. 30th. We treat the data for the last 10 days as the testing data and others as training data. We set one hour as the length of a time interval. The total number of orders and time intervals in the dataset are 5,359,944 and 4,392 respectively. And the number of stations used in the dataset is 128. The dataset can be collected from the website of Citi-Bike system[1].

5.2 Evaluation Metric

We use Rooted Mean Square Error (RMSE) and Mean Absolute Error (MAE) as the metrics to evaluate the performance of our model and the baselines, which are defined as:

$$RMSE = \sqrt{\frac{1}{z}\sum_i (y_i - \hat{y}_i)^2} \tag{8}$$

$$MAE = \frac{1}{z}\sum_{i=1}^{z} |y_i - \hat{y}_i| \tag{9}$$

where $\hat{y}_i$ and y_i denote the predicted value and ground truth respectively, and z is the number of all predicted values.

5.3 Baselines

We compare our STDI-Net with the following baselines:

- **Historical average (HA):** Historical Average (HA) predicts the future demand by averaging the historical demands.
- **Auto-regressive integrated moving average (ARIMA):** Auto-Regression Integrated Moving Average (ARIMA) is a well-known model used for time series prediction.
- **Lasso regression (Lasso):** Lasso regression is a linear regression method with L_1 regularization.
- **Ridge regression (Ridge):** Ridge regression is a linear regression method with L_2 regularization.

---

[1] https://www.citibikenyc.com/system-data.

- **Multiple layer perception (MLP):** MLP is a neural network with four hidden layers. The number of hidden units are 256, 256, 128, 128 respectively. The MLP predicts the demand matrix M^t by taking a sequence of the previous l demand matrix $[M^{t-l}, \ldots, M^{t-2}, M^{t-1}]$ as input.
- **ST-ResNet** [26]: ST-ResNet is a CNN-based model with residual blocks for traffic prediction, which used multiple CNN components to extract features from the historical data sequence.
- **DMVST-Net** [24]: DMVST-Net is a deep learning model which based on CNN and LSTM for taxi demand prediction. It also contains graph embedding to capture similar demand patterns among regions.
- **DeepSTN+** [12]: DeepSTN+ is a deep learning-based convolutional model for crowd flow prediction, which contains long range spatial dependence modeling, POI-based spatial information capturing, and a fusion mechanism for features extracted from different aspects.

Table 1. Comparison with baselines.

Method	RMSE	MAE
Historical average	10.7308	5.8374
ARIMA	10.4773	4.7005
Lasso regression	8.4947	3.6799
Ridge regression	8.4699	3.6984
Multiple layer perception	7.1888	3.3388
ST-ResNet	5.1249	2.7206
DMVST-Net	5.0595	2.3423
DeepSTN+	4.9060	2.4269
STDI-Net	**4.6339**	**2.1946**

5.4 Comparison with Baselines

Table 1 shows the testing results of our proposed model and baselines on the dataset. We can see that our STDI-Net achieves the lowest RMSE and MAE(4.6339 and 2.1946) among all the competing methods. The HA and ARIMA perform poorly, as they only consider the historical demand values for prediction. Because of the consideration of more context relationships among sequence, the linear regression methods (Lasso and Ridge) perform better than the above two methods. However, they do not extract more spatial-temporal information for prediction. The MLP further extracts features from the sequence and performs better than the above methods. However, the MLP does not model spatial or temporal dependency. The ST-ResNet achieves 5.1249 and 2.7206 for RMSE and MAE which is better than MLP due to the extracting of spatial features. Compared with ST-ResNet, DMVST-Net extracts joint spatial-temporal feature and similar demand patterns among regions, which further improve its performance for prediction. Compared with previous methods, DeepSTN+ explores spatial correlations from different aspects to reduce the prediction error. However, it doesn't consider about the influence of different time intervals. Our model further contributes a dynamic interval module which further improves the performance.

5.5   Comparison with Modules Combinations

Our full model consists of three modules for three types of information modeling. To explore the influence of different modules combinations on the task, we combine them and implement the following networks:

- **Spatial module + FC:** This network contains the spatial module of our proposed model and a fully connected layer. This network only extracts spatial features for prediction.
- **Temporal module + FC:** This network only uses the temporal module of our proposed model to capture the temporal information, and a fully connected layer is used to output the predicted results.
- **Spatial module + Temporal module + FC:** This method is the combination of the spatial module, temporal module, and a fully connected layer. In this method, we model joint spatial-temporal information without considering the influence of different time intervals.
- **Spatial module + Dynamic Interval module:** In this network, we combine the spatial module and the dynamic interval module of our proposed model, to capture spatial information, and the dynamic mappings for different time intervals.
- **Temporal module + Dynamic Interval module:** For this network, we use the temporal module and the dynamic interval module of our proposed model. This network models the temporal information, and generates the dynamic mappings for different time intervals.
- **STDI-Net:** Our proposed model, which models joint spatial-temporal information, and generates dynamic mappings for different time intervals.

Table 2 shows the results of the test. The RMSE and MAE of the spatial module + FC are 5.6558 and 2.6218 respectively, while that of the spatial module + dynamic interval module are 4.9077 and 2.3457. The results of the temporal module + FC achieve 5.2614 and 2.3914 while the RMSE and MAE of the temporal module + dynamic interval module are 4.7788 and 2.2582 respectively. We can see that compared with separate spatial or temporal module + fully connected layer, the performance of the combination with the dynamic interval module improves significantly. Furthermore, the spatial module + temporal module + FC achieves the results of 5.0832 and 2.3476, which are worse than that of our complete model. The results show that our dynamic interval module improves the performance significantly.

Table 2. Comparison with different modules combinations

Method	RMSE	MAE
Spatial + FC	5.6558	2.6218
Temporal + FC	5.2614	2.3914
Spatial + Temporal + FC	5.0832	2.3476
Spatial + Dynamic Interval	4.9077	2.3457
Temporal + Dynamic Interval	4.7788	2.2582
STDI-Net	**4.6339**	**2.1946**

5.6   Comparison with Variants of Our Model

The above experiments show that our proposed dynamic interval module achieves a good result in the demand prediction of BSS. However, we have not proved the rationality of the parameters-generated mode in the dynamic interval module. Besides, we also need to evaluate the effectiveness of the time-specific convolutional layers in our spatial module. In addition, the advantage of using *GloVe* need to be proved by comparing with the model that embed time intervals into vectors without the pre-trained *GloVe*. To address these questions, we construct the following three variants of our proposed model:

- **STDI-Net-fusion:** In this network, we apply a Linear layer in the Interval Net to transform the interval embedding vector to a feature, and then we concatenate it with the output of the temporal module. After that, a fully connected layer is used to output the predicted results.
- **Unified-Spatial Net:** This network is the variant of our proposed spatial module, which is used to evaluate the performance of applying the same filters in different temporal indexes. This model applies unified filters for each index of the sequence in all convolutional layers, and a fully connected layer is used after convolutional layers. Note that, in the Unified-spatial Net, we use the same Conv Blocks structure as our proposed STDI-Net.
- **STDI-Net-embedding:** In this model, we apply a learnable embedding layer to embed the hours' number instead of using the pre-trained *GloVe* to embed them.

Table 3 shows the results of the above three variants of our model. We can see that our spatial module + FC (5.6558 and 2.6218 for RMSE and MAE) outperforms Unified-Spatial Net (6.1493 and 2.9533 for RMSE and MAE), that means, our proposed time-specific convolution layers perform better than applying same convolutional filters in different temporal indexes. Otherwise, STDI-Net-fusion achieves 4.8149 for RMSE and 2.2995 for MAE, which are worse than our STDI-Net (4.6339 and 2.1946 respectively). Therefore, our parameters-generated mode is better than the fusion way.

Due to applying a trainable embedding layer instead of using a pre-trained model (*GloVe*), the STDI-Net-embedding (4.6154 and 2.1783) has more learnable parameters than STDI-Net (4.6339 and 2.1946). Therefore it can perform

Table 3. Comparison with variants of our model

Method	RMSE	MAE
Unified-Spatial Net	6.1493	2.9533
Spatial module + FC	**5.6558**	**2.6218**
STDI-Net-fusion	4.8149	2.2995
STDI-Net-embedding	4.6154	2.1783
STDI-Net	**4.6339**	**2.1946**

better than our STDI-Net. However, its performance has not improved significantly (0.4% and 0.7% for RMSE and MAE respectively) with additional parameters. That means, our STDI-Net can perform almost as well as STDI-Net-embedding with less parameters than it. To reduce the number of learnable weights, we apply *GloVe* to embed hours instead of using an additional embedding layer to embed them.

5.7 Influence of Sequence Length and Number of ResUnits

In this section, we explore the influence of the length of the input sequence and the influence of the number of ResUnits.

Figure 6a shows the prediction results of different input sequence length. We can see that our method achieves best performance when sequence length is set to 4. The prediction error decreases with the increasing of sequence length from 1 to 4, that means the temporal dependency plays an important roles in the task. However, as the length of sequence increases to more than 4 h, the performance of our model slightly degrades and it has a fluctuation. One potential reason is that with the length of the input sequence growing, many more parameters need to be learned, which makes the training harder.

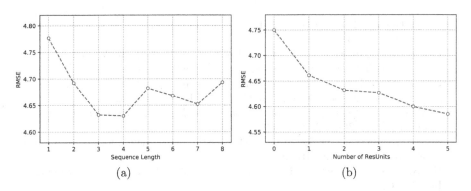

Fig. 6. (a) RMSE with respect to the length of the input sequence. (b) RMSE with respect to the number of ResUnits in a Conv Block.

In Fig. 6b, we show the performance of our model with respect to the number of ResUnits. We can see that the prediction error decreases as the number of ResUnits growing from 0 to 5. That means, with the number of convolutional layers rising from 1 to 11, the performance of our model becomes better. This due to the fact that the original feature maps are convoluted with their local correlations as layers deepen, which makes deeper layers have larger receptive fields. As we know, larger receptive fields can capture more spatial correlations. Therefore, the model can learn more spatial information as layers deepen to improve its performance.

6   Conclusion and Discussion

In this paper, we propose a novel deep learning-based method for demand prediction of Bike Sharing System (BSS). Our model considers the extraction of joint spatial-temporal feature and time-specific convolutional layers with residual links. Furthermore, we contribute a dynamic interval module to include the factor that different time intervals have a strong influence on demand prediction in BSS by generating different feature mappings for different time intervals. We evaluate our model on the NYC Bike dataset, and the results show that our model significantly outperforms the competing baselines. In the future, we will consider some other features to further improve the performance of our model, such as meteorology data, holiday data. And we will consider the more dependent relationship of stations, such as use Graph Convolutional Network (GCN) to extract the spatial feature among stations.

Acknowledgments. This work was supported in part by the National Key Research and Development Project under grant 2019YFB1706101, in part by the Science-Technology Foundation of Chongqing, China under grant cstc2019jscx-mbdx0083.

References

1. Andrychowicz, M., et al.: Learning to learn by gradient descent by gradient descent. In: NeurIPS (2016)
2. Bertinetto, L., Henriques, J.F., Valmadre, J., Torr, P., Vedaldi, A.: Learning feed-forward one-shot learners. In: NeurIPS, pp. 523–531 (2016)
3. Chiang, M.F., Hoang, T.A., Lim, E.P.: Where are the passengers?: a grid-based gaussian mixture model for taxi bookings. In: SIGSPATIAL (2015)
4. DeMaio, P.: Bike-sharing: history, impacts, models of provision, and future. J. Public Transp. **12**(4), 41–56 (2009)
5. Finn, C., Abbeel, P., Levine, S.: Model-agnostic meta-learning for fast adaptation of deep networks. In: ICML (2017)
6. He, K., Zhang, X., Ren, S., Sun, J.: Deep residual learning for image recognition. In: CVPR (2016)
7. Hochreiter, S., Schmidhuber, J.: Long short-term memory. Neural Comput. **9**(8), 1735–1780 (1997)

8. Informatik, F., Bengio, Y., Frasconi, P., Schmidhuber, J.: Gradient flow in recurrent nets: the difficulty of learning long-term dependencies. A Field Guide to Dynamical Recurrent Neural Networks (2003)
9. Ioffe, S., Szegedy, C.: Batch normalization: Accelerating deep network training by reducing internal covariate shift. In: ICML (2015)
10. Kingma, D.P., Ba, J.: Adam: a method for stochastic optimization. arXiv preprint arXiv:1412.6980 (2014)
11. Krizhevsky, A., Sutskever, I., Hinton, G.E.: ImageNet classification with deep convolutional neural networks. In: NeurIPS, pp. 1097–1105 (2012)
12. Lin, Z., Feng, J., Lu, Z., Li, Y., Jin, D.: DeepSTN+: context-aware spatial-temporal neural network for crowd flow prediction in metropolis. In: AAAI (2019)
13. Moreira-Matias, L., Gama, J., Ferreira, M., Mendes-Moreira, J., Damas, L.: Predicting taxi-passenger demand using streaming data. IEEE Trans. Intell. Transp. Syst. **14**(3), 1393–1402 (2013)
14. Pan, B., Demiryurek, U., Shahabi, C.: Utilizing real-world transportation data for accurate traffic prediction. In: ICDM (2012)
15. Paszke, A., et al.: Pytorch: an imperative style, high-performance deep learning library. In: NeurIPS (2019)
16. Pennington, J., Socher, R., Manning, C.: Glove: global vectors for word representation. In: EMNLP (2014)
17. Qiu, Z., Liu, L., Li, G., Wang, Q., Xiao, N., Lin, L.: Taxi origin-destination demand prediction with contextualized spatial-temporal network. In: ICME, pp. 760–765 (2019)
18. Shaheen, S.A., Guzman, S., Zhang, H.: Bikesharing in Europe, the Americas, and Asia: past, present, and future. Transp. Res. Rec. **2143**(1), 159–167 (2010)
19. Shekhar, S., Williams, B.M.: Adaptive seasonal time series models for forecasting short-term traffic flow. Transp. Res. Rec. **2024**(1), 116–125 (2007)
20. Sutskever, I., Vinyals, O., Le, Q.V.: Sequence to sequence learning with neural networks. In: NeurIPS, pp. 3104–3112 (2014)
21. Wang, D., Cao, W., Li, J., Ye, J.: DeepSD: supply-demand prediction for online car-hailing services using deep neural networks. In: ICDE, pp. 243–254 (2017)
22. Wang, X., Yu, F., Wang, R., Darrell, T., Gonzalez, J.E.: TAFE-Net: task-aware feature embeddings for low shot learning. In: CVPR (2019)
23. Wu, F., Wang, H., Li, Z.: Interpreting traffic dynamics using ubiquitous urban data. In: SIGSPACIAL (2016)
24. Yao, H., et al.: Deep multi-view spatial-temporal network for taxi demand prediction. In: AAAI (2018)
25. Yu, R., Li, Y., Shahabi, C., Demiryurek, U., Liu, Y.: Deep learning: a generic approach for extreme condition traffic forecasting. In: SIAM (2017)
26. Zhang, J., Zheng, Y., Qi, D.: Deep spatio-temporal residual networks for citywide crowd flows prediction. In: AAAI (2017)
27. Zhang, J., Zheng, Y., Qi, D., Li, R., Yi, X.: DNN-based prediction model for spatio-temporal data. In: SIGSPATIAL (2016)
28. Zhao, J., Xu, J., Zhou, R., Zhao, P., Liu, C., Zhu, F.: On prediction of user destination by sub-trajectory understanding: a deep learning based approach. In: CIKM 2018, pp. 1413–1422 (2018)

Simulation-Based Approaches

A Simulation-Based Approach for the Behavioural Analysis of Cancer Pathways

Agastya Silvina⬛ⓘ, Guilherme Redeker⬛ⓘ, Thais Webber⬛ⓘ,
and Juliana Bowles⁽⊠⁾ⓘ

School of Computer Science, University of St Andrews, St Andrews, KY16 9SX, UK
{as362,gr60,tcwds,jkfb}@st-andrews.ac.uk

Abstract. Cancer pathway is the name given to a patient's journey from initial suspicion of cancer through to a confirmed diagnosis and, if applicable, the definition of a treatment plan. Typically, a cancer patient will undergo a series of procedures, which we designate as events, during their cancer care. The initial stage of the pathway, from suspected diagnosis to confirmed diagnosis and start of a treatment is called *cancer waiting time* (CWT). This paper focuses on the modelling and analysis of the CWT. Health boards are under pressure to ensure that the duration of CWT satisfies predefined targets. In this paper, we first create the visual representation of the pathway obtained from real patient data at a given health board, and then compare it with the standardised pathway considered by the board to find and flag a deviation in the execution of the cancer pathway. Next, we devise a discrete event simulation model for the cancer waiting time pathway. The input data is obtained from historical records of patients. The outcomes from this analysis highlight the pathway bottlenecks and transition times which may be used to reveal potential improvements for CWT in the future.

Keywords: Cancer pathway · Cancer waiting time · Discrete event simulation · Process modelling

1 Introduction

Cancer is a condition where cells in some part of the human body reproduce at an uncontrollable rate. The cancer cells, instead of working together with the system, become another entity of the body, which could potentially jeopardise human health and well-being [6]. Patients with chronic cancer (e.g., lung cancer) have to undergo a series of treatments to attempt the eradication of the disease [10].

In the UK, before a patient undergoes a set of procedures that have been agreed upon by the board members and consultants, there is a period of waiting, usually ranging from 14 to 62 days[1]. This period of waiting before the decision

---

[1] https://www.england.nhs.uk/wp-content/uploads/2015/03/delivering-cancer-wait-times.pdf.

This research is partially supported by the DataLab.

© Springer Nature Switzerland AG 2021
J. Bowles et al. (Eds.): DataMod 2020, LNCS 12611, pp. 57–71, 2021.
https://doi.org/10.1007/978-3-030-70650-0_4

to treat the patient is known as *Cancer Waiting Time* (CWT) and has several planned activities depending on the patient's health condition, further tests evaluations and medical board meetings[2].

The CWT pathway for lung cancer treatment provided by the UK National Health Service (NHS) board is illustrated on Fig. 1. Within the first time period (first 2 weeks), patients will be referred by their general practitioner (GP) and then undergo several tests. During the next 14 to 28 days, the patient will have further tests. Once the board agrees on the first treatment, the decision will be made within the next 28 to 62 days. Usually, the waiting time for a decision should not exceed a 62 days period. However, there are many cases when that happens. Further, lung cancer has a poor prognosis: over half of people diagnosed with lung cancer die within one year of diagnosis and around 17.8% within the 5-year survival [10]. Hence, it becomes necessary to decrease the waiting time from the GP referral to their first treatment.

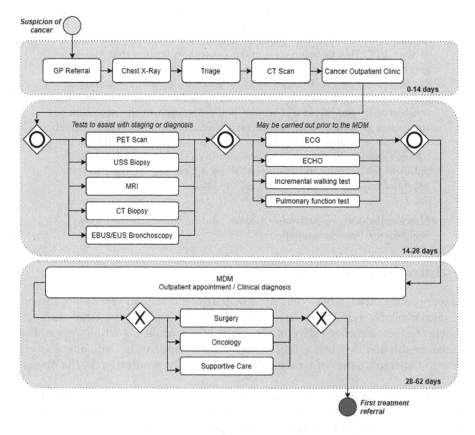

Fig. 1. Lung cancer pathway based on NHS Board

---

[2] Standards: https://www.isdscotland.org/Health-Topics/Waiting-Times/Cancer/Guidance/.

By streamlining the process of analysing the CWT dataset (e.g., through simulation) and comparing the 'actual' pathway patients experience versus what the NHS Board considers the pathway to be, we can highlight bottlenecks and transition times that exhibit high variability across patients. These insights will provide quantitative evidence that might be useful to design follow-up interventions. For example, policies to reduce the variability of specific transition times between activities may lead to overall improvements in CWT and reduction of the cumulative delays.

Discrete event simulation (DES) has been widely used in many sectors including for healthcare processes management [3,5,8]. DES allows healthcare professionals, for instance, to assess the efficiency of the existing healthcare delivery system. It has many usages ranging from forecasting the impact of changes in patient flow [5], examining the resources needed and available within a hospital [4], to observing the improvement of patient experience in an emergency department [1]. Related to this work, a DES model has been developed in the field of radiation therapy to reduce waiting time as well as to improve the treatment process planning [2]. Another recent work [7] focused on patient scheduling decisions related to chemotherapy in order to efficiently use medical resources and provide timely access to cancer treatment. Hence, DES provides the ability to investigate the complex relationship between various parameters (e.g., patient arrival rates and activities service times) through a stochastic model able to produce statistical estimates on the metrics of interest (e.g., waiting time).

The entities in a DES model (e.g., patients) are visiting service stations that compose the process, and sometimes they need to wait until service can be provided. This means that the demand for service has exceeded the capacity to provide the service readily. This information allows the healthcare professional to observe operational processes, simulating alternatives that can be used to reconfigure the existing pathway, to improve its performance, and to plan (change or reduce) its activities, without altering the present process execution while conducting such scenarios experiments [5,8]. By treating lung cancer care from the first GP referral to the first treatment as a series of discrete events, we can simulate the cancer pathway with a DES approach allowing us to understand the overall treatment process, its complexities, patient journey and bottlenecks during the pathway.

This paper is structured as follows. In Sect. 2, we present the CWT dataset and the extraction of quantitative information through database queries development. The simulation modelling approach, the generated pathway and input modelling are discussed in Sect. 3. In Sect. 4 we present the approach used to validate our simulation model. Section 5 discusses the simulation scenarios and the findings. We conclude with suggestions for further work in Sect. 6.

2   Data Analysis and Queries Development

To analyse the cancer pathway dataset compatibility with the steps established by the cancer pathway guideline as shown in Fig. 1, we acquired the dataset for lung cancer from three different hospitals within an NHS health board. The dataset contains 642 patients from 2016 to 2019 with lung cancer within NHS Lothian. It gathers the information regarding the outpatient (i.e., patient not formally admitted to the hospital), inpatient treatment (i.e., patient formally admitted to the hospital), and patients' orders (e.g., prescriptions, test's appointments). It also contains the information related to the type of the event (e.g., *services* for the outpatients, *order_item* for orders), the event start date (i.e., when the event is registered to the system), event execution date (i.e., the exact start date of the event) and event finish date.

The modelling effort proposed in this paper aims to help the health professionals to analyse lung cancer pathway behaviour as a complex process (CWT) and assess its execution issues. For the first milestone, we focus on the whole observed waiting time without splitting the events based on each waiting time category (i.e., 0–14 days, 14–28 days, 28–62 days). Even though the board states the splitting, in reality, patients do not strictly follow the procedure guideline.

The guideline establishes that several tests could be performed prior to a final decision on the treatment, at any time, and it is up to the medical professionals to define the ones appropriate to each case following the patient's case development. The overall care process is rather complex and could take considerable time to schedule appointments and tests, reschedule, execute procedures and analyse/deliver results, depending on available resources and specific test characteristics. Thus, after discussions with healthcare professionals, we use the dataset to describe the behaviour of the CWT process, and then use the gathered information to create the DES model. We are interested in calculating the time patients spend on (parts of) the pathway (i.e., added time), and the number of patients flowing throughout the process (i.e., between activities), as well as calculate the elapsed days according to each milestone on the guideline, as follows:

- We calculate the *number of patients* in the dataset and the *added service time* observed between the first GP Referral to the definitive Multidisciplinary Meeting (MDM). MDM is an important event that happens at least once before starting the patient's treatment. In this meeting, the healthcare professionals determine whether a patient needs further care. The definitive MDM is the last MDM before starting the patient' treatment (e.g., radiotherapy, surgery, palliative care).
- We calculate the *number of patients* undergoing each category of tests requested (i.e., *CT Scan, CT Biopsy, PET, Bronch/EBUS, Surgical staging/Biopsy*).
- We calculate the *added service time* observed from the first outpatient (OP) appointment (in the Cancer Outpatient Clinic) to the definitive MDM.
- We calculate the *number of patients* who have more than one outpatient (OP) appointment prior to the definitive MDM.
- We calculate the *added service time* observed between Triage to the first OP appointment.
- We calculate the *service time* per order, i.e., for each test: CT Scan, PET Scan, CT Biopsy, grouped by the type of first treatment given to the patients.

We design the SQL queries to get the information directly from the *Trak* Oracle database to calculate each requested observation. The design of these queries is similar to each other. First, we categorise the event based on the *service* (i.e., for the outpatient) and *order_item* (i.e., for orders). There are more than 1,000 different *services* and *order_items*. However, there is no list to categorise these events. Together with the health professionals, we created a list of categories. For some *services*/*order_items*, we use keywords (e.g., CT, PET). Once we get the list of the *services*/*order_items* (event), we perform a manual check. For the other events without a reliable keyword, we choose the event that was performed to a significant number of patients, i.e., more than 50 patients.

- Once we categorise the service, we calculated the *elapsed days* between the categorised events and the first treatment date.
- With the elapsed days, we determine the first (or last) events (i.e., the definitive MDM is the one which has the highest elapsed days).
- Hence, we can calculate the *added service time* and the *number of patients* between various events.

From these observations we can derive an observed pathway which is the basis of our simulation model.

3   Simulation Modelling and DES

After analysing the dataset, we simulate the CWT process by creating a discrete event simulation (DES). We want to compare the pathway in the guideline (refer to Fig. 1) and the pathway that emerged from the data. By knowing the difference between the two, we can then further investigate and perform analysis for the CWT process within the health board. In this case study, we applied a simulation modelling process [8] in four basic steps (problem statement, process activities identification, flow analysis, metric(s) of interest, and model refinement) as follows.

1. *Problem statement*: we aim to simulate the pathway from the first time patients are being referred by their general practitioner (GP)/the first time the patients are seen in the hospital until the start of their first treatment. The time elapsed between these two events is defined as cancer waiting time. We are interested in finding the events/occasions when elapsed days exceed 62 days (i.e., the recommended maximum days for cancer waiting time according to the guideline).
2. *Process activities and execution flow*: we abstract the activities and process behaviour from the guideline as shown in Fig. 1 as well as matching with the available CWT data. We determine the composition of the process in terms of entities (e.g, patients) and activities/events (e.g., CT Scan, MDM, and so on) that we assign into the appropriate simulation flow. The process starts with patient arrival event (GP referral) and ends with first treatment referral, for each patient. Each activity in the process represents a service

(an event) to a patient performed within a service time distribution. The process flow can contain one or more decision gateways, each indicating two or more output probabilities (or conditions) to follow. In our case, we present two gateways ruled by probabilities. The event scheduling process of DES tools [8] presents a time advance mechanism that guarantees that at least one event is scheduled when simulation starts and that it will consume an event list during execution. The simulation execution captures quantitative information until a defined stop criteria is reached. Usually, the arrival event configuration dictates the simulation continuance (or halt), i.e., the maximum number of entities arrivals to simulate. Also a desired simulation length (e.g., duration in days) can be defined prior to execution.

3. *Metric(s) of interest*: once all the activities of the process (i.e., events in the model) have been defined, we choose the performance metric to assess within our simulation (i.e., waiting time, elapsed days between activities, and so on). Variables and counters can be coded by the simulation analyst to provide additional quantitative results on the sample journeys, as long as required.

4. *Model refinement*: after the process flow and activities have been defined, we indicate the model parameters. They represent fitted probability distributions to be applied at each activity (event) determining their behaviour expressed as service times, and as inter-arrival time regarding the patients arrival (GP referrals). The output probabilities on gateways are acquired from further statistical analysis over the dataset concerning all patients' journey. Once these timing information are set for each component in the DES, we can run the model and perform refinements on parameters, counters, variables, and overall behaviour to match the actual process according to the validation framework adopted, until we have a coherent base model checked through a statistic measurement of the dataset.

Before we simulate the CWT, we simplify the pathway as shown in Fig. 2. The focus is on finding the process bottleneck that may represent delays on the most common procedures (events) the patients undergo from their first GP

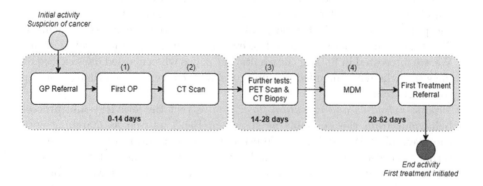

Fig. 2. Simplified lung cancer pathway obtained by dataset analysis

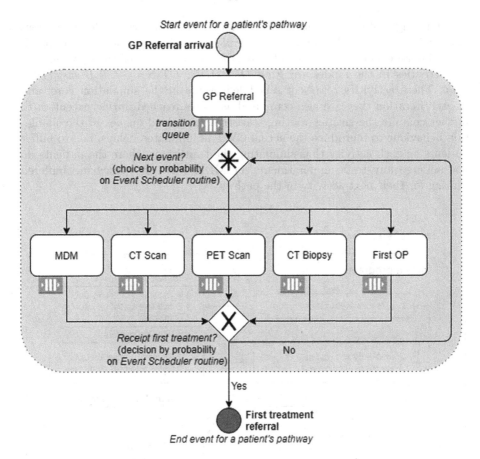

Fig. 3. Observed lung cancer pathway as a simulation (DES) model

appointment to their first treatment. Hence, for our model, we choose several events during the CWT pathway based on the number of occurrences and categorised them in four activities in which a patient can be at any time: (1) First appointment (*First OP*), such as Triage, Cancer Outpatient appointment; (2) *CT Scan* (i.e., primary test before further tests); (3) Most common further tests (i.e., *CT Biopsy* and *PET Scan*); and (4) *MDM*. The *GP referral* and *First treatment referral* are considered as start and end events in the pathway, respectively. After choosing and categorising these events, we update the current pathway. Figure 2 shows the simplified pathway with activities and events within the milestones.

Further, we compare the simplified pathway with the pathway captured from the dataset. From the dataset, we find that the CWT does not strictly follow the guideline regarding the pathway. Instead, the pathway is an iterative process as shown in Fig. 3. From our observation, any event can happen in any particular order. Tests, appointments, and discussions are events that may happen several times in a patient journey.

Thus, Fig. 3 also represents the DES model. The start event ruled by patient inter-arrival time distribution is *GP referral*. The end event ruled by a probability within an exclusive decision gateway is *First treatment referral*. The remaining activities in the model are *First OP, MDM, CT Scan, CT Biopsy, PET Scan*. These activities represent scheduled events in the simulation core, and at each iteration they are also computed as states reached during execution to further compile the entities routing statistics. We added queues in the simulation behaviour to reproduce the actual CWT accumulated delays, i.e., to buffer patients on each activity thus simulating the transitions where the patients do not undergo any tests, appointments, or MDM but surely they are buffered waiting for their next activity in the pathway.

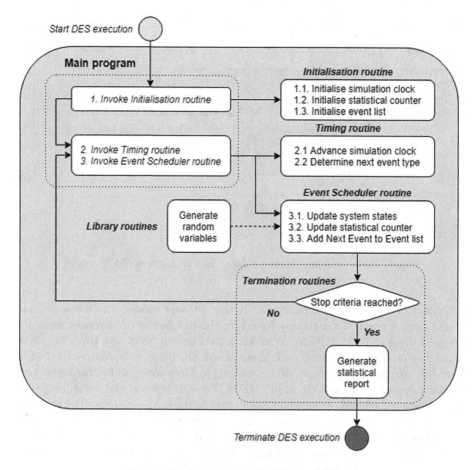

Fig. 4. Simulation core flow (DES routines)

We focus on determining the process activities (or in this case, also its events) and the process flow (i.e., including activities partial ordering) as the other

---

Algorithm 1: FIT_BEST_DISTRIBUTION

Input: *data*
Result: *best_distribution, parameters*
distributions ← list of distributions

dist_results ← []

for *dist in distributions* **do**
  parameters ← dist.fit(data)
  D, p ← kstest(data, dist, parameters)
  dist_results.append((dist, D, p, parameters))
end

best_distribution, parameters ← best(dist_results)

---

simulation parameters and components are correctly handled by the simulation framework *Salabim*[3].

Salabim is an open-source object-oriented developed for DES of complex control in logistics and production environments. It follows the methodology of process description as demonstrated in *Simula* and later in *Prosim, Must* and *Tomas*. As a python package, it allows the use of other powerful python libraries (e.g., for statistical processing, presentation, machine learning). It also has an integrated animation engine which eases the manual observation of process flow for the user (i.e., the healthcare professionals).

The model description we presented in Fig. 3 is coded within the *Salabim* simulation core, which is illustrated in Fig. 4 with important routines and main program flow.

To determine the distributions for the simulation parameters, we use the *Kolmogorov-Smirnov* test (*kstest*). The *kstest* compares the two sample statistical distributions. It is a non-parametric test which does not require the data to follow the normal distribution. When we compare the possible distributions (e.g., *normal, exponential*) to the dataset, we get the D *statistic* and p value. The D *statistic* is the maximum absolute difference between two distribution functions. By comparing the D *statistic* and p value for each distribution (i.e., minimum value), we can determine the best fit distribution for the data. The procedure is shown in Algorithm 1. The list of distributions is composed of 12 distributions, i.e., we identified six types of events, and for each event, we fit two distinct distributions. One distribution for the time needed for patients to undergo the particular event, and the second distribution is for the transition time between the current event to the next one. Table 1 shows each activity and its service time distribution provided by the dataset statistical analysis.

The execution flow (refer to Fig. 3) schedules events to patients in a FIFO (*First-in/First-out*) policy, and the flow can reach two possible decision

---

[3] More information on simulation framework can be found on https://www.salabim. org/.

Table 1. Cancer Waiting Time pathway simulation information

EVENTS/ACTIVITIES	FITTED PROBABILITY DISTRIBUTIONS
GP Referral arrival	Interval time: *norm (2.33, 1.76)*
GP Referral transition	Interval time: *genextreme (−0.36, 4.77, 4.86)*
First OP	Service time: *constant (1 day)*
First OP transition	Service time: *genextreme (−0.23, 8.53, 7.56)*
CT Scan	Service time: *genextreme (−0.73, 4.70, 4.73)*
CT Scan transition	Service time: *genextreme (−0.45, 7.25, 6.27)*
CT Biopsy	Service time: *exponweib (1.47, 1.94, −0.997, 14.92)*
CT Biopsy transition	Service time: *genextreme (−0.13, 6.36, 4.18)*
PET Scan	Service time: *genextreme (−0.037, 13.69, 4.29)*
PET Scan transition	Service time: *genextreme (−0.13, 6.36, 4.18)*
MDM	Service time: *constant (1 day)*
MDM transition	Service time: *genextreme (−0.42, 8.65, 9.18)*

gateways. The first gateway represents a decision on the test(s) a patient will undergo during the pathway (i.e., schedule new event). This one determines, from the set of events, which one is the next to be scheduled in the simulation core, following the current simulation state (i.e., current activity the patient is undergoing) and simulation time counters. The second gateway determines a two-way probability that defines whether the entity (patient) will remain in the pathway executing activities (i.e., schedule new event), or leave the simulation since it received first treatment referral after MDM (i.e., schedule the end event). For the output probabilities, we calculate the number of transition from each activity (i.e., state). For each state, we set a different probability for determining the next state (e.g., according to the dataset, more than 50% of the patients will undergo *First OP* after *GP Referral*).

Figure 5 show the transition probabilities matrix used within the first decision gateway. The second gateway presents a conditional probability determining if patient had at least one MDM in his/her pathway. According to dataset, 49% of patients get their first treatment after *MDM*.

	GP Ref	First OP	CT Scan	PET Scan	CT Biopsy	MDM	First treatment
GP Referral	−	46%	9%	16%	7%	22%	−
First OP	−	23%	36%	7%	4%	9%	21%
CT Scan	−	21%	15%	11%	2%	2%	49%
PET Scan	−	23%	19%	6%	4%	8%	40%
CT Biopsy	−	18%	67%	4%	3%	3%	5%
MDM	−	18%	72%	2%	5%	−	2%
First treatment	−	−	−	−	−	−	100%

Fig. 5. Transition matrix with routing probabilities (%)

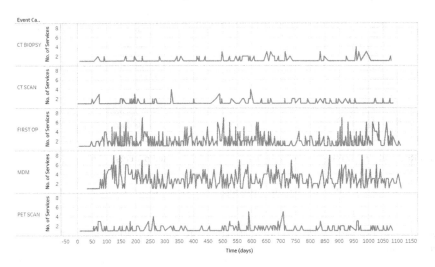

Fig. 6. Number of services for the CWT events

Even though our dataset contains no information regarding the number of resources (i.e., staff availability and the number of machines), we still incorporated the resources as parameters to guide the events scheduling. This way, we simulate varied scenarios of having more healthcare professionals and machines to the overall pathway activities. We calculate the number of resources by observing the maximum number of services and test orders that can happen in any days from our dataset. Figure 6 shows the number of services for the event we selected from 2016 to 2019, i.e., 1,150 days (3-year dataset). Though these numbers may not be an accurate representation of the number of resources, we can use it as starting point before we obtain the information (e.g., from interviews, survey or new dataset) regarding the resources capacity and availability.

4   Model Validation

The input data modelling provided fitted distributions to service times in all activities as well as patient inter-arrival rate concerning GP referrals. Also, the decision gateways probabilities are set with the compilation of all occurrences in the complete pathway, for all patients in the dataset. These input parameters were also discussed with healthcare professionals that actively participate in the CWT. After running the model for 365 simulated days, we observe the output (i.e., the sampling on the waiting time metric) in order to compare with real data, i.e., the average waiting time.

Figure 7 shows the waiting time distribution for both real data and simulation. Because the waiting time is not normally distributed, we use KS-test to compare both dataset distributions [9]. The result is $KS\text{-}statistic = 0.06984$ and $p\text{-}value = 0.152$. We know that if the KS statistic is small or the $p\text{-}value$ is high,

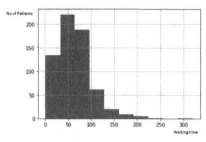
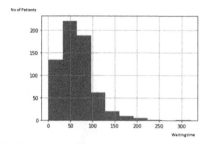

(a) Real patients' waiting time distribution   (b) Simulated patients' waiting time distribution

Fig. 7. Patients' waiting time distribution in days

then we cannot reject the hypothesis that the distributions of the two samples are the same.

Table 2. Patients' waiting time descriptive statistic

MEASURES	ACTUAL (DATASET)	SIMULATED
Mean	64.42	65.87
Std deviation	37.67	39.04
25% percentile	38	37
50% percentile	61	56
75% percentile	82	84

From the KS-test result, the *p-value* is high (more than 5% level of significance). Hence, we cannot reject that the distributions of the two samples are the same. The result of the descriptive statistic for both datasets as shown in Table 2 supports the close correspondence between the simulated and observed outcome. Therefore, our model can provide reasonable approximation and observation of the expected system behaviour.

5   Simulation Results

The purpose of creating a DES model of the CWT pathway is to simulate alternative scenarios to analyse bottlenecks and assess how to improve the current process. Table 3 shows the simulation scenarios and their respective results. We built multiple simulation models varying parameters such as Service Capacity (SC), Waiting Transition Time (WTT), and Service Time (ST). Thus, for each scenario, we modify the number of resources available (e.g., the number of machines), the transition time needed between each event, and the time needed for the service execution, respectively. The applied total simulation length is 365 days to collect statistics.

Results demonstrate that increasing in 50% the SC for *MDM* (Scenario (3)) or limiting the WTT after *MDM* in 5 days (Scenario (4)) we achieve the best improvements for patients, i.e., getting the first treatment before 62 days. Regarding Scenario (3), results show 62% of the patients started the treatment before 62 days whilst in the Scenario 4 the result is even better with 74% of patients simulated. These results show that *MDM* can be a bottleneck in the whole process because almost all patients will undergo *MDM* before getting their first treatment.

Table 3. CWT pathway simulated scenarios and their results

#	SIMULATED SCENARIOS *(varying parameters SC, WTT, and ST)*	MEAN WAITING TIME *95% CI (lower, upper)*	% *(<62days)*
(1)	50% increase SC for *First OP*	67.06 (59.78, 74.32)	56
(2)	Limit WTT after *First OP* (5 days)	63.99 (56.72, 71.25)	60
(3)	50% increase SC for *MDM*	59.85 (53.89, 65.82)	62
(4)	Limit WTT after *MDM* (5 days)	49.45 (44.14, 54.76)	74
(5)	50% increase SC for *CT Scan*	63.91 (56.97, 70.85)	59
(6)	Decrease ST on *CT Scan* (max 5 days)	64.44 (55.75, 73.13)	59
(7)	Limit WTT after *CT Scan* (5 days)	64.30 (57.61, 70.98)	58
(8)	50% increase SC for *CT Biopsy*	65.97 (59.12, 72.81)	53
(9)	Decrease ST on *CT Biopsy* (max 5 days)	69.56 (58.72, 80.40)	51
(10)	Limit WTT after *CT Biopsy* (5 days)	65.81 (58.11, 73.51)	54
(11)	50% increase SC for *PET Scan*	65.80 (54.37, 77.38)	53
(12)	Decrease ST on *PET Scan* (max 5 days)	65.03 (53.03, 77.05)	53
(13)	Limit WTT after *PET Scan* (5 days)	65.80 (54.37, 77.28)	53

We also observe that most delays are caused by the transition time instead of the service time/availability of resources (i.e., from the *First OP* and *MDM*). This is possible to check on Table 1, for instance, regarding *CT Scan* activity with probability distribution *genextreme(-0.73, 4.70, 4.73)* compared to *CT Scan* transition with distribution *genextreme(-0.45, 7.25, 6.27)*, where the service time may not be an issue in the pathway, but the transition delay between services. The later can include another tasks that may delay the CWT, like bureaucracy and scheduling, just to name a few.

Adding more resources (e.g., by increasing the service capacity) for *CT Scan*, *PET Scan* or *CT Biopsy* has less impact on the overall patient waiting time, according to the results from Scenario (5) to Scenario (13). However, comparing the improvements in those three tests services show that CT Scan has better results when adding more resources. Thus, maybe CT Scan has a bottleneck and it is the test activity that needs more resources to not exceed 62 days period. As shown in Table 3, the probability of *MDM* or *First OP* as the next state is higher when compared to the likelihood for the tests (i.e., *CT Scan*, *PET Scan*, *CT Biopsy*). Hence, the less impact.

Even though we can simulate the lung CWT events, our model has many limitations. First, we do not consider the other services (e.g., MRI, Head CT, Pulmonary function tests) by merging all of the other services into queue transition after the states. During the simulation run, due to the fitted distribution function (e.g., *exponential*, *gen-extreme*) the simulation result may contain more outliers compared to the dataset as shown in Fig. 7. Also, the number of resources in our model is based on estimations.

In the future, we can improve the simulation by incorporating more services and update the resource number and service time with the information given by the hospital (e.g., by interview or another dataset extraction). We can also improve the simulation by adding more detailed characteristics, such as adding the type of the first treatment of the patients. This may increase the simulation accuracy because the average waiting time is very based on the patients' first treatment, as shown in Table 3.

6 Conclusion

Overall, simulations scenarios can provide valuable information for improvements in the whole CWT process. Even with the model limitation such as the number of resources (e.g., number of CT Scan machines), we can highlight the process bottleneck related to the board meeting resources (e.g. doctors, professionals) availability and give a close observation regarding alternative scenarios for the lung CWT.

The main bottlenecks of the lung CWT are related to the board meeting, i.e., the MDM state and the MDM transition. Additionally, regarding the tests' activities we exposed that the CT Scan is the one which could improve the CWT if more resources were available. Once we can add more activities, such as other tests, in the pathway from collecting integral CWT dataset within hospital database, we can fine-tune the service time and number of resources. DES can help to provide insights on process bottlenecks and improve the overall cancer care for the lung CWT. In future, more detail should be added in the simulation model to gain a better understanding of the process behaviour and clarify the transition delays in CWT.

References

1. Abo-Hamad, W., Arisha, A.: Simulation-based framework to improve patient experience in an emergency department. Eur. J. Oper. Res. **224**, 154–166 (2013)
2. Aivas, I., et al.: Reducing patient wait times for radiation therapy and improving treatment planning: a discrete-event simulation model. Clin. Oncol. **29** (2017). https://doi.org/10.1016/j.clon.2017.01.039
3. Bangsow, S.: Use Cases of Discrete Event Simulation - Appliance and Research. Springer, Heidelberg (2012). https://doi.org/10.1007/978-3-642-28777-0
4. Baril, C., Gascon, V., Miller, J., Bounhol, C.: The importance of considering resource's tasks when modeling healthcare services with discrete-event simulation: an approach using work sampling method. J. Simul. **11**, 103–114 (2017)

5. Günal, M., Pidd, M.: Discrete event simulation for performance modelling in health care: a review of the literature. J. Simul. **4**, 42–51 (2010)
6. Hochhauser, J.S.T.D.: Cancer and its Management, 6th edn. Wiley-Blackwell, Hoboken (2010)
7. Liu, E., Ma, X., Sauré, A., Weber, L., Puterman, M.L., Tyldesley, S.: Improving access to chemotherapy through enhanced capacity planning and patient scheduling. IISE Trans. Healthcare Syst. Eng. **9**(1), 1–13 (2019)
8. Rossetti, M.D.: Simulation Modeling and Arena, 2nd edn. Wiley Press, Hoboken (2010)
9. Young, I.T.: Proof without prejudice: use of the Kolmogorov-Smirnov test for the analysis of histograms from flow systems and other sources. J. Histochem. Cytochem. **25**, 935–941 (1977)
10. Zappa, C., Mousa, S.A.: Non-small cell lung cancer: current treatment and future advances. Transl. Lung Cancer Res. **5**(3), 288–300 (2016). https://doi.org/10.21037/tlcr.2016.06.07

Discovering the Impact of Notifications on Social Network Addiction

Lucia Nasti$^{(\boxtimes)}$, Andrea Michienzi, and Barbara Guidi

Department of Computer Science, University of Pisa,
Largo B. Pontecorvo, 56127 Pisa, Italy
{lucia.nasti,andrea.michienzi,guidi}@di.unipi.it

Abstract. Addiction is a complex phenomenon, coming from environmental, biological, and psychological causes. It is defined as a natural response of the body to external stimuli that become compulsive needs. From the biological point of view, the brain has the central role: many neural circuits and, above all, the Dopamine System, are involved in the addiction process. Over the last decade, social network communication has become an increasingly addictive activity, for which users appear to engage in social media excessively and/or compulsively. In this work, we show that the current online social networks' notifications system triggers addictive behaviors. We prove our hypothesis simulating the mathematical modeling of the Dopamine System on real interactions among members of a set of 18 Facebook groups. In line with recent psychological studies, we find that the addicted users show a high frequency of social interactions on the platform.

Keywords: Social networks · Computational model · Internet addiction · Facebook groups

1 Introduction

Addiction is a complex phenomenon that has had different interpretations over the years. In general, we can define it as the natural response of the body to external stimuli that become a compulsive need. This condition appears as a total loss of control and repetitions of the same actions periodically, arduous to break because they create an unreal feeling of wellness [22].

Since the 1960s, researchers of diverse fields (such as medicine, sociology, and psychology) started to analyze the addiction from various points of view, underlying how many factors contribute to its development, such as biological, psychological, and environmental aspects. From a biological perspective, the brain plays a central role [18]. The Dopamine System (DS) is a group of cells originating in the midbrain whose function is to anticipate the reward. The level of dopamine, a neurotransmitter, increases in reaching a stimulus, originating a sense of pleasure. However, in an addiction context, this mechanism breaks and induces to search for a higher or more frequent reward. Consequently, the

© Springer Nature Switzerland AG 2021
J. Bowles et al. (Eds.): DataMod 2020, LNCS 12611, pp. 72–86, 2021.
https://doi.org/10.1007/978-3-030-70650-0_5

effect of dopamine decreases, causing tolerance and withdrawal symptoms. As well as the biological aspects, the environmental factors, such as the impact of age, gender, and social background, have a crucial influence on the spread of addiction, as shown in [1]. Some particular habits are popular in social groups because people, especially the younger ones, tend to imitate reciprocally, and this behaviour is generally known as emulation.

In the last decade, the introduction of new technologies, like smartphones and 5G, and the advent of Social Media, are changing the way of how people communicate. In particular, Social Media are one of the most used Internet applications, with more than 3 billion of users, where people can create virtual contacts by increasing the number of connections and frequency of contact. Social Media completely changed the social life of people facilitating their interactions.

Indeed, as described in [8,16], platforms, such as Facebook, are popular communication tools, used for many activities as maintenance of online and offline relationships, oneself promotion, gaming and marketing. Over the last decade, the engagement between users and social networks has become pervasive to the point of being a problematic phenomenon, characterized by compulsive behaviours (loss of control, mood modification and so on). For this reason, researchers belonging to different fields have started to analyze these behaviours as a new kind of addiction.

In this context, we study Internet addiction, namely the excessive Internet (and technology) use that may interfere with daily life, and the way it spreads through the interaction on social networks.

We start our work simulating the mathematical model of Dopamine System [14,15] on a dataset extracted from Facebook containing the interactions of 18 real social groups. We associate the DS model to each member of the group; then, we use the real interactions to simulate the exchange of messages among the members. Thus the stimuli are the messages sent to and received from the other users. Consequently, each individual has his/her dopamine level, and by analyzing the intensity of interaction, we identify the users that are susceptible to become addicted.

Then, analysing the real communication data, we are able to show that there are intrinsic mechanisms, like notifications, which repeatedly engaging the users, may contribute to the development of social networks addiction.

The rest of this paper is organized as follows. In Sect. 2, we introduce the problem of the Internet addiction, mentioning the sociological aspects of this phenomenon, then we describe the network communication model, which we consider for our work, and the mathematical model of the Dopamine System. In Sects. 3 and 4 we describe, respectively, the characteristics of the dataset we collect and how we perform the simulations. Finally, in Sects. 5 and 6 we draw our conclusions and discuss future work.

2   The Internet Addiction

In few years, the impact of Internet and technology has fundamentally changed the way we relate and communicate with each other [23]. People, especially the younger ones, tend to prefer online communication, choosing text messages to communicate with their peers [7]. Moreover, social network platforms offer a great variety of services and apps that improve the engagement with the users, whose number will be approximately of 3 billion in 2021 as estimated in [20].

Adopting a computer-mediated communication has multiple consequences on users life, such as the loss of empathy and the increase of stress [13], and, as underlined in [3], there is growing scientific evidence suggesting that the excessive and compulsive use of social networking sites may result in symptoms traditionally associated with substance-related addictions, such as salience, mood modifications, tolerance, withdrawal, relapse, and conflict.

In order to bring more clarity to this phenomenon, researchers have started to investigate Internet addiction, trying to understand which mechanisms affect the user's behaviour. Indeed, users show different attitudes to this communication form, which mainly depends on their level of stress, sense of isolation and inadequacy [17].

As pointed out in [5], the Internet addiction can be analyzed according to biological, social and psychological factors. Recent research suggests that *age* influences particularly social media addiction [2]: younger users are more likely to engage in online activities. Among social factors, the authors in [5] propose: *gender*, *intensity of use*, *user's met needs*, and *social comparison*. Gender influences the nature of online activities; while intensity, met needs, and social comparison identify how social user needs an intense and frequent use of social networks to establish new relationships and compare themselves to other individuals. Finally, *stress*, *empathy*, *conscientiousness*, and *depression* are the most common psychological factors predicting the Internet addiction. In particular, as described in [11], the stress increment affects the social media use. In [12], instead, researchers study how users, who do not exhibit the ability to share and understand others' emotions, are more inclined to use social media rather than in-person contact for their social interactions.

These factors together can be used to predict a sort of susceptibility to Internet addiction. However, in this context, the main issue is represented by the objective difficulty to quantify accurately their effects on user behaviour. Indeed, parameters as stress or empathy cannot be measured quantitatively. Therefore, in this work, we proceed applying a novel approach, which studies the Internet addiction analyzing only the structure and the mechanisms at the basis of social network sites.

2.1   The Network Communication Model

Online Social Groups (OSGs) are becoming increasingly important social networks because they represent a new opportunity for user participation and engagement. Formally, a group is described as two or more individuals who are connected by and within social relationships [6]. In the online world, we can find several examples of OSG, such as the Facebook Groups, the hashtag communities of Twitter or Instagram, or the Steemit communities. The common factor of all these proposals is that these groups form around an interest or a topic, such as an artist, or a sport which is of interest among all the members of the group.

Inside an Online Social Group, users can write contents (generally called *post*) with which then other users can interact. Interactions happen in two forms: via written interactions (or *comments*), or via more immediate *reactions*. An immediate reaction is a quick way to express a feedback towards a specific post. Usually, they take the form of positive feelings, such as the *"Like"* button in Facebook, or the *"Heart"* buttons of Twitter and Instagram. This form of feedback is largely used by users because of the ease with which they can be expressed. Although common, immediate reactions are not always relevant, since sometimes they are expressed mindlessly by users. On the other hand, comments remain the most relevant because they require a non trivial intellectual effort to be produced, and therefore are perceived as more meaningful if compared to a single immediate reaction. Moreover, comments do not necessarily target a specific content, but they can be considered as additional considerations to a discussion, thus targeting all the people involved in the same conversation.

Users can express reactions to comments as well, and that comments can be further commented, creating an arbitrarily deep structure of comments which can be organised as a tree. Notifications in OSGs advise the members of a group that new content has been published (as a comment or a reaction). We identify three cases in which the notification system is triggered:

- **New content:** a new content is created, and all users of the group (except the creator of the content) receive a notification concerning the newly created content;
- **Reaction:** a user expressed a reaction towards a specific content or comment. Only the user that created the content or comment will receive a notification;
- **New comment:** a new comment was created, therefore all users participating to the discussion are notified;

In Fig. 1, we represent the scheme of the notification system, in which the user U_1 is the author of the original post, for which all the other members of the group $(m_1...m_n)$ receive a notification. If the U_1's post receives a comment or a reaction, only U_1 receive a notification, while any replies to a previous comment (with a comment or a reaction) involves a notification for U_1 and the author of the comment (in the scheme represented as U_2).

2.2   The Mathematical Model of Dopamine System

From a biological point of view, the Dopamine System (DS) is one of the neurological circuits mainly involved in the addiction context. As shown in [21], the Dopamine System is part of the reward pathways in the brain, and so all the positive feelings obtained in response to positive reinforcement, which means achieving something when we perform an action.

In the case of addiction, there are different consequences affecting the brain, such as compulsion, loss of control, and negative emotional state, which depend

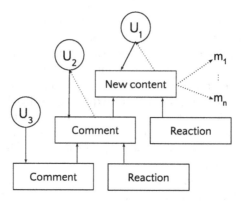

Fig. 1. The scheme of the notification system implemented in social networks. U_1 is the user that writes a new content, which implies a notification to all group's members $(m_1, ..., m_n)$. If another user (U_2) replies (with a comment or a reaction), only U_1 will receive a notification. If U_2 receives a comment or a reaction, the notifications will be sent to U_2 and U_1. In the scheme, the solid edges represent the act of express a comment or a reaction; the dotted edges the notification path.

on the increasing amount of dopamine. These effects are exactly the same regardless the kind of addiction. Then, in order to investigate this phenomenon, the authors in [14,15] extend and simplify the mathematical model of the Dopamine System, proposed by Gutkin et al. in [10] to analyze the nicotine addiction. Such a model describes the main neurological processes involved in addiction phenomena and it has been validated against experimental data [4].

The model in [14,15] describes, in an abstract way, the interaction between dopamine and neurological receptors that lead to persistent changes in brain structures (due to neuronal plasticity) that really occur in the case of addiction. The authors represent the "memorization" of the received stimuli, which can result in tolerance and withdrawal symptoms, implementing threshold-based switches, with simpler differential equations defined by cases. As a result, the model consists of two differential equations:

- *Dopamine concentration.* The following differential equation describes the dynamics of the variable D representing the dopamine concentration in the prefrontal cortex:

$$\frac{dD}{dt} = \alpha \left(-D + k + \begin{cases} 1, & if \ r - M \geq \theta_p \\ 0, & if \ \theta_n \leq r - M \leq \theta_p \\ -\frac{D*M}{2}, & if \ r - M \leq \theta_n \end{cases} \right)$$

The dynamics of D is calculated by considering the following parameters:
  - k is the basal production rate of dopamine;
  - r is the perceived stimulus;
  - M is the memory of the stimulus, whose value is given by the second differential equation;

- θ_p is the positive threshold, in the simulation is set to 80;
- θ_n is the negative threshold, in the simulation is set to -30;
- $\alpha = 0.3$ is a unique time-scaling parameter.

Apart from standard decay and basal production, the differential equation describes the dynamics of the dopamine concentration by considering three cases given by the comparison of the current stimulus r with the memory M and the two thresholds (both chosen by performing simulations). When the stimulus is largely greater than the memory, the dopamine concentration increases. When the stimulus and the memory are comparable the dopamine concentration does not increase. Finally, when the stimulus is largely smaller than the memory, the dopamine concentration decreases with a rate that depends both on D and on M.

- *Memory.* The second differential equation describes, in an abstract way, the opponent process (in psychology defined as a contrary emotional reaction to a previous stimulus) that is modeled as a "memorization" process of previous stimuli.

$$\frac{dM}{dt} = \alpha \left(-M + \left\{ \begin{array}{ll} \frac{r-M}{2}, & if \ r > M \\ 0, & otherwise \end{array} \right. \right)$$

Dopamine and memory take different times to reach "high" values: Memory requires some time to reach values comparable to the stimulus r, but when it reaches such a level, it contrasts the increase of dopamine concentration in the brain.

In this work, we identify the notifications, described in details in Sect. 2.1, with the stimulus r that triggers the user in the visit of social network platforms. Indeed, these messages engage the users, notifying them that the discussions of the group were enriched by additional contents or that someone expressed a feedback. To better describe the communication model, we assign different intensities to each action we observe in the dataset (reported in details in Sect. 3):

- **Posting a new content**: when a user writes a new content, all the group's members (including the author of the content) receive a stimulus of intensity 100, that is comparable to the stimulus considered in the model presented in [14, 15] in normal conditions;
- **Writing a comment**: when a user writes a new comment, she/he will receive a stimulus of intensity 100;
- **Receiving a comment**: since comments are the most exhaustive form of feedback, all the members receiving a comment will receive a stimulus of intensity 150;
- **Receiving a reaction**: all the users will receive a stimulus of intensity 15 for each obtained reaction;

To establish if a user shows a susceptible behaviour to addiction, we considered properly the memory level, because it represents the tolerance and so the phenomenon that better characterizes the addiction. In the model described in [14, 15], the selected threshold is $M \geq 15$, because at that point in the performed simulations, the users showed peaks and consequently decreases in dopamine trend. In our work, we will run experiments in order to find the Memory threshold that better characterized our networks, as we will describe in details in Sect. 4.

3 Dataset

Table 1. General description of the Facebook groups.

Group	Category	Users	Days	Start	End	Posts	Comments	Reactions
Ed1	Education	2,668	388	01/01/17	24/01/18	3,555	63,350	60,463
Ed2		9,506	317	06/04/17	18/02/18	5,271	77,933	350,781
Ed3		4,156	393	25/01/17	22/02/18	5,060	41,480	144,764
Sp1	Sport	1,308	249	27/08/17	03/05/18	5,588	3,823	1,456
Sp2		1,065	370	04/02/17	09/02/18	708	3,421	106,622
Sp3		11,017	28	13/02/18	14/03/18	6,353	79,998	332,727
Sp4		8,585	249	27/08/17	03/05/18	5,588	162,283	340,676
Wo1	Work	3,107	406	02/01/17	12/02/18	1,444	19,007	47,492
Wo2		1,170	418	04/01/17	26/02/18	945	16,891	12,124
Wo3		2,134	318	13/06/17	27/04/18	4,809	3,296	6,479
Wo4		1,097	485	03/01/17	04/05/18	2,651	2,382	4,577
En1	Entertainment	2,133	130	30/09/17	08/02/18	5,009	65,205	182,315
En2		1,526	123	22/10/17	23/02/18	3,777	32,235	85,891
En3		7,300	120	02/01/18	03/05/18	4,904	72,631	266,666
En4		2,578	178	09/09/17	06/03/18	3,543	33,098	56,227
Ne1	News	2,022	111	07/10/17	26/01/18	155	9,777	66,668
Ne2		8,355	91	08/11/17	07/02/18	3,397	282,358	341,091
Ne3		795	406	02/01/17	12/02/18	1,133	5,476	2,675

The dataset we use for our simulations consist of the timestamped activity of 18 heterogeneous Facebook groups, which can be grouped in 5 categories, according to their description. The dataset consists of the 17 Facebook groups already described in [9], plus another group that falls under the Sport category. Table 1 contains the most relevant information of the groups contained in the dataset. The Table shows the label we use to identify the groups (Group) and their category (Category), the number of users that interacted during the observation (Users), the length of the observation in days (Days) along with the date of the start (Start) and end (End) of the observation, and lastly the total number of posts retrieved (Posts) and their comments (Comments) and reactions (Reactions). The dataset is relevant because it contains all the information needed for our model described in Sect. 2.1.

The users are unevenly distributed among the groups and range from 795 of Ne3 to 11, 017 of Sp3. The observations have different length as well, ranging

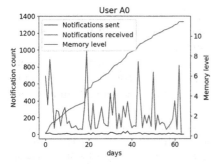

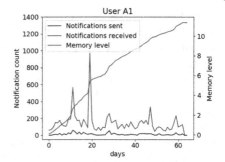

Fig. 2. Notification and memory level of user A0.

Fig. 3. Notification and memory level of user A1.

from 28 days of Sp3 to 485 days of Wo4. The different length of the observations is due to the activity of the groups, indeed in some groups (see Wo2) the activity was so low that we were able to read all the history of the group. On the other hand, in the case of Sp3 there was so much activity that we were able only to read the activity of about one month. We also report the number of posts, comments and reactions per group to give the reader an idea concerning the activity of each group. As expected, the number of posts is usually lower than the number of comments, which is, in turn, usually lower than the number of reactions. This is due to the fact that starting a conversation thread requires much intellectual effort, while reactions are more immediate and easy to express.

4   Simulations

The activity of the groups presented in Sect. 3 was retrieved, and the DS, presented in Sect. 2.2, was simulated according to the notifications defined in Sect. 2.1. Being aware that the original model was designed to detect addictive behaviours in a slightly different scenario, we needed a parameter tuning and validation session. We decided to run the simulations on a test group to select the correct parameters according to clearly addicted behaviours based on user activity.

The group chosen for the parameter tuning is En3 because it shows average properties. After a preliminary analysis of the activity of the users in the group, we decided to focus on users who showed an unusual (i.e. high) number of notifications per day to detect potentially addicted users. This choice was driven by the fact that users encouraged to check the status of the group multiple times per day are more likely to develop an addictive behaviour. Indeed, as described in [5], one of the factors detecting this kind of addiction is represented by the *intensity*, which is directly linked to the compulsory behaviour that usually characterized the addicted user.

At the end of this preliminary screening, two users were found that receive more than 100 notifications daily. The simulation of the DS of the two users can be found in Figs. 2 and 3. Their names and ids are replaced with arbitrary strings (*AO*, and *A1*) to prevent possible privacy disclosures. In both cases, we see that the notifications received are far more than the ones sent. Moreover, despite receiving a notification causes the DS to update the Memory level, simply counting the notifications does suffice to detect addictive behaviours. This is given by the fact that not all notifications produce the same stimulus, as described in Sect. 2.2.

To establish if a user became addicted, we considered properly the memory level, because it represents the tolerance and so the phenomenon that better characterizes the addiction. We decided to set to 10 the memory level to detect users that are in an addicted state, because at that point in the performed simulations, the users showed peaks and consequently decreases in dopamine trend.

5   Results

Figure 4 shows the distribution of notifications sent, notifications received, Memory and Dopamine at the end of the simulations for each user of the dataset at the end of the simulations. The histograms concerning the number of notifications sent and received show that most users are not greatly involved in the activities of the group. On the other hand, there are also few users with a very high involvement which managed to interact a lot with other users of the group, suggesting us that they may have developed addiction (see Table 2 for a more detailed view). Our supposition is confirmed by the distribution of the Memory of the users at the end of the simulation. Indeed, we see that tens of users achieved a Memory level of at least 10.

A more detailed view of the 84 addicted users, divided by groups, can be found in Table 2. The table shows, for each group, the number of users found to have developed addiction (Memory $\geq$10), and their average number of notifications (sent or received), Memory and Dopamine levels at the end of the simulations. The Table shows that in seven groups none of the users developed addiction, in eight groups up to 3 users developed addiction, and in the remaining groups En1, Sp4, and Ne2 respectively 9, 21 and 37 users were found addicted. Interestingly enough, in the Work category no users were found addicted, while in the categories Education and Entertainment at least one user per group was found addicted. This suggests us that social media addiction is not tied, or at least more common, in specific group categories rather than others.

We now explore more in detail the users who were found with highest number of notifications, Memory, and Dopamine (see Table 3). The user with the highest notification count (TN) is the addicted uses of Ne1 which exceeds 68,000 notifications. Its Memory is almost three times the threshold we set for considering a user addicted. Interestingly enough, this user is not also the user with the most severe addiction. Indeed, the user with the highest Memory level (TM) belongs to the group Ne2 and has a Memory level of 39.50, more than 10 points higher. The number of notifications is of comparable magnitude, but lower of approximately 2000 units. Lastly, the user with the highest Dopamine (TD) belongs to

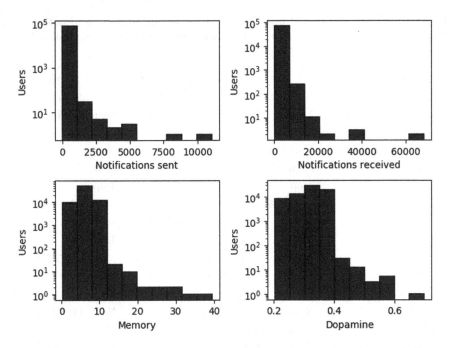

Fig. 4. Notification sent and received, Memory, and Dopamine distribution of all users in all groups.

the group Ne2 as well. While this user has a high Memory level, reaching 35, the number of notifications is much lower with respect to the other two users, barely reaching 40,000. This is a clear sign that the number of notifications is not proportional to the Memory of the users. Indeed, comparing the plots in Figs. 8, 9 and 10, representing the number of notifications sent and received, and the levels of Dopamine of the users TN, TM and TD respectively, we can notice that the frequency and the peaks of the stimuli have the highest impact on the development of the addiction. Moreover, none of the three users shows withdrawal symptoms, since the level of Dopamine tends to increment, which means that they do not interrupt the use of the platform.

Figure 5 shows the bivariate distribution of the notifications sent and received by each user. Green dots mark users who belong to the *safe* groups (Ne3, Sp1, Sp2, Wo1, Wo2, Wo3, Wo4), i.e. where no users were found to be addicted. Yellow markers are users who belong to the *risky* groups (Ed1, Ed2, Ed3, Ne1, En2, En3, En4, Sp3), i.e. where only up to three users were found to be addicted. Orange dots mark users who belong to the *dangerous* groups (Ne2, En1, and Sp4), i.e. groups with more than 3 addicted users. Addicted users are highlighted with a red marker in the plot to make them easier to spot. The peculiar distribution is given by the fact that users belong to a set of 18 different groups and each "band" of points corresponds to the users of a group. The plot shows that close to 5,000 notifications received groups from all the three categories can be found,

Table 2. Number of addicted users per group. The average number of notification, Memory and Dopamine levels of the addicted users divided in each group is also shown.

Group	Addicted		Avg	Group	Addicted		Avg
Ed1	3	Nots	15,675.3	En4	1	Nots	9,722.0
		Mem	17.65			Mem	10.32
		Dop	0.50			Dop	0.38
Ed2	2	Nots	11,758.5	Sp1	0	Nots	-
		Mem	10.62			Mem	-
		Dop	0.39			Dop	-
Ed3	3	Nots	15,751.3	Sp2	0	Nots	-
		Mem	12.08			Mem	-
		Dop	0.40			Dop	-
Ne1	1	Nots	68,681.0	Sp3	3	Nots	13,515.3
		Mem	28.68			Mem	11.67
		Dop	0.45			Dop	0.41
Ne2	37	Nots	13,805.9	Sp4	21	Nots	11,131.61
		Mem	14.80			Mem	11.57
		Dop	0.43			Dop	0.41
Ne3	0	Nots	-	Wo1	0	Nots	-
		Mem	-			Mem	-
		Dop	-			Dop	-
En1	9	Nots	18,420.3	Wo2	0	Nots	-
		Mem	15.56			Mem	-
		Dop	0.45			Dop	-
En2	2	Nots	15,389.0	Wo3	0	Nots	-
		Mem	13.67			Mem	-
		Dop	0.42			Dop	-
En3	2	Nots	13,172.0	Wo4	0	Nots	-
		Mem	11.40			Mem	-
		Dop	0.39			Dop	-

confirming that the number of notifications alone is not a good measure of the addiction of users. Although, it must be noted that all addicted users tend to receive a large amount of notifications: 7000 or above.

We now focus more in detail on the users found addicted and their Memory and Dopamine levels at the end of the simulation. Figure 6 shows the Notifications bivariate distribution of addicted users, but the top 30% of users per Memory level at the end of the simulation are highlighted with a yellow marker, and the top 10% is highlighted with a red marker. The plot shows that the

Table 3. Simulation values of users with highest notification count, Memory and Dopamine.

	Top Nots	Top Mem	Top Dop
Nots	68,681	66,297	40,399
Mem	28.68	39.50	35.20
Dop	0.45	0.56	0.69
Group	Ne1	Ne2	Ne2

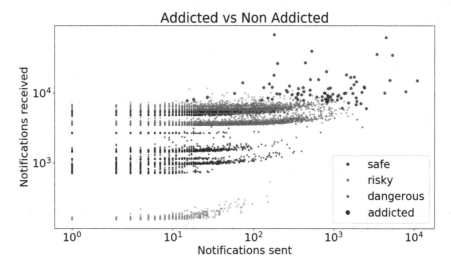

Fig. 5. Notification sent and received, Memory, and Dopamine of all users in all groups. (Color figure online)

most severe cases of addiction are connected to an higher number of notifications, mostly received. However, the plot also shows that there is no correlation between the notifications sent and received. This is counter-intuitive because one would expect that the more a user sends notification (and interacts with other people), the more other users are encouraged to interact with her/him. However, as described in [19], passive activities are the most popular ones.

Figure 7 shows the Dopamine-Memory bivariate distribution of addicted users, but the top 30% of users per notification count are highlighted with a yellow marker, and the top 10% is highlighted with a red marker. In this distribution we see that at low Memory levels correspond low levels of Dopamine (see black and yellow markers). Additionally, an higher notification count is usually bound to an higher Memory (and Dopamine) level. On the other hand, the nodes marked as the top nodes per notifications does not confirm this trend, and are instead more scattered. Interestingly enough, the three markers corresponding to the users who were found with the highest notification count (TN), highest

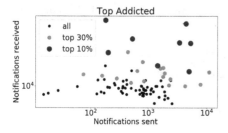

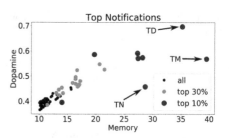

Fig. 6. Users with highest memory. (Color figure online)

Fig. 7. Users with most notifications. (Color figure online)

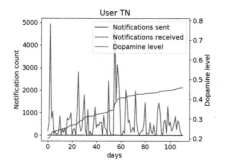

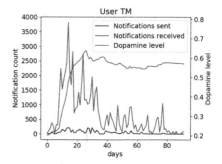

Fig. 8. Notifications and dopamine level for user TN.

Fig. 9. Notifications and dopamine level for user TM.

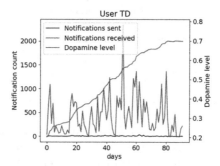

Fig. 10. Notifications and dopamine level for user TD.

Memory level (TM) and highest Dopamine level (TD) (see Table 3), are the users that distances the most from the others.

6   Conclusions

Addiction is a complex phenomenon, which has several consequences on the brain and the behaviour of people. In the last decade, the introduction of new technologies and the advent of Social Media have changed the way of how people communicate, giving rise a new kind of addiction, namely the social network addiction, for which users engage in different online activities excessively and/or compulsively.

In order to investigate this phenomenon, researchers have started to study Internet addiction, to unveil the mechanisms affecting the user's life. In this context, the applied approaches are based on the analysis of different factors, such as biological, social and psychological aspects.

The sociological and psychological factors can be used to predict the susceptibility to Internet addiction. However, it is difficult to measure accurately how they affect the user's behaviour. Therefore, in this work, we apply a novel approach, which studies the Internet addiction analyzing only the structure and the mechanisms at the basis of social network sites. In particular, simulating the computational model of Dopamine System and using the real data of 18 groups of Facebook, we are able to study how the notifications affect significantly the user's behaviour.

Our work can be further developed in different ways. In the future, we want to extend our analysis considering other typologies of Facebook groups and, in particular, monitoring their activities for longer periods. Moreover, we plan to collect also data of different social networks, such as Twitter and Instagram, to compare the results of our analysis and study how the user's behaviour is different according to the used platform. Besides, we want to investigate deeper the role of the *intensity* on the addiction development.

The Dopamine System is also linked to the human perception of the satisfaction, stimulating the attention, the memory and the learning. Therefore, it is possible to extend ulteriorly our work to test satisfaction of the user in human-computer interactions.

References

1. Andreassen, C.S., Pallesen, S., Griffiths, M.D.: The relationship between addictive use of social media, narcissism, and self-esteem: findings from a large national survey. Addict. Behav. **64**, 287–293 (2017)
2. Andreassen, C.S., Torsheim, T., Brunborg, G.S., Pallesen, S.: Development of a Facebook addiction scale. Psychol. Rep. **110**(2), 501–517 (2012)
3. Balcerowska, J.M., Bereznowski, P., Biernatowska, A., Atroszko, P.A., Pallesen, S., Andreassen, C.S.: Is it meaningful to distinguish between Facebook addiction and social networking sites addiction? Psychometric analysis of Facebook addiction and social networking sites addiction scales. Curr. Psychol. 1–14 (2020)
4. Corrigall, W.A., Franklin, K.B., Coen, K.M., Clarke, P.B.: The mesolimbic dopaminergic system is implicated in the reinforcing effects of nicotine. Psychopharmacology **107**(2), 285–289 (1992). https://doi.org/10.1007/BF02245149
5. Dailey, S.L., Howard, K., Roming, S.M., Ceballos, N., Grimes, T.: A biopsychosocial approach to understanding social media addiction. Hum. Behav. Emerg. Technol. **2**(2), 158–167 (2020)
6. Forsyth, D.R.: Group Dynamics. Cengage Learning, Boston (2018)

7. Greenfield, S.: Mind Change: How Digital Technologies Are Leaving Their Mark On Our Brains. Random House, New York (2015)
8. Griffiths, M.D., Kuss, D.J., Billieux, J., Pontes, H.M.: The evolution of internet addiction: a global perspective. Addict. Behav. **53**, 193–195 (2016)
9. Guidi, B., Michienzi, A., De Salve, A.: Community evaluation in Facebook groups. Multimedia Tools Appl. **79**(45), 33603–33622 (2019). https://doi.org/10.1007/s11042-019-08494-0
10. Gutkin, B.S., Dehaene, S., Changeux, J.P.: A neurocomputational hypothesis for nicotine addiction. Proc. Natl. Acad. Sci. U.S.A. **103**(4), 1106–1111 (2006)
11. Hou, X.L., Wang, H.Z., Guo, C., Gaskin, J., Rost, D.H., Wang, J.L.: Psychological resilience can help combat the effect of stress on problematic social networking site usage. Personality Individ. Differ. **109**, 61–66 (2017)
12. Jiao, C., Wang, T., Peng, X., Cui, F.: Impaired empathy processing in individuals with internet addiction disorder: an event-related potential study. Front. Hum. Neurosci. **11**, 498 (2017)
13. Kuss, D.J., Griffiths, M.D.: Online social networking and addiction? A review of the psychological literature. Int. J. Environ. Res. Public Health **8**(9), 3528–3552 (2011)
14. Nasti, L., Milazzo, P.: A computational model of internet addiction phenomena in social networks. In: Cerone, A., Roveri, M. (eds.) SEFM 2017. LNCS, vol. 10729, pp. 86–100. Springer, Cham (2018). https://doi.org/10.1007/978-3-319-74781-1_7
15. Nasti, L., Milazzo, P.: A hybrid automata model of social networking addiction. J. Log. Algebraic Methods Program. **100**, 215–229 (2018)
16. Przepiorka, A., Blachnio, A.: Time perspective in internet and Facebook addiction. Comput. Hum. Behav. **60**, 13–18 (2016)
17. Raskin, R., Terry, H.: A principal-components analysis of the narcissistic personality inventory and further evidence of its construct validity. J. Pers. Soc. Psychol. **54**(5), 890 (1988)
18. Roberts, A.J., Koob, G.F.: The neurobiology of addiction: an overview. Alcohol Res. Health **21**(2), 101 (1997)
19. Ryan, T., Chester, A., Reece, J., Xenos, S.: The uses and abuses of Facebook: a review of Facebook addiction. J. Behav. Addict. **3**(3), 133–148 (2014)
20. Statista: Number of social network users worldwide from 2010 to 2021 (in billions) (2019). www.statista.com/statistics/278414/number-of-worldwide-socialnetwork-users/
21. Volkow, N.D., Koob, G.F., McLellan, A.T.: Neurobiologic advances from the brain disease model of addiction. N. Engl. J. Med. **374**(4), 363–371 (2016)
22. West, R., Brown, J.: Theory of Addiction. Wiley, Hoboken (2013)
23. Zhao, S., Grasmuck, S., Martin, J.: Identity construction on Facebook: digital empowerment in anchored relationships. Comput. Hum. Behav. **24**(5), 1816–1836 (2008)

A Simulation Study on Demand Disruptions and Limited Resources for Healthcare Provision

Juliana Bowles[1], Ricardo M. Czekster[2]([⊠]), Guilherme Redeker[1], and Thais Webber[1]

[1] School of Computer Science, University of St Andrews, St Andrews KY16 9SX, UK
{jkfb,gr60,tcwds}@st-andrews.ac.uk
[2] School of Computing, Newcastle University, Newcastle upon Tyne NE1 7RU, UK
ricardo.melo-czekster@ncl.ac.uk

Abstract. Philanthropic hospitals in Brazil are in great part funded by the government and are daily accessed by a large portion of the population. As the Brazilian economy faces deep cuts in healthcare, managers are adjusting budgets and focusing on less expensive alternatives such as process improvements. Hospitals are even more impacted by the recent COVID-19 pandemic with widespread disruption on operational processes forcing them to stretch resources. Thus, it brings an opportunity to evaluate the actual performance of these settings under different scenarios where analysts may address bottlenecks and the impact on resources. Our focus is to quantify the capacity of an emergency department to support patient demand with limited resources in pre and post-pandemic scenarios. We use a 12-month longitudinal dataset consisting of pre-pandemic emergency occurrences and assigned resources.

Keywords: Healthcare processes · Emergency department · Process simulation · COVID-19

1 Introduction

Healthcare is a multidimensional domain posing interesting challenges to researchers. Over time, a wealth of studies was carried out on how to combine computing with medical practices while taking into account high quality patient care, balancing budget and available resources [6,12]. Despite technological advances and the use of data science or analytics in healthcare sectors across the globe, in some countries those enhancements are far from becoming palpable, as scarce resources and low budget must meet strict objectives mostly within public hospitals [8,12]. It remains a challenge to redesign complex business processes for performance using what-if scenarios coupled with resource management [3,6].

This research was partially supported by a Scottish Funding Council GCRF grant 2019/20.

J. Bowles et al. (Eds.): DataMod 2020, LNCS 12611, pp. 87–103, 2021.
https://doi.org/10.1007/978-3-030-70650-0_6

Simulation allows the artificial creation of the most likely scenarios management would face, assigning resources' service time and adjusting capacity to circumvent monetary and physical limitations [15]. These models provide the investigation of key metrics of interest such as average throughput, waiting time, process total capacity, and resource utilisation [10,17], to mention a few. A recent literature review highlighted the importance of the application of Modelling and Simulation (M&S) specifically to improve operation of emergency wards known as Accidents & Emergency (A&E) departments [16]. Authors revealed a growing interest on the use of *Discrete Event Simulation* (DES) as a performance analysis tool in 81% out of 254 selected papers. Recent studies have applied DES to situations where resource management scenarios exploration was essential to reduce operational costs and increase performance [2,14].

One challenge of tackling Brazilian healthcare is to create a set of comprehensive what-if scenarios to help improve business processes with resource-aware capabilities, especially after the recent Coronavirus pandemic (COVID-19) [5,11]. According to the World Health Organisation (WHO), Brazil registered 1,085,038 cases of COVID-19 with 50,617 confirmed deaths by 23 June 2020 [18]. Even before the global pandemic, A&E was one of the most crowded departments in Brazilian hospitals. Such developing countries struggle to cope with resource scarcity as in some Brazilian regions difficulties were already a serious predicament prior to COVID-19. It is worth noticing that clinical staff and managers must cope with restrictive resources to meet demand of both patients infected with COVID-19 and those in need of urgent medical assistance.

The focus of this work is to compile information, model, and analyse the ability of an A&E department to support patient demand with limited resources. We have explored pre-pandemic and post-pandemic simulation scenarios for A&E settings with increasing daily patient demand, combining available staff (medical doctors and nurses) among different patient arrival rates. Our aim was to investigate the effects of a disrupted demand, for example, that brought forth by COVID-19, to quantify and assess bottlenecks on A&E operational process and then estimate resource utilisation and queues behaviour. Finally, it is our aim to raise awareness on the possibility of improving resource allocation and patient care in healthcare facilities using M&S for performance assessment.

This paper is structured as follows. Section 2 covers the issues faced by a Southern Brazilian hospital within the A&E department while Sect. 3 presents our M&S and key measures of interest. Section 4 shows simulation scenarios in pre-pandemic settings with effects on resource allocation and patient waiting time, and numerical analysis of post-pandemic scenarios with demand disruption. Section 5 concludes the work with suggestions and further work.

2   Southern Brazilian Hospital Settings

Our case study is a general public emergency care process on a Southern Brazilian hospital (*Hospital Santa Cruz*-HSC) considered a reference hospital for cardiac surgeries and traumatology. We focus on the A&E department as target business process for analysis due to high patient demand and equally high amounts of investments needed per year in medical supplies and resources. In 2015, for instance, HSC had performed approximately $221,500$ patient attendances in the A&E. HSC offers diagnose and treatment of a host of medical procedures such as paediatric and surgery care, among other healthcare services.

The hospital is equipped with a modern medical imaging centre, one inpatient wing, a recovery centre, and an A&E ward operating in two 7-h and one 10-h daily shifts: i) 00:00 to 06:59; ii) 07:00 to 13:59; and iii) 14:00 to 23:59. A minimal number of Medical Doctors (MD) and nurses are allocated following a pre-arranged schedule. About the IT (*Information Technology*) infrastructure, the hospital invested in an *Enterprise Resource Planning* (ERP) software, which is customised to the hospital needs to maintain data digitised in its business processes [7]. A wealth of sub-processes deals with patient arrival and with the outcomes based on clinical decisions. And, to stress things further, Brazilian health regulation mandate a clinical decision in A&E units to take place within 24 h.

The hospital underwent serious operational changes to tackle performance, something that is happening since 2015, including IT department remodelling. The effort encompassed all sectors and started from mapping key business processes as well as quantifying available resources. The initiative involved interactive work among stakeholders and managers, staff and performance analysts to discuss improvements in practices and prioritisation. As support tools, they conduct face-to-face meetings, structured interviews, and ERP data analysis.

Furthermore, they have started using the Business Process Model & Notation (BPMN)[1] [4] to visually model the business processes with standardised graphical elements and annotations to represent and describe the flow of activities in detail. It is worth mentioning that BPMN offers the possibility of a shared understanding of business processes between administrators and simulation analysts [4], among other advantages.

Recently, the COVID-19 crisis has overwhelmed healthcare organisations across the globe undermining the capacity of operational processes [11,18]. Thus, it is crucial for hospitals like HSC to prepare for emergent demand disruptions and promote effective decisions to keep patients and staff safe. HSC administrators have reorganised the healthcare services during and post-pandemic especially for most critical processes in A&E and in the Intensive Care Unit (ICU). The following subsections present the BPMN models elaborated before the emergence of COVID-19 disrupting the A&E care processes.

2.1 A&E Triage System

The hospital uses the Manchester Triage System (MTS) for clinical risk management as a fundamental system to be applied when the demand exceeds available clinical resources [9]. It helps organising patient flows in A&E wards, considering

---

[1] Object Management Group (OMG) technology standards detailed information on: https://www.omg.org/spec/BPMN/2.0/About-BPMN/.

primarily each patients' needs and to ensure high quality care in a timely manner. The triage is performed by a certified trained nurse that assigns a colour to the incoming patient according to a protocol that evaluates the case severity. Figure 1 presents the BPMN model representing the MTS process.

On patient arrival, a nurse conducts a *basic health assessment* on the patient, collecting data (temperature, pressure, weight) and a questionnaire on current symptoms. Each case's severity classification is simplified in the BPMN model in two major patient groups: Urgent cases (comprising Red and Orange), and Non-Urgent cases (Yellow, Green, and Blue). The simplification was applied due to few Immediate or Very Urgent care cases retrieved from the ERP software. The bulk is composed of Non-Urgent cases where a significant amount of daily cases cease limited resources in a daily basis.

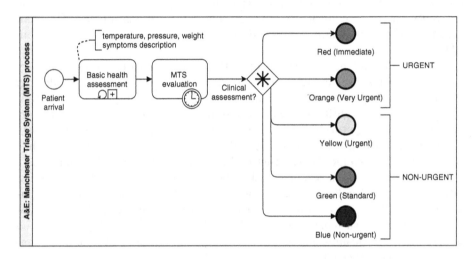

Fig. 1. Manchester Triage System (MTS) process performed by trained nurse. (Color figure online)

During the pandemic a pre-triage desk promptly identified COVID-19 patients redirecting them to a new specialised ward whilst the other cases were directed to the usual A&E. The hospital also moved staff temporarily across departments (e.g., to the ICU, inpatient care ward), keeping only two MDs for A&E patients not related to COVID-19. The pre-triage on patient arrival only took a few minutes each, which can be considered negligible to the analysis of patient waiting time within the usual operation of the A&E. During pandemic, the above-mentioned pre-triage contributed to the reduction on patient arrival (i.e., those seeking consultation) in the usual (pre-pandemic) A&E.

2.2   Usual Pre-pandemic A&E Patient Care Process

Patient arrival is a start event in the care process that represents ingress in the system (e.g., by ambulance or as walk-in patient). Depending on severity, the colour (Red or Orange) is assigned right before the patient reaches the premises (e.g., immediate or very urgent cases). If it is an immediate case, the patient is automatically classified as Red (urgent case, emergency) and goes straight to a stabilisation sub-process (Fig. 2). After stabilisation (or treatment of an urgent case), one out of three actions happens to patients: i) hospitalisation (ICU or other); ii) Surgery; or iii) discharged with (or without) prescription; also includes 'deceased', i.e., the patient has left the process nevertheless.

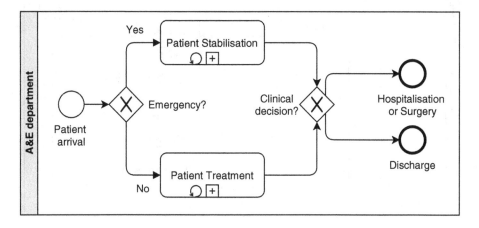

Fig. 2. A&E macro process.

The urgent cases are contrasted with those non-urgent cases such as patients experiencing minor cuts or burns, mild headaches, or exhibiting amenable cold symptoms, just to name a few. In a non-urgent case, the patient himself goes to Patient Treatment sub-process (Fig. 3).

The patients enter in the activity of Admission registering where the clerk collects more general data (personal data, health details, and other important information such as symptoms and comorbidities). Then, the patient is routed to the Risk assessment activity, where a nurse collects health data using medical devices and a trained nurse performs MTS process.

The patient then goes to a waiting area until an MD is available for consultation (Consult doctor activity). The MD could request more tests (e.g., blood screening, medical imaging, etc.), so the patient goes to Request tests activity; or MD could prescribe medication with immediate administration or just put patient in observation period (Medication & therapeutics activity) within hospital premises. In both cases, patients should wait for the activities to complete, and sometimes they may return for new consultation with the same MD (or next in the shift) until their treatment process reaches an outcome.

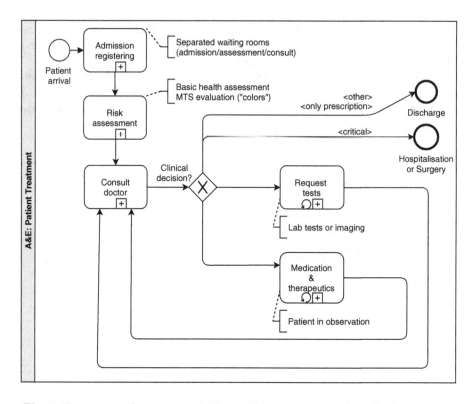

Fig. 3. Treatment sub-process activities until it reaches one of the final outcomes.

3   Applied Modelling and Simulation in the A&E

Modelling and Simulation (M&S) [17] is a broadly used approach to model systems or processes using primitives that extract quantitative performance indices for analysis. Simulation models based on *Discrete Event Simulation* (DES) use abstractions and concepts to describe and map processes into descriptive workflows [13, 15]. The one provided by the BPMN models shown in Sect. 2 indicates how activities are interconnected and depicts the alternative flows (gateways with decision to be taken according to conditions) present in the process model.

From BPMN models we can manually (or automatically) derive simulation models [1, 4] and execute them in simulation tools based on DES, for instance, the *Arena Software*[2] [15]. Arena provides an integrated framework for building simulation models in a wide variety of applications from industry to healthcare. It is worth mentioning that the execution of simulation models within any DES framework can help revealing bottlenecks and key resources in almost any process flow model with timing information.

---

[2] Rockwell Arena software information: https://www.arenasimulation.com/.

Before the pandemic outset, we have conducted a comprehensive process analysis within the hospital following four basic iterative steps. We aimed to obtain qualitative and quantitative information about processes behaviour and then apply DES technique. Figure 4 describes the planned steps from initial meetings with stakeholders (*Step 1*) towards to the actual simulation of the healthcare processes using a simulation tool (*Step 4*). During development (*Step 2* and *Step 3*), the simulation analysts, IT professionals, and stakeholders had interacted to discuss best strategies to deal with ERP data as well as on key modelling aspects.

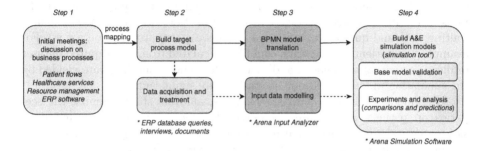

Fig. 4. Planned activities for applying DES in healthcare settings.

The *Step 2* produced the BPMN models presented on Sect. 2. A comprehensive data acquisition (from documents, textual logs, traces, process monitoring, ERP data) and treatment activity was deemed necessary to: i) detect and filter outliers; ii) process invalid observations due to lack of data inputs by clinical staff; iii) understand how entities and resources are interacting in the process and how the ERP software is processing the entries, and; iv) discover how the actual process operates. In the event of data inconsistencies (e.g., invalid or missing numbers, outliers), analysts should use appropriated statistical techniques to overcome the issues [15]. Arena software also provides a statistical tool named *Arena Input Analyser* [15] that is a built-in tool to provide basic statistical properties (e.g., minimum, maximum, mean, standard deviation, and so on) as well as probability distribution fitting to datasets, which is conducted on *Step 3* and applied on *Step 4*.

On *Step 3*, BPMN models are ready to be translated to simulation models. The flow is directly mapped to DES in terms of structure because both have similar elements (activities, start/end events, and decision gateways). After data acquisition on *Step 2*, the input data modelling activity provides a probability distribution function to parametrise the simulation models (patient arrival rate, activities service times, resources' capacity, and rotation probabilities on decision gateways). Thus, model parametrisation depends on acquiring sets of input data from reliable sources, including database sets and personnel interviews to review inconsistencies. In our case study, we have chosen to model the decision gateways with constant probabilities for output flows. For example, it was verified in the dataset that around 50% of patients' clinical path have followed an outcome of 'Discharge'. Thus, the majority of A&E patients were discharged without needing further tests, or medication applied on site.

The *Step 4* is the refinement of the simulation model (DES) translated from the BPMN model, adding timing information such as the probability distribution expressions, also resources quantity and behaviour, i.e., adding the parameters obtained on *Step 3* input data modelling. Our previous research [4] has proposed BPMN models embedded with a structured format for text annotations to improve simulation design and what-if scenario management. At the *Step 4* analysts can make use of several statistical tools and validation approaches they see fit to their experiments. In the end, a baseline model is evaluated towards the measures of interest (e.g., average resource utilisation, queuing analysis such as waiting time and queue size, and total process capacity, to mention a few). For example, the patient waiting time could be calculated from the acquired dataset or discussed with stakeholders, and then its difference from the figure yielded by the simulation model should not be statistically significant.

After model validation with stakeholders, analysts start planning the scenarios on patient arrival rates, resource allocation, service times, and decision gateways' probabilities. During scenarios execution, analysts observe the process behaviour and statistical calculations are summarised in performance indices [17]. The analysts can then evaluate these indices for multiple *what-if* scenarios. Performance scenarios enable stakeholders to interpret and act on changes or suggest modifications that would probably be less costly, or use fewer resources for the same or higher desired output. M&S offers a way to diminish the impact of physical changes and show managers how simple adjustments could yield better outcomes [15]. Next section details the *Input data modelling* (*Step 3*), and the simulation scenarios and analysis (*Step 4*).

3.1   Input Data Modelling for the Pre-pandemic Simulation

During the data acquisition activity (*Step 2*) across hospital IT infrastructure, we inspected 221,664 daily operation logs to use as real parameters for the baseline model. We have pointed out the following issues in the dataset:

1. Seasonality aspects: we have analysed the one-year dataset to determine whether or not the seasons (or the day of the week) were affecting our study, accumulated monthly;
2. Arrival patterns: we investigated the rates of arrival (10,185 entries), according to severity, and per hour of the day, accumulated monthly;
3. Consultation times for medical staff: we were interested into determining the average time spent per medical staff on patients care according to severity.

Figure 5 presents seasonality aspects by month for each aggregated group - *Urgent* and *Non-urgent* (refer to Fig. 1). It shows the percentage on the total number of occurrences observed throughout the duration of the study (12 months), matching the occurrences described in the BPMN model (refer to Fig. 3).

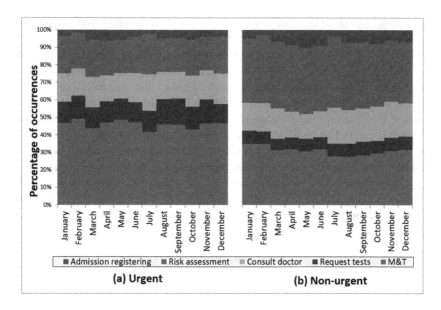

Fig. 5. Seasonality (by month) for Urgent (a) and Non-urgent (b).

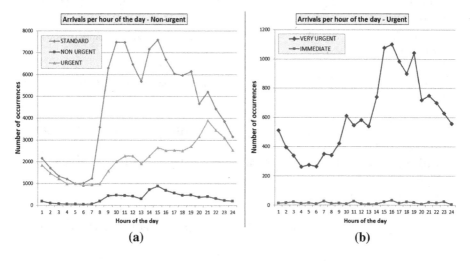

Fig. 6. Arrivals per hour (accumulated monthly) in Non-urgent (a) and Urgent (b).

Regarding to patient arrival patterns (per hour of the day), Fig. 6 shows the number of arrivals for *Urgent* and *Non-urgent* cases. It presents a low number of occurrences prior to the beginning of the day (i.e., before 6:00), which increases as the day passes, and decreases towards the end. Figure 6(a) shows an interesting behaviour after 12:00 where the incidence increases considerably when taking into account the totality of occurrences. However, because those cases concern

Urgent cases, the total number is considered very low (around 300 occurrences), so no actual interpretation is effective for these cases.

Table 1 relates the inter-arrival time and the human resources to known probability distributions. We used the *Arena Input Analyser* tool that operates over a list of data points acquired from the data. Probability distributions were generated for each activity in the simulation flow. We show the descriptive statistics from the dataset before data treatment. It indicates the present of outliers, which supposedly incurred from ERP software misuse (most probably by human error while inputting data) or business process related particular issues, concerning their daily operation. We computed the probability distribution expressions after data treatment step and used the values to parametrise the simulation models.

We direct attention to the variability of MDs' service time for both Consultation and M&T activities, since the amplitude is high, e.g. from 0.2 to 2, 400 min and from 1 to 1, 220 min, respectively.

Table 1. Statistical analysis in the input data modelling step.

Resource (Task)	Data points	Min.	Max.	Mean	Std. Dev.	Probability distribution (scale in minutes)
Patient inter-arrival	10,185	0	119	15.5	19.2	`-0.001 + EXPO(15.5)`
Desk clerk (Admission Reg.)	66,702	0	44	0.713	1.02	`-0.5 + GAMM(0.563, 2.16)`
Qualified Nurse (Risk Assessment)	67,297	0	35	0.513	0.903	`-0.5 + EXPO(1.01)`
Nurse (Request Tests)	843	0	202	2.56	10.3	`-0.001 + EXPO(2.56)`
Medical Doctor (Consultation)	33,174	0.2	2,400	50	159	`WEIB(13.1, 0.505)`
Medical Doctor (M& T)	43,463	1	1,220	4.2	15	`0.999 + WEIB(0.216, 0.259)`

*GAMM (Gamma Prob. Distribution), *EXPO (Exponential), *WEIB (Weibull).*

We have performed a time analysis for the top five MDs by time intervals (of 5 min), dividing consultation duration in nine categories ranging from 0–4 min to 40–44 min. The most usual consultation duration is of 0–4 min, followed by 5–9 min, and then 10–14 min. Beyond 15 min very few occurrences are present for Non-urgent cases. We discovered that doctors and staff use the information system only to close or report occurrences, allowing patients to move along the process as quick as possible. After interviews, MDs described their actual consultation period with the patient around 15 min on average. The remaining categories had low frequency, i.e., from 45–49 min or more, could be considered as outliers in the dataset according to administrators (i.e., adverse events occurring during consultation, or even a particular operation of the ERP software).

As mentioned earlier, using data points from ERP data is crucial determining baseline parameters and asserting model validity when performing experiments. Preliminary simulation experiments set the statistical parameters and analysts can check whether the baseline model is simulating the current process operation or need further improvement. Figure 7 illustrates the structured annotations documented in the BPMN model to guide the simulations construction.

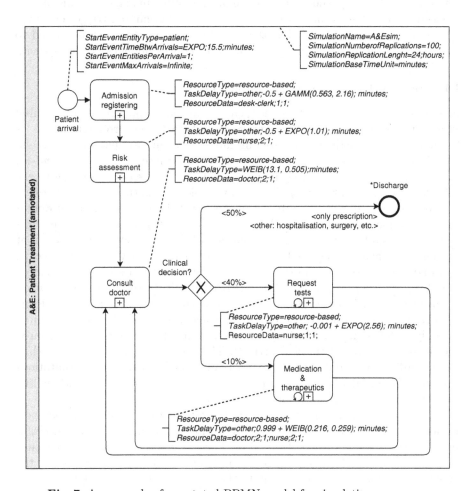

Fig. 7. An example of annotated BPMN model for simulation purposes.

4   Pre-pandemic and Post-pandemic Scenarios Simulation

The pre-pandemic scenario modelled the busiest hour for key human resources in the A&E, i.e., selecting the parameters for the worst case present in the real-case hospital before COVID-19 outset, then aligning the next *what-if* scenarios accordingly. We considered three simulation scenarios for arrival rates (pre-pandemic, pandemic and post-pandemic) and compiled the results in Fig. 8, 9, 10, and 11. We have assumed inter-arrival time of incoming patients to be constant throughout the workday, as well as service time. The values come from input data modelling step (Fig. 7). As output, we were interested in performance indices such as patient waiting time, number of patients waiting for service, and resource (MDs, nurses) utilisation. The Clerk utilisation in the A&E process is not considered as an issue by hospital managers after management installed a service totem. It has optimised patient check-in and organised triage screening. Staff interviews pointed out that the hospital's major concern was related to consultation waiting room and on urgent care services provided to the patient.

4.1   Pre-pandemic Scenario Simulation

The pre-pandemic scenario (baseline scenario) uses an exponentially distributed inter-arrival time based on the average time between occurrences yielded as 15.5 min by the statistical fitting tool in Table 1. The most requested resource in the whole process is the MD as confirmed by earlier interviews (*Step 1 and 2*), and thus it is replicated in the simulation behaviour (*Step 4*) according to the *MD utilisation* plot in Fig. 8(a). The two available MDs in the *Patient Treatment sub-process* operate in a shared-based routine on their activities (Consult doctor and Medication & therapeutics – M&T), both being dedicated 100% of the time in their A&E shift catering patients. Thus, if an MD is not consulting a patient at a given time, then she/he could be working in the M&T activity, and vice-versa.

In addition, two nurses work on their respective activities (Risk Assessment and Request tests) also in a shared-based mechanism. Results on Nurse utilisation in Fig. 8(d) show that the A&E nurses could stay idle in pre-pandemic settings since they mostly execute Risk assessment activities during their shifts, and only perform M&T depending on consultation outcome, thus they are shared only if there is demand (patient arrival). The probability of M&T is less than 10% according to the dataset. The majority of patients seeking out consultations (around 90%) are discharged with prescriptions or requested tests, without the need of monitoring or medication administration *in situ*.

During interviews, managers and staff mentioned other sub activities performed by nurses and doctors (e.g., filling forms, preparing medications, cleaning/preparing rooms) during their shifts. These sub activities are not explicitly described in the BPMN mapping of the A&E Patient Treatment process, so the resource utilisation indice refers only to the performance on modelled activities. We have validated our simulation approach matching the baseline model result (pre-pandemic scenario) with the dataset statistical analysis, focusing on the average number of patients waiting during peak hours, i.e., the average queue size (in peak operation hours) within 95% confidence interval. The *patient waiting time* is the key performance indice we have collected for the three distinct scenarios under evaluation. Results in Fig. 9(a) demonstrate an average number of 17.48 patients in queue waiting consultation and in Fig. 10(a) the average patient waiting time around 2.8 h in the pre-pandemic setting. Moreover,

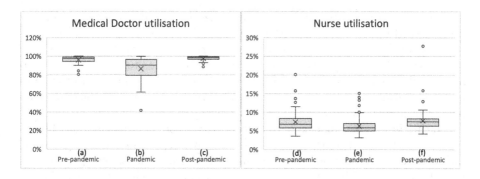

Fig. 8. Resource utilisation simulation results.

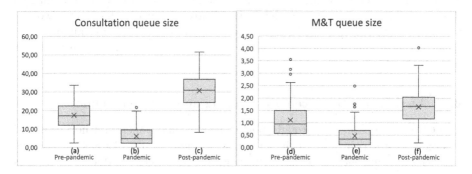

Fig. 9. Patient queue simulation results.

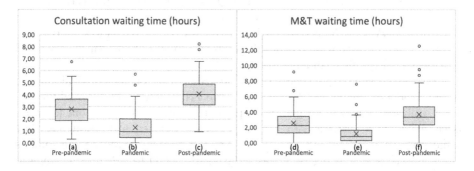

Fig. 10. Patient waiting time simulation results.

Fig. 9(d) and Fig. 10(d) provide the simulation results on M&T. Comparatively, patients undergoing treatment after consultation also presented an elevated waiting time as shown in consultation outcomes, i.e., the waiting time was around 2.56 h despite an average number of 1.10 patients waiting in queue. This simulation provided that the *total patient waiting time* is 4.33 h (in average), confirmed by the managers for their worst-case scenario of observed waiting time.

For improving waiting time and queue size for the pre-pandemic scenario, we suggested the addition of another MD. The new scenario speeds up the Consultation queue in the A&E, where the *total patient waiting time* was reduced from 4.33 to 2.06 h (in average) and the queue from 17.48 to 7.83 patients waiting consultation. The performance bottleneck still persists in the waiting time on Consultation activity, however, for the managers perspective, has increased patient overall satisfaction.

During interviews, managers mentioned that their knowledge about bottlenecks in A&E operation was acquired mostly by daily *in situ* observations and casual patient satisfaction enquiries made in waiting rooms often by temporary staff. They highlighted that the waiting rooms capacity were struggling to accommodate the pre-pandemic demand (mostly in peak days) and the total waiting time was rightly inferred by the baseline simulation. Although managers discussed that the baseline model lacks of adverse events that could worsen the patient waiting time, for instance, when systems become unavailable (e.g., reception totem malfunction) or healthcare services are overloaded (e.g., delays in exam results delivery).

4.2   A&E Disruption Scenarios During and Post-pandemic

The COVID-19 pandemic brought new challenges and policies for hospitals and emergency care regarding their services provision. In the A&E for instance, activities *in situ* such as consultations were dramatically reduced. Managers reported a 50% reduction on face-to-face assistance to patients, and scheduled resources (MDs and nurses) started performing new activities concerning the urgent actions needed by the pandemic (e.g extra time to put protective equipment or cleansing). An isolated service ward separated from A&E was set to treat only COVID-19 infections. MDs in the A&E received new shared tasks, however their priority were to consult patients arriving at the emergency ward as expected in the pre-pandemic scenario.

Our second simulation scenario is a 50% reduction on inter-arrival time in A&E (exponent. distr. as 23.25 min). Figure 8(b) shows a high variability on MDs' utilisation, so the reduction on patients arrival provided room for MDs is shared in new activities. In Fig. 8(e) Nurses reduced utilisation, i.e. they could operate in a reduced number in A&E or having shared responsibilities on new activities. Waiting time was reduced from 2.80 to 1.28 h on average in Consultation activity during pandemic as observed in Fig. 10(b), and queue size from 17.48 to 6.12 patients on Fig. 9(b). Regarding M&T in Fig. 10(e) and Fig. 9(e), waiting time was reduced to 1.17 h representing a 50% drop in services provided with less than one queued patient during workdays. Both reductions were caused by the decrease in urgent care (less people on the streets, fewer car/work related accidents) and by the patients' concern on being contaminated when accessing the hospital premises (avoiding visits). The simulation results showed that MDs and nurses (A&E capacity) were sufficient to assist non-urgent cases which are not related to COVID-19 during the pandemic.

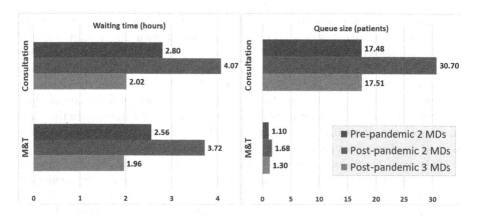

Fig. 11. Comparison of pre-pandemic and post-pandemic scenarios.

A post-pandemic effect on hospital operations is predicted by managers and MDs with bottleneck even more evident especially on A&E and other services interrupted such as cancer treatments, surgeries scheduling, and several others. The arrival rates were suppressed during pandemic period and when services return to normal operation more patients will seek care for their health issues in minor and major cases. We have increased the inter-arrival patient time by 25% in the post-pandemic scenario in comparison with pre-pandemic, assigning an exponentially distributed value of 11.63 m. This increase represents mostly non-urgent patients (e.g., patients with minor to moderate injuries, mild symptoms, or those in the identified risk group for COVID-19) that avoided the hospital premises during the pandemic. Figure 8(c) shows MDs' utilisation will be close to 100% all the time, meaning that after post-pandemic wave slows down, resources in the A&E are to be increased to reduce their utilisation rate to levels similar to pre-pandemic settings. Nurses suffered an increase on utilisation rate but still less than 8% (in average).

Patient waiting time for consultation has doubled in post-pandemic scenario with two MDs, from 2.80 h to 4.07 h as shown in Fig. 11. The queue size has increased from 17.48 to 30.70 patients similarly, which represents an even worst scenario to be faced regarding patient experience in the waiting rooms. For that reason, we have simulated an alternative post-pandemic scenario increasing capacity to three MDs and the simulation results presented in Fig. 11. It showed an improvement in waiting time (about 2 h for consultation) that could be compared to pre-pandemic scenario with two MDs (2.80 h), and also queue size was computed as 17.51 patients, in average.

5   Conclusion

M&S is crucial to accurately model diverse situations in healthcare. When models are parametrised with actual data, they provide valuable insights to managers as to how to best allocate (limited) resources or cope with increasing demand, to mention a few advantages. This is especially relevant with major unanticipated events such as what the world is now witnessing with COVID-19. Emerging countries are particularly interested in such results as the situation has only worsened after the pandemic. The problem will persist even after the pandemic subsides, as there as no vaccines for the whole population and, on top of that, it is unfeasible to think about a 100% coverage that could exterminate the virus throughout the globe. It is thus only reasonable to prepare for a constant increase in these respiratory issues cases with higher contagion levels.

This work highlighted the importance of M&S on actual settings and the need for better collecting input data for more consistent quantitative measures. It seems like this is a solved problem, however, in emerging countries buying less expensive ERPs, this is very challenging and a source of concern. Hospital nurses and MDs were trained to input better data into the ERP software and interact with the modelling sector to improve the process models even further.

As limitations of our work we may cite that it could fall short in terms of adaptability to new situations, i.e., it has a fixed evaluation quality that it is hard to circumvent whenever a crisis or an anticipated behaviour is bound to occur. In this sense, we hope that the models could be quickly revised and re-executed, where specialised personnel would pinpoint shortcomings on the process and advise the medical staff in a timely manner.

Our work has considered pre and post-pandemic scenario analysis varying inter-arrival time and resource allocation to specific tasks in A&E of a sizeable hospital in Brazil. The results have discussed the impact of the pandemic on the hospital A&E department, helping managers devise new operational strategies to cope with demand and address better allocations.

As future work, we aim to expand the model with other activities and assign resources to tasks to increase the modelling opportunities of more realistic settings. We also would like to review service times and suggest improvements to management as to deadlines so MDs and nurses could meet to increase operational efficiency due to adversities, and deal better with process bottlenecks.

Acknowledgements. We thank HSC managers and staff for the research opportunity and the time spent on interviews as well as sharing datasets from their healthcare system. We are grateful to Dr Sandra Quickert and Dr Marco B. Caminati for discussions on input data analysis.

References

1. Antonacci, G., Calabrese, A., D'Ambrogio, A., Giglio, A., Intrigila, B., Ghiron, N.L.: A BPMN-based automated approach for the analysis of healthcare processes. In: Proceedings of the 25th International Conference on Enabling Technologies: Infrastructure for Collaborative Enterprises (WETICE), pp. 124–129. IEEE Computer Society (2016)
2. Baril, C., Gascon, V., Vadeboncoeur, D.: Discrete-event simulation and design of experiments to study ambulatory patient waiting time in an emergency department. J. Oper. Res. Soc. **70**(12), 2019–2038 (2019)

3. Bisogno, S., Calabrese, A., Gastaldi, M., Ghiron, N.L.: Combining modelling and simulation approaches: how to measure performance of business processes. Bus. Process Manag. J. **22**, 56–74 (2016)
4. Bowles, J., Czekster, R.M., Webber, T.: Annotated BPMN models for optimised healthcare resource planning. In: Mazzara, M., Ober, I., Salaün, G. (eds.) STAF 2018. LNCS, vol. 11176, pp. 146–162. Springer, Cham (2018). https://doi.org/10. 1007/978-3-030-04771-9_12
5. Carenzo, L., et al.: Hospital surge capacity in a tertiary emergency referral centre during the COVID-19 outbreak in Italy. Anaesthesia **75**(7), 928–934 (2020)
6. Costa, L.B.M., Filho, M.G., Rentes, A.F., Bertani, T.M., Mardegan, R.: Lean healthcare in developing countries: evidence from Brazilian hospitals. Int. J. Health Plan. Manag. **32**, e99–e120 (2017)
7. Czekster, R.M., Webber, T., Jandrey, A.H., Marcon, C.A.M.: Selection of enterprise resource planning software using analytic hierarchy process. Enterp. Inf. Syst. **13**(6), 895–915 (2019)
8. Doniec, K., Dall'Alba, R., King, L.: Brazil's health catastrophe in the making. Lancet **392**, 731–732 (2018)
9. FitzGerald, G., Jelinek, G.A., Scott, D., Gerdtz, M.F.: Emergency department triage revisited. Emerg. Med. J. **27**(2), 86–92 (2010)
10. Günal, M., Pidd, M.: Discrete event simulation for performance modelling in health care: a review of the literature. J. Simul. **4**, 42–51 (2010). https://doi.org/10.1057/ jos.2009.25
11. Heymann, D.L., Shindo, N.: COVID-19: what is next for public health? Lancet **395**(10224), 542–545 (2020)
12. Hussain, M., Malik, M.: Prioritizing lean management practices in public and private hospitals. J. Health Organ. Manag. **30**(3), 457–474 (2016)
13. Law, A., Kelton, W.: Simulation Modeling and Analysis, 3rd edn. McGraw-Hill, New York (2000)
14. Pongjetanapong, K., Walker, C., O'Sullivan, M., Lovell-Smith, M., Furian, N.: Exploring trade-offs between staffing levels and turnaround time in a pathology laboratory using discrete event simulation. Int. J. Health Plan. Manag. **34**(2), e1119–e1134 (2019)
15. Rossetti, M.D.: Simulation Modeling and Arena, 2nd edn. Wiley Press, Hoboken (2010)
16. Salmon, A., Rachuba, S., Briscoe, S., Pitt, M.: A structured literature review of simulation modelling applied to emergency departments: current patterns and emerging trends. Oper. Res. Health Care **19**, 1–13 (2018)
17. Sokolowski, J.A., Banks, C.M.: Principles of Modeling and Simulation: A Multidisciplinary Approach. Wiley, Hoboken (2011)
18. WHO: World health organisation, covid-19 dashboard, country: Brazil (2020). https://covid19.who.int/region/amro/country/br. Accessed 23 June 2020

A Formal Model for Emulating
the Generation of Human Knowledge
in Semantic Memory

Antonio Cerone$^{(\boxtimes)}$ (ID) and Graham Pluck

Department of Computer Science, School of Engineering and Digital Sciences,
Nazarbayev University, Nur-Sultan, Kazakhstan
{antonio.cerone,graham.pluck}@nu.edu.kz

Abstract. The transfer of information processed by human beings from
their short-term memory (STM) to their semantic memory creates two
kinds of knowledge: a semantic network of associations and a structured
set of rules to govern human deliberate behaviour under explicit attention. This paper focuses on the memory processes that create the first
of these two kinds of knowledge. Human memory storage and processing are modeled using the Real-time Maude rewrite language. Maude's
capability of specifying complex data structures as many sorted algebras
and the time features of Real-Time Maude are exploited for (1) providing a means for formalising alternative memory models, (2) modelling
in silico experiments to compare and validate such models. We aim at
using our model for the comparison of alternative cognitive hypothesis
and theories and the analysis of interactive systems.

Keywords: Cognitive science · Human memory models · Formal
methods · Rewriting logic · Real-Time Maude

1 Introduction

Human *semantic memory* is a core aspect of declarative *long-term memory
(LTM)*, comprised of propositional information, specifically word meanings and
facts. An example of semantic memory being the fact that a penguin is a bird.
Clearly, such information must be acquired from the environment, such as reading, or formal education.

In terms of information flow within the human memory system, sensations of
the environment (e.g., sounds heard) are first processed by modality-specific sensory stores, which we globally call *sensory memory*. Items attended in those sensory stores persist for very short time periods and are then passed to a temporary
short-term memory (STM) limited capacity store (about 7 items [21], usually

Work partly funded by Project SEDS2020004 "Analysis of cognitive properties of interactive systems using model checking", Nazarbayev University, Kazakhstan (Award
number: 240919FD3916).

J. Bowles et al. (Eds.): DataMod 2020, LNCS 12611, pp. 104–122, 2021.
https://doi.org/10.1007/978-3-030-70650-0_7

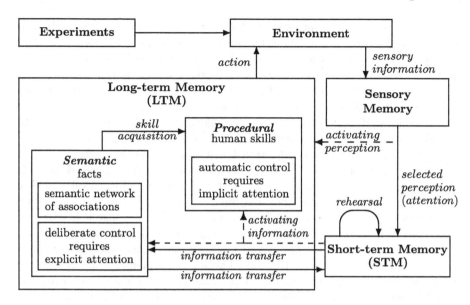

Fig. 1. Human memory architecture

called *chunks* [24], for healthy adults), with rapid access and rapid decay. From STM information passes to LTM, which has a virtually unlimited capacity and where information is organised in structured ways, with slow access but little or no decay. Finally, within LTM, information repeatedly used in practice activities may move from semantic memory to *procedural memory*, thus determining skill acquisition. In fact, the transfer from semantic memory to procedural memory refers to our skills and consists of rules and procedures that we unconsciously use to carry out tasks, particularly at the motor level.

This structure of human memory is depicted in Fig. 1, where continuous arrows show transfer of information between memory components while dashed arrows denote information stored in the source component that activate memory processing in the target component.

In previous work [12] we considered the transfer of information from semantic memory to STM as a means to retrieve knowledge stored in semantic memory, in order to perform in silico experiments in which an emulated human subject answers questions that refer to specific knowledge domains. Such previous work builds up from the definition of the Behaviour and Reasoning Description Language (BRDL) [11] and its implementation for the emulation of human reasoning [13] as well as from earlier work, which was based on the Human Behaviour Description Language (HBDL), a subset of BRDL, and proposed and partly implemented an approach to the modelling of automatic and deliberate human behaviour while interacting with an environment consisting of heterogenous physical components [9,10].

A similar approach to ours was developed by Broccia *et al.* [5], who, driven by the specific objective of modelling human multitasking, used Real-time Maude to extend our initial untimed framework [9]. In their work, however, time is used to model non-cognitive aspects, such as the duration of the task, which is an interface-dependent outcome of the interaction process, and external aspect, such as the delay due to the switching from one task to another. In contrast to Broccia *et al.* we focus on the human component and model the duration of the mental process, which is an important aspect of human cognition.

In this paper we focus on the transfer of factual knowledge from STM to semantic memory and model this memory process using Real-Time Maude [25, 26]. The large time gap between the rapid decay of the information stored in STM (of the order of seconds [22]) and the little or no decay of the information in semantic memory (and in LTM, in general) has pushed research in cognitive psychology to look for something in between. In fact, nowadays, among cognitive scientists there is a tacit acceptance of an intermediate memory stage that somehow bridges the gap between STM and LTM, a form of memory that operates in the range of minutes to a few hours and, possibly, extending even further in time. Alan Dix calls this intermediate level *mezzanine memory* and believes it likely to be carried through long-term potentiation [17,18] while modern neuroscience locates it in the hippocampus [18,19].

The minutes-hours magnitude of decay time makes it difficult to study mezzanine memory in an experimental setting: too long to observe decay within a single experimental session and too short to measure the effect of the decay between two consecutive experimental sessions. For this reason there is little mention of such a kind of intermediate memory in the literature. In *reading comprehension* it is sometime called *long-term short-term memory*, while other time it is identified with *working memory* and is thus seen as a different level of memory that overlaps with both STM and LTM. For example in the context of reading a book, there is an interplay between what we store in STM from what we are currently reading, the recall of what we have read in the same chapter several minutes before, and the more long-term memory of the book plot, which can date back to several days, when we read previous chapters.

A more extreme position is the 'Levels of Processing' framework of Craik and Lockhart [16]. They argue that deeper (semantic) processing causes slower decay, but they are talking of a unitary memory store which encompasses both STM and LTM processes. Nevertheless, as they consider only one memory store, their reduced decay rate argument applies to short-term storage. This idea of 'deeper processing' is equivalent to elaborative rehearsal.

In this work we aim at proposing an in silico approach to filling the experimental gap between STM and LTM. Although it is hard to carry out experiments on human subjects to validate hypotheses about the mezzanine memory or, more in general, about the mechanism underlying the transfer of information between STM and LTM, we expect that the in silico emulation of such experiments would produce important insights into this matter. Moreover, this approach would, in some sense, blur the difference between experimental investigation and case study-based investigation. In fact, the in silico emulation would allow the researcher to consider a large amount of data and a specific human memory model for a single individual, and perform an intensive analysis within a much shorter time than in a real-life case study.

The rest of this paper is organised as follows. The Real-Time Maude code illustrated in this paper can be downloaded from a GitHub repository[1]. Section 2 briefly introduces informal cognitive models of the information transfer from STM to LTM from the cognitive psychology literature, with reference to maintenance rehearsal and elaborative rehearsal. Section 3 first provides a brief highlight of Real-Time Maude and refers to the sections of the paper where the different aspects of the language are illustrated. Then it extensively presents the Real-time Maude formal models for the information to be processed and for its STM and semantic memory stores. Section 4 is devoted to the formal models of memory processes: perception in Sect. 4.1, maintenance rehearsal in Sect. 4.2, elaborative rehearsal in Sect. 4.3, and the actual learning process that consolidates knowledge in semantic memory in Sect. 4.4. Section 5 illustrates our formal models using the two cases of *rote learning*, in Sect. 5.1, and *effective learning*, in Sect. 5.2. Section 6 concludes the paper.

2   Cognitive Models for Information Transfer

The sequential processing from STM to LTM is captured by several cognitive models, most commonly, the Multistore Model [1] and Working Memory Model [3], however, both are equivalent in proposing structural distinctions between phonologically-coded STM storage for verbal content and a separate LTM. The STM and LTM distinction is known partially through cognitive neuroscience, as it is observed that brain lesions can selectively impair either phonological STM capacity or LTM contents (either semantic or episodic). Furthermore, severe reductions in STM capacity caused by brain lesions, such as the inability to hold more than two items in phonological STM simultaneously, also prevent the acquisition of new semantic memory entries in LTM [4]. Thus, indicating that items for storage in semantic memory must first be processed within phonological STM.

The mechanism by which information transfers from STM to semantic memory is *elaborative rehearsal* [2]. This involves using the items within STM to access existing entries within semantic memory. This deep processing, based on semantics, increases the chance that the items will become stored in LTM, probably by strengthening their appropriate connection within the nexus of semantic entries. This elaborative rehearsal within STM, which induces transfer to LTM, can be contrasted with *maintenance rehearsal*. This latter form of processing can be seen as phonological looping of the items to renew their representations within STM, thereby delaying signal decay.

---

[1] http://github.com/AntonioCerone/Publications/tree/master/2020/DataMod/ Cognition.

As shown in Fig. 1, among the sensory information briefly stored in sensory memory, attention selects some and transfers it to STM. Information in STM can then be used

- to activate the deliberate control in semantic memory or the automatic control in procedural memory, or,
- after elaborative rehearsal, to create associations as well as deliberate control rules in semantic memory.

Moreover, information can be retrieved from semantic memory and transferred to STM. Furthermore, the repeated use of rules for deliberate control in semantic memory produces skill acquisition and the resultant creation of rules for automatic control in procedural memory. In previous work we have formally modeled human behaviour under deliberate and automatic control [13] as well as information retrieval from semantic memory [12].

3   Real-Time Maude Models of STM and Semantic Memory

Real-Time Maude [25,26] is a formal modeling language and high-performance simulation and model-checking tool for distributed real-time systems. It is based on Full Maude, the object-oriented extension of Core Maude, which is the basic version of Maude. Real-Time Maude makes use of

- algebraic equational specifications in a functional programming style to define data types;
- labeled rewrite rules to define local transitions;
- tick rewrite rules to advance time in the entire system state.

Maude *equational logic* supports declaration of *sorts*, with keyword `sort` for one sort, or `sorts` for many. A sort `A` may be specified as a subsort of a sort `B` by `subsort A < B`. Operators are introduced with the `op` (for a single definition) and `ops` (for multiple definitions) keywords:

$$\text{op } f \; : \; s_1 \ldots s_n \; \text{->} \; s.$$
$$\text{ops } f_1 \; f_2 \colon \; s_1 \ldots s_n \; \text{->} \; s.$$

Operators can have user-defined syntax, with underbars '_' marking the argument positions and '' ' ' to denote a space. Some operators can have *equational attributes*, such as `assoc`, `comm`, and `id`, stating that the operator is associative, commutative and has a certain identity element, respectively. Such attributes are used by the Maude engine to match terms *modulo* the declared axioms. An operator can also be declared to be a constructor (`ctor`) that defines the carrier of a sort. Axioms are introduced as equations using the `eq` keyword or, if they can be applied only under a certain condition, using the `ceq` keyword, with the condition introduced by the `if` keyword. Variables used in equations are placeholders in a mathematical sense and cannot be assigned values. They must be declared with the keyword `var` for one variable, or `vars` for many. The use of the `owise` (or `otherwise`) equational attributes in an equation denotes that the axiom is used for all cases that are not matched by the previous equations. All Maude statements are ended by a dot.

In the rest of this section we define the formal infrastructure that we use to model STM, semantic memory and the information items stored in them. Some additional details about Core Maude data types are illustrated in Sect. 3.2. The Full Maude syntax for classes is illustrated in Sect. 4 while the syntax for messages as well as labelled rewrite rules and Real-Time Maude tick rewrite rules are illustrated in Sect. 4.1.

3.1   Facts, Questions and Goals

Humans, throughout their lives, acquire knowledge of the *facts of the real world* and are able to refer to them and reason about them using *declarative proposi-tions*. Since a declarative proposition is just a natural language description of a fact, we will often use the word 'fact' also to denote the declarative proposition that describes it. Moreover, human beings reason about facts, and organise such facts in their semantic memory triggered by *questions* that are put to them, or they put to themselves.

We model a *fact* in Real-Time Maude as follows:

```
a "dog" is a "animal".
```

The article 'a' is used for any noun, although this is ungrammatical when the noun starts with a vowel as in the case of 'animal'. Other examples of facts are:

```
a "animal" can "breathe"
a "dog" can "move"
a "dog" can "bark"
a "cat" cannot "bark"
a "cat" is not a "dog"
```

In such examples `"animal"`, `"dog"` and `"cat"` are categories, `"breathe"`, `"move"` and `"bark"` are attributes and `is a`, `can`, `is not a` and `cannot` are types to be applied to attributes. Categories may also be used as attributes as in `a "dog" is a "animal"`. The application of a type to an attribute, such as `is a "animal"` or `can "breathe"`, is called *typed attribute*.

A *question* may be of several kinds [12]. In this paper we consider only `can` questions and `is a` questions, such as:

```
can a "dog" "breathe" ?
is a "dog" a "animal" ?
```

The two questions, which have the same structure, will be answered by one declarative proposition, by stating the fact either negatively or positively.

A *goal* specifies what a human being aims at achieving as the result of an activity. Goals drive deliberate behaviour, which exploits the knowledge in semantic memory, but do not affect automatic behaviour, which exploits the knowledge in procedural memory [9,10,13]. In deliberate behaviour, goals activate *attention*, a selective processing activity that aims to focus on one aspect of the environment while ignoring others, thus allowing the human mind to focus on goal-relevant stimuli in the environment (*explicit attention*). Another form of attention, called *implicit attention*, is grabbed by sudden stimuli that are associated with the current mental state or carry emotional significance, thus determining automatic behaviour. For the purpose of this paper we only consider explicit attention.

We model a goal by considering two aspects: a *domain of knowledge* to which we refer and what we gain once the goal is achieved. For example, rehearsing facts of our knowledge about dogs may be our goal. Then `"dogs"` is the domain and `"rehearsed"` is what we gain as the achievement of our goal. Moreover, the goal of rehearsing a fact will activate our explicit attention to focus on the presence of fact descriptions in the environment, such as a written statement describing a fact.

3.2   Modelling Basic Information Items and Goals

We model *basic information items* (facts and questions) and *goals* in Real-Time Maude as follows:

```
sorts Fact Question Domain BasicItem Item Goal .
subsorts Fact Question < BasicItem < Item .
subsort Goal < Item .

sorts BasicItemSet ItemSet EmptyItemSet .
subsort BasicItem < BasicItemSet .
subsorts EmptyItemSet < BasicItemSet < ItemSet .
subsort Item < ItemSet .
op none : -> EmptyItemSet [ctor] .
op _;_ : BasicItemSet BasicItemSet ->
            BasicItemSet [ctor assoc comm id: none format (b o n b)] .
op _;_ : ItemSet ItemSet -> ItemSet [ctor ditto] .
op _;_ : EmptyItemSet EmptyItemSet -> EmptyItemSet [ctor ditto] .
op goal : Domain BasicItemSet Nat Nat -> Goal [ctor] .
```

Sorts `Facts`, `Question` and `Goal` model facts, questions and goals, respectively. The first two are subsorts of `BasicItem`. Sorts `BasicItem` and `Goal` are subsorts of `Item`.

Both `BasicItem` and `Item` are organised into sets by defining the two sorts `BasicItemSet` and `ItemSet` using the `;` user-defined infix operator, which is given the appropriate equational attributes for the properties that characterise sets. The `ditto` equational attribute is a short form for all attributes of the previous sort declaration. The `format` equational attribute is used to format the output with spaces, colours and newlines in order to make it more readable. By declaring `BasicItem` as a subsort of `BasicItemSet` and `Item` as a subsort of `ItemSet` we implicitly define singletons of sorts `BasicItemSet` and `ItemSet`.

However, the **none** empty set needs to be explicitly introduced as the only element of sort `EmptyItemSet`, which is subsort of `BasicItemSet`, in turn subsort of `ItemSet`.

The sorts `Category` and `Attribute` include Maude-predefined sort `String` as a subsort:

```
sorts Category Attribute TypedAttribute .
subsort String < Category < Attribute .
subsort String < Domain .
```

This allows us to freely use any string, which is enclosed by double quotes in Maude syntax, as a category or attribute, while leaving open the option to use other representations in possible extensions of the module. The elements of sorts `TypedAttributes`, `Facts` and `Questions` are instead defined using constructors, since they have special relationships between each other and need to be manipulated in special, distinct ways by the Maude engine. Attribute types **can** and **is a** as well as facts and questions constructed using them are modeled as follow:

```
ops can_ is'a_ : Attribute -> TypedAttribute [ctor] .
ops cannot_ is'not'a_ : Attribute -> TypedAttribute [ctor] .
op a__ : Category TypedAttribute -> Fact [ctor] .
ops can'a__? is'a__? : Category Attribute -> Question [ctor] .
op _is'negative'of_ : TypedAttribute TypedAttribute -> Bool .
```

One of these special relationships is the negation: **cannot** and **is not** are the negations of **can** and **is**, respectively. Negation is expressed as an infix boolean operator **is negative of**.

Goals are defined using the constructor **goal**. In addition to the two aspects mentioned in Sect. 3.1, the knowledge domain, of sort `Domain`, and the achievement, of sort `BasicItemSet`, the constructor **goal** has two additional arguments of sort `Nat`. The first `Nat` argument models the number of times the goal is planned to be achieved, for example, the number of time we want to rehearse a given fact. The second argument is the *goal determination*, namely how determinate we are in achieving the goal. However, the usage of this argument is beyond the purpose of our paper.

3.3 Modelling Explicit Attention and Goal Achievements

In order to model the explicit attention we need to extract achievements from the goals. We use the operators `isAchievement` and `explicitAttention`, which are defined as follows:

```
sort Achievement .
subsort Achievement < BasicItem .
ops foundAnswer rehearsed : -> Achievement [ctor] .
ops isAchievement explicitAttention : BasicItem ItemSet -> Bool .

vars BI1 BI2 : BasicItem .    var BIS : BasicItemSet .
var IS : ItemSet .    var D : Domain .    vars DET REP : Nat .
eq isAchievement(BI1, goal(D, (BI2 ; BIS), DET, REP) ; IS) =
```

```
            BI1 == BI2 or isAchievement(BI1, IS) .
eq isAchievement(BI1, IS) = false [owise] .

var Q : Question .   var F : Fact .
eq explicitAttention(Q,
              goal(D, (foundAnswer ; BIS), DET, REP) ; IS) = true .
eq explicitAttention(F,
              goal(D, (rehearsed ; BIS), DET, REP) ; IS) = true .
eq explicitAttention(BI1, IS) = false [owise] .
```

For the purpose of our paper we only consider two achievements: foundAnswer, which drives attentions to questions to be answered, and rehearsed, which drives attentions to facts to be rehearsed.

3.4 STM—Short-Term Memory

STM is normally used as a buffer where the information that is needed for processing activities is temporarily stored. In our previous work [12] we modeled the mechanism for emptying STM when the stored information is no longer needed by associating a *decay time* with each information item stored in STM. A fixed value of decay time was associated with the information item at the moment this was first stored in STM, then decreased according to the passing of time and, when it was down to 0, the item was removed from STM. We now extend this model by separating the actual *lifetime* of an information item from its decay time at the current time of its lifetime. These two time aspects of an STM-stored information item are the two time arguments of the constructor chunk_decay_of_, which is defined as follows:

```
sorts Chunk ShortTermMemory .
subsort Chunk < ShortTermMemory .

op chunk_decay_of_ : ItemSet TimeInf TimeInf -> Chunk [ctor] .
op emptySTM : -> ShortTermMemory [ctor] .
op _;_ : ShortTermMemory ShortTermMemory ->
    ShortTermMemory [ctor assoc comm id: emptySTM format (b o n b)] .

eq chunk ITEM:Item decay 0 of T:TimeInf = emptySTM .
```

Another extension with respect to our previous model is the use of the notion of *chunk*. Information items can be aggregated to form chunks whereby STM capacity refers to the number of chunks rather than the number of information items. The exact mechanism of chucking in human memory is poorly understood. However, it is thought that conjoining items by their associations within LTM (e.g. common word collocations), such that a person's past experience would influence the chunk selection, is part of the mechanism, as it is a form of data compression where pieces of information are renamed under a new label, such as '6' and '1' being labeled as '61' [24].

As shown in the Maude code above, operator chunk_decay_of_, whose syntax is user-defined, associates two possibly infinite times with the aggregate set of information item that forms the chunk (an element of sort `Chunk`). The sort `TimeInf` extend the sort `Time` with value `INF` to model an infinite time. Obviously, an infinite decay time means no decay at all; although this is unrealistic for human STM, it may be useful in testing and calibrating newly defined models. The sort `ShortTermMemory` defines sets of chunks (of sort `Chunk`, which is a subsort of sort `ShortTermMemory`) using the constructor `;`. The nullary operator `emptySTM` defines an STM that does not contain any information, that is, an empty set of chunks. The equation on the constructor `chunk_decay_of_` ensures that if the decay time has reached zero, the chunk is removed from STM.

Both times specified in the chunk are initialised with a standard decay time, whose value is fixed *a priori* when the chunk is first stored in STM. Then the first time argument (decay time) decreases according to the passing of time whereas the second argument (lifetime) does not change as long as the chunk is passively kept in STM without being used. However, if the chunk is used to carry out maintenance rehearsal or to access information in semantic memory, then also the lifetime may increase, thus consolidating the information chunk and paving the way for its transfer to semantic memory. This modelling approach is consistent with the cognitive neuroscience finding that the phonological looping of items renews their representations within STM, thereby delaying signal decay. In Sect. 4.2 and Sect. 4.3 we present formal models of this mechanism for maintenance rehearsal and elaborative rehearsal, respectively.

3.5   Semantic Memory

Semantic memory has been modeled in our previous work to represent knowledge about rules that govern human behaviour [9,10,13], acquired inference rules [13] and facts of the real world [12,13]. In this paper we focus on fact representation and explain our approach using a case study taken from our previous work [12].

A *fact representation* in semantic memory is modeled as follows:

```
sorts FactRepresentation SemanticMemory .
subsort FactRepresentation < SemanticMemory .

op emptySemantic : -> SemanticMemory .
op _:_|-_->|_ : Domain Category Time TypedAttribute ->
    FactRepresentation [ctor format (!r o b o r o b o)] .
op __ : SemanticMemory SemanticMemory ->
    SemanticMemory [ctor assoc comm id: emptySemantic format (o n o)] .
op _is`negated`in_ : Fact SemanticMemory -> Bool .
```

The finite time that appears as one of the arguments of the fact representation constructor is the retrieval time (RT) of the fact from semantic memory. As an example, the fact that 'a dog is an animal' is represented within the semantic domain `"dogs"` as

```
"dogs" : "dog" |- 1 ->| is a "animal"
```

and this form of generalisation can be retrieved from semantic memory in 1 time unit. The more specific category of a generalisation (e.g., `"dog"`) inherits all typed attributes of the more generic category (e.g., `"animal"`) unless the attribute is redefined at the more specific category level. Therefore,

```
"animals" : "animal" |- 1 ->| can "move"
```

which is an association of a category with a typed attribute, specifies that 'an animal can move' and, since an animal is a generalisation of a dog, such a typed attribute is inherited by the category `"dog"` ('a dog can move').

Fact representations are defined as elements of the sort `FactRepresentation`. The semantic memory is modelled by the sort `SemanticMemory`, which is defined as a set of fact representations. The constructor __ denotes that sets of fact representations are created by justapposition, with no written operator. The constructor `emptySemantic` denotes an empty semantic memory.

4   Modelling Memory Processes

In this section we show how the different memory components are put together as a Full Maude class object and, in Sect. 4.1, 4.2, 4.3 and 4.4 how tick rewrite rules are used to model memory processes.

A declaration class $C \mid att_1 : s_1, \ldots, att_n : s_n$ declares a class C with attributes att_1 to att_n of sorts s_1 to s_n. An *object* of class C is represented as a term $< O : C \mid att_1 : val_1, \ldots, att_n : val_n >$ of sort `Object`, where O, of sort `Oid`, is the object's *identifier*, and where val_1 to val_n are the current values of the attributes att_1 to att_n.

We model the structure of human memory using the following Real-Time Maude class:

```
class HumanMemory | shortTermMem : ShortTermMemory,
                    semanticMem : SemanticMemory .
```

STM is modelled by the field `shortTermMem`. Semantic memory is modelled by the field `SemanticMem`. Note that this model has been simplified for the purpose of this paper and does not include some other memory components, such as procedural memory, and memory attributes, such as the cognitive load.

4.1   Perception

Although sensations of the environment are initially processed by *sensory memory* before being passed to STM, in our model we assume that *perceptions* available in the environment are selected using attention and directly transferred to STM. In order to model perceptions we use Full Maude messages. A message is an element of the pre-defined sort `Msg` and has the same syntax as an operation but, in addition, is also an element of the pre-defined sort `Configuration`. The system state is a term of sort `Configuration`, and is a *multiset* of objects and messages. Multiset union is denoted by an associative and commutative juxtaposition operator, so that rewriting is *multiset rewriting*.

Therefore, a perception is modelled as a message using the constructor `perc` as follows:

```
sorts Perception TimedBasicItem FutureBasicItem .
subsorts Perception < Msg .

op _for_ : BasicItem TimeInf -> TimedBasicItem [ctor] .
op perc : TimedBasicItem -> Perception [ctor] .
var BI : BasicItem .
eq perc(BI for 0) = none .
```

The persistence of a perception in the environment is modeled by the constructor for. Note that the time may be infinite to denote that the perception persists forever. The equation ensures that if the persistence time has reached zero, the perception is removed from the configuration (none is the empty configuration).

The processing of information within memory components and the transfer of information between components are modeled using Real-Time Maude tick rewrite rules. Labeled rewrite rules

$$\text{rl } [l] : t \Rightarrow t' \quad \text{or} \quad \text{crl } [l] : t \Rightarrow t' \text{ if } cond$$

define local transitions from state t to state t'. Tick rewrite rules

$$\text{rl } [l] : \{t\} \Rightarrow \{t'\} \text{ in time } \Delta \quad \text{or} \quad \text{crl } [l] : \{t\} \Rightarrow \{t'\} \text{ in time } \Delta \text{ if } cond$$

advance time in the *entire* state t by Δ time units.

The following rewrite rule models the storage in STM of information perceived from the environment:

```
crl [perception-explicit-storage] :
    (perc (BI for T))
    < H : Human | shortTermMem : STM >
    REST
=>
    < H : Human | shortTermMem :
        (chunk BI decay DECAY-TIME of DECAY-TIME) ; idle(STM,TP) >
    (perc (BI for (T monus TP)))
    REST
in time TP
if TP := tp(perc (BI for T)) /\ IS := removeTime(STM) /\
    explicitAttention(BI, IS) /\ not isItemIn(BI, IS) .
```

The basic information BI, which is available in the environment for the time T, is stored in STM if it is not already there (not isItemIn(BI, IS)) and the untimed content IS of STM drives explicit attention on it (explicitAttention(BI, IS)). As we have seen in Sect. 3.3, the explicitAttention operator checks whether the structure of BI has a matching information in a goal stored in STM. Operator tp gives the time for storing the information in STM. As suggested by Kolers [20] we assign 100 milliseconds (ms) as the time to move orthographic information to a phonological storage, such as the one represented by STM, by defining operator tp as a constant.

4.2   Maintenance Rehearsal

As mentioned in Sect. 1 there is no agreement on what fills in the decay time gap between STM and LTM. However, in order to explain how learning occurs through maintenance rehearsal, Burgess and Hitch [6,7] claim the existence of two learning mechanisms operating in parallel during STM storage. This is part of a model of working memory [4]. That model includes a 'fast' short-term learning process that is the basis of STM and is associated with trace decay, and a 'slow' learning process that gradually leads to LTM (in the same cells), but enhances within STM. These dual learning processes are said to operate in parallel, and are biologically plausible. They are used to explain the Hebb Repetition effect, which is that if the same list is repeated several times, recall from STM is improved, suggesting a longer-range learning mechanism (longer than rehearsal resetting the decay level). As that model emphasises rehearsal as being the basis of the fast learning mechanism, it would be reasonable to assume that the parallel slow learning mechanism would be delaying decay.

The following rewrite rule models the effect of the learning mechanism proposed by Burgess and Hitch:

```
crl [perception-explicit-maintenance] :
   (perc (BI for T))
   < H : Human | shortTermMem : (chunk BI decay T1 of T2) ; STM >
   REST
=>
   < H : Human | shortTermMem :
      (chunk BI decay T2 of maintenance-effect(T2)) ; idle(STM,TP) >
   (perc (BI for (T monus TP)))
   REST
in time TP
if TP := tp(perc (BI for T)) /\ T2 < STM-TO-LTM-THRESHOLD /\
   IS := removeTime(STM)  /\  (rehearsed, IS) .
```

The operator isAchievement, which was defined in Sect. 3.3, is used to activate the rehearsal loop when the untimed content IS of STM includes a goal having rehearsed as its achievement.

Burgess and Hitch's 'fast' short-term learning process is controlled by the T1 decay time, while the parallel slow learning mechanism is represented by an increase in the T2 information lifetime. Such an increase can be set in a way that can accommodate a specific hypothesis or theory by using appropriate equations to define operator maintenance-effect. For example, we can model a small, constant increase at each rehearsal loop or we may implement Naveh-Benjamin and Jonides' suggestion [23], that the first rehearsal is the most important, because it involves producing the rehearsal plan, with subsequent loops of that plan adding little to the transfer to LTM.

Finally, the decay time T1 is reset to the current lifetime T2 (before increase) and the condition on the STM-TO-LTM-THRESHOLD keeps the rehearsal process alive until the appropriate threshold for transferring to LTM is reached.

4.3   Elaborative Rehearsal

Suppose that we know that a "animal" can "move" but we do not know that a "dog" is a "animal". Once we read this new fact, which thus enters our STM, elaborative rehearsal could be activated by questions about dogs that require the retrieval of animal's attributes. The question can a "dog" "move" ? would allow us to use the just read new fact (a "dog" is a "animal") to retrieve the answer as an attribute of category "animal". As explained in Sect. 2, the usage of information within STM to access existing entries within semantic memory would increase its chance to become stored in semantic memory.

In our previous work [12], we introduced a tick rule for answering a can question that explored the knowledge in semantic memory to answer a question stored in STM, but without using any fact possibly stored in STM in the retrieval process. The following tick rewrite rule extends our previous tick rule by (1) using information stored in STM in combination with the knowledge in semantic memory in order to answer the question; (2) modifying the lifetime of the facts stored in STM that are used in the retrieval process.

```
crl [retrieval-can-elaborative-is-a] :
   < H : Human |
     shortTermMem : (chunk goal(D, foundAnswer, N1, N2) decay T1 of T2) ;
                    (chunk (can a C A ?) decay T3 of T4) ; STM,
     semanticMem : S >
   REST
=>
   < H : Human |
     shortTermMem : NEW-GOAL-CHUNK ;
                    (chunk F decay DECAY-TIME of DECAY-TIME) ;
                    idle(NEW-STM, T),
     semanticMem : S >
   idle(REST,T)
in time T
if F := a C can A /\ IS := removeTime(STM) /\ not isItemIn(F, IS) /\
   T := canRetrievalTime(C, A, S, IS) /\ T <= MAX-RETRIEVAL-TIME /\
   NEW-STM := elaborativeRetrieval(C, A, S, STM) /\
   not ( F is negated in S ) /\ not isItemIn(a C cannot A, IS) /\
   NEW-GOAL-CHUNK := if N1 > 0
         then (chunk goal(D, foundAnswer, N1 monus 1, N2)
                  decay DECAY-TIME of DECAY-TIME)
         else emptySTM fi .
```

The retrieval time T is calculated using the canRetrievalTime operator, which searches in the semantic memory S for a fact representation with category Cn and typed attribute can A, where either $Cn = C$ or Cn is a generalisation of C through a chain of facts

a C is a C1,   a C1 is a C2,   ...   a C(n − 1) is a Cn

which either have representations in semantic memory or are in STM.

The operator elaborativeRetrieval performs a similar search in semantic memory but with the purpose of modifying the lifetime of all facts stored in

STM that are used in the process. As in the case of maintenance rehearsal, it is unknown to which extent to modify the lifetime. Again, we can then set such a modification in a way that can accommodate a specific hypothesis or theory. This is achieved by appropriately defining an operator `elaborative-effect`, similar to `mantainence-effect`, and use it within the definition of the operator `elaborativeRetrieval`.

4.4   Transfer from STM to Semantic Memory

The following rule models the transfer of information from STM to Semantic Memory.

```
crl [from-STM-to-LTM-fact] :
   < H : Human |
     shortTermMem : (chunk goal(D, rehearsed, N1, N2) decay T1 of T2) ;
                    (chunk (a C TA) decay T3 of T4) ; STM,
     semanticMem : S >
   REST
=>
   < H : Human |
     shortTermMem : STM,
     semanticMem : (D : C |- 1 ->| TA) S >
   REST
if T4 >= STM-TO-LTM-THRESHOLD .
```

Since the cognitive psychology literature does not provide any information on possible values of the `STM-TO-LTM-THRESHOLD` threshold, we should give an estimation depending on the specific hypothesis or theory we consider in defining the lifetime increments in the cases of maintenance rehearsal and elaborative rehearsal. For instance, if we follow Naveh-Benjamin and Jonides' hypothesis [23], that the first rehearsal loop is the most important, then a reasonable decay time cut-off could be the time taken to get the phonological code into STM. In Sect. 4.1 we considered Kolers' suggestion [20] that the time to move orthographic information to a phonological storage in STM should require approximately 100 ms. However, the conversion of the ortographical format into the phonological format suitable for the storage is achieved by subvocalization which, according to Mueller and Krawitz [22], requires between 1.5 and 2 s. This is in accordance with the original Collins and Quillian experiments [15], which used a two second presentation to their human participants. Therefore, a reasonable threshold should be at least 3 or 4 s, by considering 1.5–2 s for the initial transfer and another 1.5–2 s for the first rehearsal loop.

5   In Silico Experiments

In order to perform in silico experiments we need to define an infrastructure to plan experiments and make them actual at the specified time. We call *planned experiment* the presentation of a single piece of orthographic information (orthographic representation of a fact or a question) to a human subject, together with the time that must pass before it is actually presented.

The experimental infrastructure is modeled as follows:

```
sorts FutureBasicItem SingleExperiment Experiment .
subsort SingleExperiment < Experiment < Msg .
op _in_ : TimedBasicItem Time -> FutureBasicItem [ctor] .
op exp : FutureBasicItem -> SingleExperiment [ctor] .
op noExp : -> Experiment [ctor].
op repeat_times'starting'in_:_ : Nat Time SingleExperiment -> Experiment .

var T : Time .    var E : SingleExperiment .
eq repeat 0 times starting in T : E = none .
eq repeat 1 times starting in T : E = E .
```

A single experiment is modeled as a message `exp((BI for PT) in FT)`, where FT denotes in how many time units the experiment is scheduled and PT denotes the number of time units the perception of the basic information BI persists in the environment. A sequence of experiments is modeled as a message `repeat N times starting in TI : E`, where experiment E is repeated for N times and the sequence starts in TI time units. Two simple rewrite rules generate single experiments from a sequence defined using the `repeat_times'starting'in_:_` operator and a perception from a single experiment.

5.1 Rote Learning

In rote learning, maintenance rehearsal is used for achieving the transfer of the information from STM to semantic memory. For example, if the time is given in milliseconds,

```
repeat 10 times starting in 5000 :
        ((a "dog" is a "animal") for 2000) in 3000
```

models an experimental session that starts in 5 s and in which a human subject is presented the sentence 'a dog is an animal' 10 times, every 3 s, each time for 2 s. Every rehearsal loop increases the fact lifetime in STM until the threshold for transferring to semantic memory is reached so that a representation of the fact is created in semantic memory.

5.2 Effective Learning

In order to model effective learning, we have to make sure that the fact to be learned is first stored in STM and then used to retrieve information from semantic memory. For example

```
((a "dog" is a "animal") for 2000) in 5000
repeat 10 times starting in 3000 :
        ((can a "dog" "move" ?) for 2000) in 3000
```

models an experimental session that starts in 5 s and in which a human subject is first presented the fact 'a dog is an animal' once and is then presented the question 'can a dog move?' 10 times, every 3 s, each time for 2 s. The retrieval process needed to answer the question starts by using the fact in STM and ends by using the representation of the fact a "animal" can "move" in semantic memory. The repeated use of fact a "dog" is a "animal" increases its lifetime in STM until the threshold for transferring to semantic memory is reached so that a representation of the fact is created in semantic memory.

6   Conclusion and Future Work

In this paper we presented an approach to the formal modelling of memory processes underlying the transfer of information from STM to LTM, with focus on the consolidation of factual knowledge in semantic memory. We have tested our approach on a simple experimental setting. In our future work we aim at investigating how our approach can cope with more complex experimental settings.

A number of hypotheses and theories from cognitive psychology have been considered as good candidates to be investigated within our approach. Such hypotheses and theories are normally conceptual in nature, with only vague, controversial quantitative characterisations. For example, STM decay time has been traditionally proposed to be 2 s, but some argue that it is much longer, between 4 and 10 s [22]. Other suggest less than 3 s and Campoy proposes an average estimate of 2,700 ms [8]. Although there are no specific theories that describe mezzanine memory, the manipulation of the chunk lifetime supports the emulation of processes that fill the time gap between STM and semantic memory.

In fact, our in silico experiments can be used to compare such alternative hypotheses and theories, or even contribute to the formulation of new theories, as we aim in the case of mezzanine memory, as part of our future work. One way to carry out such a comparison is to determine and test alternative quantitative implementations of conceptual hypotheses or theories, as we proposed for Burgess and Hitch's parallel learning mechanisms [6,7], in Sect. 4.2, and for Naveh-Benjamin and Jonides' hypothesis [23], in Sect. 4.4. Another way is the direct comparison of alternative estimates form cognitive psychology or neuroscience. This is the case for STM decay time and for Mueller and Krawitz's conversion of the ortographical format into the phonological format.

As part of our future work, the results of in silico experiments may also be compared with real datasets to evince which model best mimics reality. In addition to a manual comparison, we aim at the generalisation of an approach from our previous work [14] in which 'formal validation' is achieved by converting a dataset into a formal representation that can be composed in parallel with the system model. In the context of this paper, the system model is actually the human memory model. Model-checking would then be used to verify properties that may only hold when the dataset matches the in silico experiment.

Finally, the human memory model of a user can be combined with the model of the used computer system. Such an overall model can be formally verified using Real-time Maude model-checking features. This is also part of our future work.

References

1. Atkinson, R.C., Shiffrin, R.M.: Human memory: a proposed system and its control processes. In: Spense, K.W. (ed.) The Psychology of Learning and Motivation: Advances in Research and Theory II, pp. 89–195. Academic Press (1968)
2. Atkinson, R.C., Shiffrin, R.M.: The control of short-term memory. Sci. Am. **225**(2), 82–90 (1971)
3. Baddeley, A.: The episodic buffer: a new component of working memory? Trends Cogn. Sci. **4**(11), 417–423 (2000)
4. Baddeley, A., Papagno, C., Vallar, G.: When long-term learning depends on short-term storage. J. Mem. Lang. **27**(5), 586–595 (1988)
5. Broccia, G., Milazzo, P., Ölveczky, P.C.: Formal modeling and analysis of safety-critical human multitasking. Innovations Syst. Softw. Eng. **15**(3–4), 169–190 (2019). https://doi.org/10.1007/s11334-019-00333-7
6. Burgess, N., Hitch, G.J.: Memory for serial order: a network model of the phonological loop and its timing. Psychol. Rev. **106**(3), 551–581 (1999)
7. Burgess, N., Hitch, G.J.: A revised model of short-term memory and long-term learning of verbal sequences. J. Mem. Lang. **55**(4), 627–652 (2006)
8. Campoy, G.: Evidence for decay in verbal short-term memory: a commentary on Berman, Jonides, and Lewis (2009). J. Exp. Psychol. Learn. Mem. Cogn. **38**(4), 1129–1136 (2012)
9. Cerone, A.: A cognitive framework based on rewriting logic for the analysis of interactive systems. In: De Nicola, R., Kühn, E. (eds.) SEFM 2016. LNCS, vol. 9763, pp. 287–303. Springer, Cham (2016). https://doi.org/10.1007/978-3-319-41591-8_20
10. Cerone, A.: Towards a cognitive architecture for the formal analysis of human behaviour and learning. In: Mazzara, M., Ober, I., Salaün, G. (eds.) STAF 2018. LNCS, vol. 11176, pp. 216–232. Springer, Cham (2018). https://doi.org/10.1007/978-3-030-04771-9_17
11. Cerone, A.: Behaviour and reasoning description language (BRDL). In: Camara, J., Steffen, M. (eds.) SEFM 2019. LNCS, vol. 12226, pp. 137–153. Springer, Cham (2020). https://doi.org/10.1007/978-3-030-57506-9_11
12. Cerone, A., Murzagaliyeva, D.: Information retrieval from semantic memory: BRDL-based knowledge representation and Maude-based computer emulation. In: Cleophas, L., Massink, M. (eds.) SEFM 2020. LNCS, vol. 12524, pp. 159–175. Springer, Cham (2021). https://doi.org/10.1007/978-3-030-67220-1_13
13. Cerone, A., Ölveczky, P.C.: Modelling human reasoning in practical behavioural contexts using Real-Time Maude. In: Sekerinski, E., et al. (eds.) FM 2019. LNCS, vol. 12232, pp. 424–442. Springer, Cham (2020). https://doi.org/10.1007/978-3-030-54994-7_32
14. Cerone, A., Zhexenbayeva, A.: Using formal methods to validate research hypotheses: the Duolingo case study. In: Mazzara, M., Ober, I., Salaün, G. (eds.) STAF 2018. LNCS, vol. 11176, pp. 163–170. Springer, Cham (2018). https://doi.org/10.1007/978-3-030-04771-9_13
15. Collins, A.M., Quillian, M.R.: Retrieval time from semantic memory. J. Verbal Learn. Verbal Behav. **8**, 240–247 (1969)

16. Craik, F.I., Lockhart, R.S.: Levels of processing: a framework for memory research. J. Verbal Learn. Verbal Behav. **11**(6), 671–684 (1972)
17. Dix, A.: Personal communication (2019)
18. Fiebig, F., Lansner, A.: Memory consolidation from seconds to weeks through autonomous reinstatement dynamics in a three-stage neural network model. In: Liljenström, H. (ed.) Advances in Cognitive Neurodynamics (IV). ACN, pp. 47–53. Springer, Dordrecht (2015). https://doi.org/10.1007/978-94-017-9548-7_7
19. Kesner, R.: Parallel processing of spatial and temporal information in rodents and humans: role of the hippocampus. In: Call, J., Burghardt, G.M., Pepperberg, I.M., Snowdon, C.T., Zentall, T. (eds.) APA Handbooks in Psychology®. APA Handbook of Comparative Psychology: Basic Concepts, Methods, Neural Substrate, and Behavior, pp. 517–538. American Psychological Association (2017)
20. Kolers, A.P.: A pattern-analyzing basis of recognition. In: Cermak, L.S., Craik, F.I. (eds.) Levels of Processing in Human Memory, pp. 363–384. Psychology Press, Hove (2014)
21. Miller, G.A.: The magical number seven, plus or minus two: some limits on our capacity to process information. Psychol. Rev. **63**(2), 81–97 (1956)
22. Mueller, S.T., Krawitz, A.: Reconsidering the two-second decay hypothesis in verbal working memory. J. Math. Psychol. **53**(1), 14–25 (2009)
23. Naveh-Benjamin, M., Jonides, J.: Maintenance rehearsal: a two-component analysis. J. Exp. Psychol. Learn. Mem. Cogn. **10**(3), 369 (1984)
24. Norris, D., Kalm, K., Hall, J.: Chunking and redintegration in verbal short-term memory. J. Exp. Psychol. Learn. Mem. Cogn. **46**(5), 872–893 (2019)
25. Ölveczky, P.C.: Real-Time Maude and its applications. In: Escobar, S. (ed.) WRLA 2014. LNCS, vol. 8663, pp. 42–79. Springer, Cham (2014). https://doi.org/10.1007/978-3-319-12904-4_3
26. Ölveczky, P.C., Meseguer, J.: Semantics and pragmatics of Real-Time-Maude. Higher-Order Symb. Comput. **20**(1–2), 161–196 (2007)

Analysis of COVID-19 Data with PRISM: Parameter Estimation and SIR Modelling

Paolo Milazzo[(✉)] [iD]

Department of Computer Science, University of Pisa,
Largo B. Pontecorvo, 3, 56127 Pisa, Italy
paolo.milazzo@unipi.it

Abstract. We propose a pipeline for the stochastic analysis of a SIR model for COVID-19 through the stochastic model checker PRISM. The pipeline consists in: (i) the definition of a modified SIR model, able to include governmental restriction and prevention measures through an additional time-dependent coefficient; (ii) parameter estimation based on real epidemic data; (iii) translation of the modified SIR model into a Continuous Time Markov Chain (CTMC) expressed using the PRISM input language; and (iv) stochastic analysis (simulation and model checking) with PRISM.

Keywords: PRISM model checker · SIR models · COVID-19

1 Introduction

The impact that the COVID-19 (or better, SARS-COV-2) pandemic is having on the population around the world is recorded in increasingly large and varied databases. The spread of the virus is tracked on a daily basis almost everywhere in the world, but the effects of the epidemics can be observed also in datasets in the contexts of healthcare, mobility, finance, and many others. The analysis of COVID-19 epidemic data could help in understanding the dynamics of the contagion, evaluating the effect of restriction and prevention measures taken by national and local governments and predicting the effect of alternative measures.

Epidemic phenomena are often studied by means of a *SIR model* [8]. This happened also for COVID-19 pandemic, with several extensions of the model proposed to take into account its peculiarities [2,5–8]. SIR models typically describe epidemics as *deterministic* dynamical systems, through Ordinary Differential Equations (ODEs). For a more realistic description of the epidemic dynamics, *stochastic fluctuations* are often to be taken into account. This happens, in particular, when a *small number* of infected individuals are present in the population, causing the disease spread to depend tightly on the probability of such few individuals to meet and infect other people. In order to deal with these stochastic events, SIR models can be reformulated in terms of *Continuous Time Markov Chains (CTMCs)*. This can be done essentially by interpreting

© Springer Nature Switzerland AG 2021
J. Bowles et al. (Eds.): DataMod 2020, LNCS 12611, pp. 123–133, 2021.
https://doi.org/10.1007/978-3-030-70650-0_8

infection and recovery rates, already used in ODEs, as parameters of exponential distributions. The obtained CTMC can then be analyzed through suitable methods which include, for example, stochastic simulation.

PRISM [1] is one of the most used probabilistic/stochastic model checkers. It can be used to study dynamical properties of a CTMC through an *exhaustive exploration* of all possible behaviors. Dynamical properties can be expressed as temporal logic formulae (for CTMCs, PRISM supports the CSL temporal logic [3]). Properties assessment consists then in an exhaustive exploration of the CTMC state space This may require a long sequence of matrix multiplications giving the probability distribution of each possible state at discrete time steps.

Stochastic model checking allows studying properties of a dynamical systems in a very systematic way. Property assessment does not provide only information about the possible systems behaviors: given a dynamical property (e.g. reachability of a given state, causality between events or possibility of oscillation), a stochastic model checker computes the probability that the system behavior will satisfy it. This analysis is not performed on a bunch of simulation results, but by taking all possible behaviors into account. Of course, the main limitation of stochastic model checking techniques is often due to size of the state space (state explosion problem). Moreover, in the case of stiff systems, property assessment may require a huge number of matrix multiplications. In some cases, these limitations can be overcome by using suitable model specification tricks.

In this paper, we describe preliminary processing and modelling activities that allow a SIR model of the COVID-19 pandemic to be analyzed with PRISM. Our approach actually consists in the following pipeline:

1. Definition of a *modified SIR model* (based on ODEs) that allows taking into account restriction and prevention measures (e.g. lockdown);
2. Parameter estimation using standard Python libraries (NumPy and SciPy);
3. Translation of model into a CTMC expressed in the PRISM input language;
4. Analysis with PRISM.

We will use real data about the spread of COVID-19 in the Tuscany Region (Italy) to show the pipeline steps. However, our aim is not to perform a deep analysis of such data with PRISM, but to show how it is possible to obtain, from data, a PRISM model that can be analyzed efficiently. Hence, although we will show some inferences and analysis results, the intended contribution of this paper is mostly methodological.

2   SIR Epidemic Models and COVID-19

Epidemic phenomena are often studied by means of a *SIR model* [8]. The SIR acronym summarizes the classes of individuals into which the population is partitioned. They are: *Susceptible*, individuals who can be infected; *Infected*, individuals who have been infected and that can infect susceptible ones; and *Recovered*, individuals who passed the infection phase and can no longer infect others.

The dynamics of epidemic phenomena is described by means of a system of Ordinary Differential Equations (ODEs). In its simplest formulation, the model includes one equation for each class of individuals. The population size is assumed constant over time and it is *normalized* in $[0, 1] \subseteq \mathbb{R}$. Hence, variables $S, I, R \in [0, 1]$ with $S + I + R = 1$ describe the *ratios* of each class of individual in the population. Moreover, the model is based on the following assumptions:

– infection and recovery are the only relevant events: other events related to reproduction, death, migration, etc., are not taken into account;
– disease is transmitted by personal contacts between individuals of I and S classes (*horizontal transmission*);
– contacts between individuals are random, i.e. the number of infections is proportional to both I and S;
– after infection and recovery, individuals become resistant to the disease.

Therefore, the model is described by this small system of differential equations:

$$\begin{cases} \frac{dS}{dt} = -\beta SI \\ \frac{dI}{dt} = \beta SI - \gamma I \\ \frac{dR}{dt} = \gamma I \end{cases} \tag{1}$$

where β is the *infection coefficient*, describing the probability of infection after the contact of a healthy individual with an infected one, and γ is the *recovery coefficient*, describing the rate of recovery of each infected individual (in other words, $1/\gamma$ is the time one individual requires for recovering). Note that:

– S can only decrease, and R can only increase;
– if $\beta < \gamma$ (i.e., $\beta/\gamma < 1$), I can only decrease (since $S \leq 1$);
– if $\beta > \gamma$ (i.e., $\beta/\gamma > 1$), the behavior of I depends on S. It initially increases if $S > \gamma/\beta$.

Many extensions of the SIR model are available in the literature, and have been proposed to study different infection schemes, the effects of vaccinations or the influence of information. In order to apply the SIR model to the COVID-19 epidemic and, in particular, in order to analyze data collected during the first few months of the epidemic, it is necessary to take into account prevention measures (e.g. lockdown) that have been enforced by the national governments. Hence, we propose a variant of the SIR model which includes a time dependent coefficient $p(t)$ expressing the effect of such measures on the infection rate.

Our *modified SIR model* is hence defined as follows:

$$\begin{cases} \frac{dS}{dt} = -\beta SIp(t) \\ \frac{dI}{dt} = \beta SIp(t) - \gamma I \\ \frac{dR}{dt} = \gamma I \end{cases} \tag{2}$$

where $p(t) \in [0, 1] \subset \mathbb{R}$ is used to scale down the infection coefficient β in accordance with the strength of the enforced prevention measures at time t. A value of $p(t)$ close to 0 represents strong prevention, while $p(t) = 1$ means no prevention at all. Let us consider the first few weeks of the epidemics, and let us assume that lockdown has been enforced at time t_{lock}. With some degree of approximation, we can describe $p(t)$ as a piecewise linear function as follows:

$$p(t) = \begin{cases} 1 & \text{if } t < t_{lock} \\ p_{lock} & \text{if } t \geq t_{lock} \end{cases} \tag{3}$$

with $p_{lock} \in [0,1] \subset \mathbb{R}$ modeling the effect of lockdown on infection coefficient.

3   Parameter Estimation

Now, we face the problem of estimating parameters for the modified SIR model presented in (2). In particular, if we assume $p(t)$ to be expressed by a piecewise linear function as in (3), we have to estimate values for β, γ, and p_{lock}.

By focusing on the Tuscany Region, we can estimate such parameters by applying standard optimization methods in order to fit real epidemic data. We use COVID data published on a daily basis by the Regional Health Agency of the Tuscany Region[1]. The dataset[2] includes data on infections, deaths, hospitalizations, etc., collected every day in the whole region starting from February 24th, 2020. Moreover, data on infections are available also disaggregated by province.

We focus on the time period of March-May 2020, corresponding to the initial spread of the infection and the lockdown phase. More precisely, we consider the time interval between day 20 (March, 15th) and day 75 (May, 9th). We choose not to consider data from the first 20 days since the number of detected infections in that period is extremely small, and probably unreliable.

In order to take into account geographical distribution of the population in the Tuscany Region, we choose to use the (modified) SIR model at the level of provinces. This choice will mitigate the assumption of the SIR model that the population is uniformly distributed in the territory, and that all individuals can freely meet with each other. Moreover, this will allow us to evaluate and compare differences in the disease spread in different provinces.

Tuscany consists of ten provinces. Some of them (e.g. Prato and Firenze) have a high population density, while others (e.g. Grosseto and Siena) are large and less populated. Since population density could have a correlation with the infection rate, considering data at the level of provinces could lead to more accurate parameter estimations.

The Python scripts we developed for parameter estimation purposes are available as a Jupyter Notebook on GitHub[3]. In order to estimate the parameters of the SIR model for the different provinces, we use functionalities provided by standard Python packages. In particular, we use the `optimize.curve_fit` function of the SciPy library, to find optimal values for coefficients β, γ and p_{lock}.

We apply `curve_fit` twice: the first time to estimate β and γ on the basis of the pre-lockdown data (hence, by assuming $p(t) = 1$)), and the second time to estimate p_{lock} by assuming β and γ as estimated before and by using lockdown data. As value for t_{lock} in (3), namely, as time for the enforcement of lockdown measures, we choose 45, namely April 9th. Actually, in Italy the lockdown state

---

[1] Agenzia Regionale di Sanita (ARS), https://www.ars.toscana.it/.

[2] Freely available at http://dati.toscana.it/dataset/open-data-covid19.

[3] GitHub repository: https://github.com/Unipisa/SIR-covid.

has been reached through a sequence of governmental measures taken in the period between March 5th (schools closed) and March 22nd (national lockdown). The effects of such measures on the epidemic dynamics started to become evident more than two weeks later, hence around April, 9th.

Let us assume a Python function `ModelSolution(t,beta,gamma,prev,x0)` that uses the `odeint` solver provided by the SciPy package to solve ODEs of the modified SIR model in (2), with `t` a sequence of time point for which to solve the ODEs, `beta` and `gamma` corresponding to β and γ, respectively, `prev` a constant value for $p(t)$, and `x0` an array of initial conditions (i.e., initial values for S, I and R). We define function `f1` and we pass it to `curve_fit` as follows:

```
f1 = lambda t,beta,gamma: ModelSolution(t,beta,gamma,1,x0)
p1 = curve_fit(f,t1,pre_lockdown_data,bounds=(0,[np.inf,1]))
```

The result `p1` contains two optimal values for β and γ with $\beta \in [0,\infty)$ and $\gamma \in [0,1]$, that fit pre-lockdown data.

Now, we define function `f2` and we pass it to `curve_fit` as follows:

```
f2 = lambda t,prev: ModelSolution(t,p1[0][0],p1[0][1],prev,x0)
p2 = curve_fit(f,t2,lockdown_data,bounds=(0,1))
```

Result `p2` contains now an optimal value for p_{lock}, fitting lockdown data.

For both optimizations, it is important to point out our choice for the initial condition array `x0`. More precisely, it is important to clearly explain how we relate variables S, I and R with real data. The number of infected individuals reported in the dataset is the number of persons that resulted positive to a SARS-COV-2 test. After the test, these persons are then isolated and have a very small probability of infecting other people. So, individuals reported as infected in the dataset have a role in the epidemic that is actually more similar to that of a recovered individual than of an infected one. The "real" infected individuals are instead those that have been infected, but have not been identified yet through a specific SARS-COV-2 test. These behave mostly as healthy individuals and infect other people. Unfortunately, these "real" infected individuals are hidden in the population and their number is unknown. In the initial array `x0` for the first optimization step, we choose to set the initial value of I as the triple of the number of positive persons reported on March, 15th. This because we assume that in the initial phases of the epidemic only a small part of the positive individuals were identified. The condition array `x0` for the second optimization step simply correspond to the final state reached after the first optimization.

Parameters resulted from the described estimation process are reported in Table 1. Apart form the Arezzo province, whose estimated parameters look

Table 1. Parameters estimation.

	β	γ	p_{lock}		β	γ	p_{lock}
AREZZO	0.229187	0.251815	0.994549	MASSA CARRARA	0.102454	0.084304	0.000098
FIRENZE	0.145179	0.097259	0.001654	PISA	0.122128	0.127283	0.472081
GROSSETO	0.129687	0.144080	0.487087	PRATO	0.130999	0.119076	0.145995
LIVORNO	0.107479	0.104104	0.317674	PISTOIA	0.078007	0.099515	0.991426
LUCCA	0.120928	0.111307	0.004195	SIENA	0.077028	0.069914	0.000231

like outliers, all provinces exhibit an infection coefficient β in the interval $[0.077, 0.145]$ and a recovery coefficient γ in $[0.06, 0.127]$. Provinces with a high population density, such as Firenze and Prato, actually correspond to highest infection coefficients. The estimation of p_{lock} is instead less regular, thus suggesting that something could be improved about the modelling of the lockdown effect. Inaccuracies could also be caused by the low quality of measurements in the first period of the pandemic. Anyway, the estimated p_{lock} values provide useful qualitative information about the areas in which lockdown has given better results.

Figures 1 and 2 show numerical simulation results of the modified SIR model (only the curves of I and R are depicted) compared with the real data about cumulative number of infected individuals (dots). The curve of I is actually a *prediction*, since, as we already explained, we use I to represent "real" infected individuals that are hidden in the population. The shape of this curve, that in many cases shows an edge at the start of lockdown, demonstrates the positive effect of such a prevention measure.

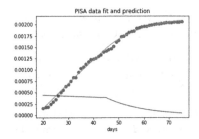

Fig. 1. Data fitting and predictions (Pisa province)

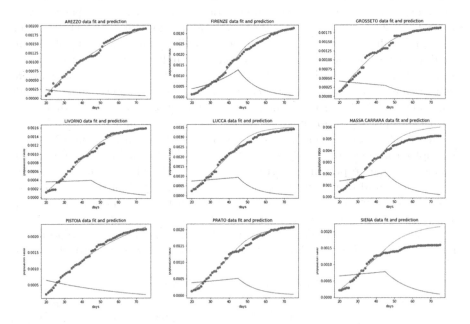

Fig. 2. Data fitting and predictions (other provinces)

4   Translation into CTMC and Analysis with PRISM

The next step we perform is to translate our extended SIR model into a stochastic model, by discretizing variables and by considering infection and recovery rates as parameters of a Continuous Time Markov Chain (CTMC). This allows us to obtain a model that is, in principle, more accurate in capturing the epidemic dynamics, by taking into account random fluctuations that may have a significant role in the case of small numbers of infected individuals.

Dynamical properties of the obtained CTMC could then be analyzed using the stochastic model checker PRISM [1,9]. Stochastic model checking, compared for instance to analysis by stochastic simulation, allows computing in a systematic way the probability of occurrence of emerging behaviors with specific properties of interest. The main problem of model checking is, however, its poor scalability to models with a very large state space. A stochastic SIR model representing a population of hundreds of thousand of individuals (like in a Tuscan province) can be very likely affected from this kind of scalability problems.

A way to solve scalability issues can be to resort to *statistical* model checking methods: a variant of stochastic model checking which provides approximate results by exploiting stochastic simulation result. PRISM itself has built-in statistical model checking facilities. However, before considering this solution, there are a few modelling tricks that can significantly reduce the state space.

PRISM describes CTMC states through a set of *bounded integer variables*. Since ODEs of the SIR model are based on real variables, the first step we have to perform is to *discretize* the model. Hence, we assume a discretization constant SIZE and we replace the variables domain $[0.0, 1.0] \subset \mathbb{R}$ with $[0..SIZE] \subset \mathbb{N}$.

This leads to the following naive CTMC specification in PRISM input language, where model parameters are defined by the beta, gamma and plock constants (initialized with estimations for the province of Pisa), SIZE is the discretization constant, s, i and r are the model variables (again, initialized with values from data collected on the province of Pisa) and we have two transitions describing events of infection and recovery, respectively.

```
ctmc

const double beta = 0.122128; const double gamma = 0.127283;
const double plock = 0.472081; const int SIZE = 100000;

module SIR_Pisa

s : [0..SIZE] init 99936;
i : [0..SIZE] init 48;
r : [0..SIZE] init 16;

[] i>0 & i<SIZE & s>0 -> beta*s*i*plock/SIZE : (s'=s-1)&(i'=i+1);
[] i>0 & r<SIZE -> gamma*i*plock : (i'=i-1)&(r'=r+1);

endmodule
```

The problem of this translation is that, by assuming SIZE = 100000, the state space turns out to include 10^{15} *potentially reachable states*, which make the model computation and analysis by PRISM unfeasible.

A first refinement of the model can be obtained by observing that one of the three variables s, i and r can be pruned. Indeed, as in the original ODEs we had $S + I + R = 1$, in the PRISM counterpart we always have s + i + r = SIZE. Removing, for instance, s will require to make a small change to the definition of the first transition, where s has to be replaced by SIZE-(i+r).

Pruning variable s immediately reduces the state space, bringing it to a size of 10^{10} states. However, this is still too huge for PRISM.

As a second refinement, we choose to introduce an upper bound to the number of infected and of recovered individuals. For example, we choose these numbers to be always smaller than 500. As shown in the following CTMC specification, where also the first refinement is implemented, this can be obtained by adding a new constant BOUND that is then used to define the domain of the two variables i and r. Moreover, we have to explicitly change the model transition to describe the behavior in the case the upper bound is reached. The two transitions of the naive translation have to be enabled only when i and r are strictly smaller than BOUND. Moreover, it is necessary to introduce a third transition that, in case the number of recovered individuals reaches the upper bound, allows an infected individual to recover (i.e. it decreases i by one) without increasing r.

```
ctmc

const double beta = 0.122128; const double gamma = 0.127283;
const double plock = 0.472081; const int SIZE = 100000; const int BOUND = 500;

module SIR_Pisa

i : [0..BOUND] init 48;
r : [0..BOUND] init 16;

[] i>0 & i<BOUND -> beta*(SIZE-(i+r))*i*plock/SIZE : (i'=i+1);
[] i>0 & r<BOUND -> gamma*i*plock : (i'=i-1)&(r'=r+1);
[] i>0 & r=BOUND -> gamma*i*plock : (i'=i-1);

endmodule
```

The addition of the upper bound actually makes the model approximated. However, if the upper bound is high enough to make the probability of the variables to reach it negligible, we have that the approximation will have no influence on the probabilities of dynamical properties assessed through model checking. We remark that the assumption on the small number of infected individuals was one of the motivations for the use of a stochastic modelling approach. In the case of big numbers, that could lead to unfeasible models with large state spaces, the whole stochastic approach would be poorly motivated, since with big numbers stochastic fluctuations would become much less relevant.

Upper bounds significantly reduce the state space, that now turns out to include "only" 250000 *states*. This makes model construction and analysis with PRISM very fast, in particular (and this is *very important*) if either the *sparse* or the *explicit* engines are selected in the relevant PRISM settings menu.

As examples of analyses performed with PRISM, we show in Fig. 3 some results of stochastic simulation and model checking performed using parameters of the Pisa province and by comparing lockdown and no-lockdown scenarios.

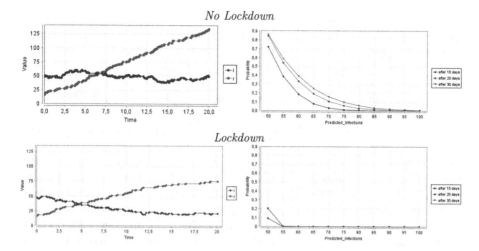

Fig. 3. Analysis of the Pisa model with PRISM (examples). On the left, a single run of a stochastic simulation. On the right, probabilities, computed by stochastic model checking, of reaching given numbers of infected individuals after 10, 20 and 30 days. The CSL property used for model checking is P=? [F<XX i=Predicted_Infections], where XX is 10, 20 or 30, and Predicted_Infections takes values as in the graph.

Simulations show that lockdown can effectively reduce the number of infected individuals, leading to a slow down of the disease spread. As before, this model allows understanding the dynamics of hidden infected individuals. Model checking is used to make predictions on the future number of infected individuals, by computing probabilities of reaching different threshold values in 10, 20, 30 days.

Stochastic model checking can be used to make predictions about reachable population states in an accurate, systematic and efficient way. This makes this technique a good candidate for real time epidemic monitoring and decision support. Moreover, the modified SIR model could be extended to describe also, for instance, age classes, hospitalizations, new therapies or vaccinations. In this case, it would be possible to use stochastic model checking as a tool to evaluate hypotheses about these new aspects, for instance by computing the probability of disease eradication when alternative vaccination strategies are followed.

5   Conclusions

In this paper we proposed a *pipeline* for the stochastic analysis of a SIR model for COVID-19 through the stochastic model checker PRISM. The whole pipeline is informative: in the parameter estimation phase, the estimated parameters themselves provide useful information about the different dynamics in different areas (e.g., provinces) and about the effectiveness of restriction and prevention measures such as lockdown. Moreover, by performing numerical simulation of the deterministic models used for parameter estimations we were able to predict the dynamics of hidden positive individuals.

PRISM allows defining a stochastic SIR model in *a dozen lines of code*. An optimized model can be analyzed in a *few minutes*. The analysis performed through the model checking features of PRISM is *exhaustive*, and not based only on a few simulation runs. These positive performance results have been obtained by applying a couple of modelling tricks (variable pruning and upper bounds) that allowed state space of the model constructed by PRISM to be reduced by several orders of magnitude. The introduction of upper bounds to the values of variables actually introduces a small approximation in the model, that is negligible in practically relevant cases. As a consequence, we believe that this approach aimed at making the analysis with PRISM feasible is in this case preferable to approaches based, for instance, on statistical model checking techniques. Indeed, the latter techniques would base the model checking analysis on stochastic simulation results, losing exhaustivity.

This paper aimed at proposing the modelling and analysis methodology. Developments of the approach could include improving the modelling of the restriction measures by considering more accurate definitions of the $p(t)$ function in the modified SIR model. Function $p(t)$ could be defined in order to gradually change after the enforcement of prevention measures, or in order to depend on the current infection trend (if the number of infected individual increases, people tends to be more cautious). Moreover, extensions of the model including age classes, hospitalizations, new therapies or vaccinations could be defined. Further work would include performing a deeper analysis of COVID data with PRISM, also by taking some of these additional aspects into account, even when some parameters about these aspects are not precisely known [4].

Acknowledgements. This work is supported by the Università di Pisa under the "PRA – Progetti di Ricerca di Ateneo" (Institutional Research Grants) - Project no. PRA_2020-2021_26 "Metodi Informatici Integrati per la Biomedica".

References

1. PRISM Probabilistic Model Checker. https://www.prismmodelchecker.org/
2. Acemoglu, D., et al.: A multi-risk SIR model with optimally targeted lockdown. Tech. rep., National Bureau of Economic Research (2020)
3. Aziz, A., Sanwal, K., Singhal, V., Brayton, R.: Verifying continuous time Markov chains. In: Alur, R., Henzinger, T.A. (eds.) CAV 1996. LNCS, vol. 1102, pp. 269–276. Springer, Heidelberg (1996). https://doi.org/10.1007/3-540-61474-5_75
4. Barbuti, R., Levi, F., Milazzo, P., Scatena, G.: Probabilistic model checking of biological systems with uncertain kinetic rates. Theor. Comput. Sci. **419**, 2–16 (2012)
5. Calafiore, G.C., Novara, C., Possieri, C.: A modified SIR model for the COVID-19 contagion in Italy. arXiv preprint arXiv:2003.14391 (2020)
6. Chen, Y.C., Lu, P.E., Chang, C.S.: A time-dependent SIR model for COVID-19. arXiv preprint arXiv:2003.00122 (2020)
7. D'Arienzo, M., Coniglio, A.: Assessment of the SARS-CoV-2 basic reproduction number, R0, based on the early phase of COVID-19 outbreak in Italy. Biosaf. Health **2**, 57–59 (2020)

8. Kermack, W.O., McKendrick, A.G.: A contribution to the mathematical theory of epidemics. Proc. R. Soc. Lond. Ser. A Contain. Pap. Math. Phys. Character **115**(772), 700–721 (1927)
9. Kwiatkowska, M., Norman, G., Parker, D.: PRISM 4.0: verification of probabilistic real-time systems. In: Gopalakrishnan, G., Qadeer, S. (eds.) CAV 2011. LNCS, vol. 6806, pp. 585–591. Springer, Heidelberg (2011). https://doi.org/10.1007/978-3-642-22110-1_47

A Formal Model for the Simulation and Analysis of Early Biofilm Formation

Antonio Cerone[1]([⊠])[ID] and Enrico Marsili[2][ID]

[1] Department of Computer Science, School of Engineering and Digital Sciences,
Nazarbayev University, Nur-Sultan, Kazakhstan
antonio.cerone@nu.edu.kz
[2] Department of Chemical and Materials Engineering, School of Engineering
and Digital Sciences, Nazarbayev University, Nur-Sultan, Kazakhstan
enrico.marsili@nu.edu.kz

Abstract. Biofilms are structured communities of bacterial cells adherent to a surface. This bacterial state is called *sessile*.

This paper focuses on the modelling of the transition between planktonic and sessile state using Real-time Maude as the modelling language. With more and more bacteria joining the sessile community, the likelihood of producing a biofilm increases. Once the percentage of bacterial cells that adheres to the surface reaches a threshold, which is specific for the considered bacterium species, a permanent biofilm is formed. An important challenge is to predict the time needed for the formation of a biofilm on a specific surface, in order to plan when the material infrastructure that comprises such a surface needs to be cleaned or replaced. We exploit the model-checking features of Real-time Maude to formally prove that a regular cleaning or replacement of the infrastructure prevents the biofilm formation.

Keywords: Biofilms · Formal methods · Rewriting logic · Real-Time Maude

1 Introduction

Biofilms are microstructured bacterial communities that live at interfaces. They are the most common mode of life for microorganisms in both terrestrial and marine environments. Usually, biofilms thrive at liquid/solid interfaces like the inner surface of water pipes [29] and catheters [28], or in soil and sediments [10]; biofilms play a beneficial role in wastewater treatment, where they increase organic carbon degradation and contaminant removal. However, biofilms harbor pathogens and protect them from antimicrobial agents, thus posing serious threats in health settings. Biofilms consist of bacterial cells encased in self-produced extracellular polymeric substances, collectively termed biofilm matrix.

This work was partially funded by the Faculty Development Competitive Research Grant Program (Grant number 110119FD4537), Nazarbayev University, Kazakhstan.

J. Bowles et al. (Eds.): DataMod 2020, LNCS 12611, pp. 134–151, 2021.
https://doi.org/10.1007/978-3-030-70650-0_9

The biofilm matrix is composed of carbohydrates, proteins and extracellular DNA. The relative proportion of these components is species-dependent and varies with biofilm age and nutrient concentration [17].

The biofilm life cycle is illustrated in Fig. 1. Biofilm formation initiates when single planktonic cells enter in contact with a surface, usually solid. Following this initial interaction, several steps can be described, including reversible attachment, irreversible attachment, microcolonies formation, and biofilm maturation, in which complex microstructures are formed and the biofilm reach its maximum thickness. In the planktonic-sessile transition, cells lose their flagella and start producing extracellular polymeric substance. The biofilm life cycle ends with biofilm detachment or dispersal, where part of the cells transitions from biofilm to planktonic state and move downstream to seed other sections of the surface. The biofilm life cycle has been validated with microscopy, transcriptomics and metabolomics analysis [30].

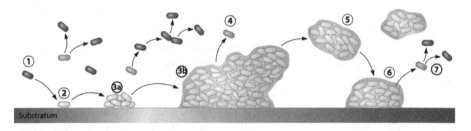

Fig. 1. Biofilm life cycle: (1) Plaktonic phenotype; (2) Newly attached planktonic cells ("settler" biofilm); (3a) Fully mature biofilm stage (biofilm phenotype); (4) Newly single cells dispersed from the biofilm (newly dispersed phenotype); (5) Detached biofilm aggregates (biofilm phenotype); (6) Reattached biofilm aggregates (biofilm phenotype); (7) Newly dispersed phenotypes cells from the biofilm giving rise to planktonic phenotype cells.

The biofilm early formation is largely dependent on the concentration of bis-(3'-5')-cyclic dimeric guanosine monophosphate (c-di-GMP), a secondary messenger that is ubiquitous in the bacterial world. Enzymes that synthesize c-di-GMP or degrade it are found in great numbers, indicating its importance as a regulator of many bacterial functions. C-di-GMP contributes to determine motility, biofilm formation, and production of multiple proteins in microorganisms. It binds to a large variety of effector components and controls targets involved in transcription and formation of large cellular and extracellular structures.

In the biofilm life cycle, the most important step is the initial attachment, in which the cells transition from free-swimming state (so-called *planktonic*) to *sessile* state, in which they attach to solid surface, lose their motility and start producing the extracellular matrix, in addition to the normal growth process [9]. Modelling of initial biofilm formation is important to predict the extent of biofilm growth on removable biomedical devices (e.g., catheters) and drinking water pipes, thus allowing for planned cleaning or replacement of biofilm-contaminated parts and minimising the risk of infections [11]. The effectiveness of cleaning treatment depends also on biofilm concentration, thus the formal modelling of initial biofilm formation will contribute to optimising the frequency and the duration of antimicrobial application in biomedical devices and water systems.

A number of biofilm models have been developed during the last 30 years. They can be roughly divided into continuum and discrete models.

Continuum models simulate biofilms in a quantitative and deterministic way [16]. However, such models may result in high computational complexity, particularly for multispecies biofilms and when considering multiple substrates [3]. Early continuum models focused on cell growth and microstructure formation. Modern continuum models concern the effect of fluid dynamics on colony formation and are validated with time-resolved single cell imaging to reveal important details on cell-fluid interactions at different biofilm ages [23].

Discrete models, on the other hand, are very successful in representing the multidimensional heterogeneity of biofilm, but introduce elements of randomness and stochastic effects into the solutions [16]. *Agents-based models*, based on several platforms, eventually integrated (e.g., NetLogo, MatNet), are especially popular because of their simplicity and low computational requirements. However, they may become highly sophisticated when integrating multiscale and constraint-based metabolic modelling [7].

Hybrid biofilms models are the most recent. They support the simulation of discrete bacterial cells within a multiphase continuum consisting of extracellular polymeric substance (EPS) and water as separate interacting phases. These models support the prediction of bacterial colony formation. The distribution of bacterial growth and EPS production is sensitive to the pore spacing between bacteria and the consumption of nutrients within the bacterial colony [12].

Although formal methods have been widely used in systems biology [6], to the best of our knowledge, no formal models of biofilms have been reported in the literature. After Păun's work on P-Systems [24], rule-based systems have been widely used in the modelling of biological systems, due to the natural way in which they can express chemical reactions and biological interactions. The use of a rule-based systems in combination with a formal analysis tool allows us to generate a model that focuses on the individual bacterial cells, whose behaviour can be defined using simple rules, assuming that the cell properties are known, rather than using a computationally expensive multidimensional continuum. We use Real-Time Maude [19,21], a toolset that comprises a rule-based formal modelling language, which uses rewriting logic [18] to model system state transitions, and high-performance simulation and model checking engines, which support formal analysis.

The rest of this paper is organised as follows. Section 1.1 provides a brief highlight of Real-Time Maude and refers to the sections of the paper where the different aspects of the language are illustrated. The Real-Time Maude code for the model, the experiments and the formal analysis can be downloaded from a

GitHub repository[1]. Section 2 presents our approach for modelling a bacterial population and its evolution, the process of biofilm formation as well as preventive interventions. Section 3 illustrates our approach using an example inspired by the information about a specific microorganism, *Pseudomonas aeruginosa*, which is available in the literature [1,25,31]. It exploits the example to illustrate both in silico experiments and the use of the model-checking features of Real-time Maude to predict the outcome of the experiments and analyse intervention plans. Section 4 concludes the paper with further considerations on our approach and ideas for future work.

1.1 Real-Time Maude

Real-Time Maude [19,21] is a formal modeling language and high-performance simulation and model checking tool for distributed real-time systems. It is based on Full Maude, the object-oriented extension of Core Maude, which is the basic version of Maude [20]. Real-Time Maude makes use of

- algebraic equational specifications in a functional programming style to define data types;
- labeled rewrite rules to define local and global transitions;
- tick rewrite rules to advance time in the entire system state.

In this paper we do not go into the details of Real-Time Maude syntax but we focus on rewrite rules and commands for simulation and formal analysis. In this section we provide high-level information on the Core Maude data type definition and Full Maude classes, subclasses and objects. Labelled rewrite rules for defining global transitions and Real-Time Maude tick rewrite rules are illustrated in Sect. 2. Commands for simulation and formal analysis are illustrated in Sect. 3.

A Core Maude *data type* is defined using an algebraic *signature*, that is, a set of declarations of *sorts*, *subsorts*, and *operators*. Operators are defined in an equational way as well as by using special tags to declare common properties, such as commutativity, associativity, having a specific identity and constructors. *Constructors* are the carriers of the sort, in the sense that they define in a unique way each member of the sort.

In Full Maude, a *class* declaration

$$\text{class } C \mid att_1 \colon s_1, \ \ldots, \ att_n \colon s_n \,.$$

declares a class C with attributes $att_1, \ldots, att_n$ of sorts $s_1, \ldots, s_n$, respectively. An *object* of class C in a given state is represented as a term

$$< O : C \mid att_1 : val_1, ..., att_n : val_n >$$

of sort `Object`, where O, of sort `Oid`, is the object's *identifier*, and where val_1, $\ldots$, val_n are the current values of the attributes $att_1, \ldots, att_n$, respectively.

---

[1] github.com/AntonioCerone/Publications/tree/master/2020/DataMod/Biofilms.

A *subclass* inherits all the attributes and rules of its superclasses. The class declaration syntax is also used for subclasses and supports the definition of new attributes specific to the subclass.

Real-Time Maude specifications are organised in *modules*, which can be imported by other modules and, as we will see in Sect. 3, be referred by the commands for simulation and formal analysis.

2 Biofilm Formation Model

We use Real-Time Maude to model a bacterial population as a multiset of objects of a class `Bacterium` with three attributes:

`state` which can be either `planktonic` or `sessile`;

`toDuplication` which is a natural number representing the remaining lifetime in minutes of a cell before duplication;

`c-di-GMP-internal` which is a natural number representing the concentration of c-di-GMP inside a single cell and is expressed in nanomoles (nM)

We also use a single object of a class `Population` to collect the global data of the entire population of bacteria. The class `Population` consists of the following attributes:

`state` which can be one of the following values, whose meaning is illustrated in Fig. 2: `creation`, `next-time`, `ready-to-reproduce`, `ready-to-die` and `attributes-updated`.

`size` which is a natural number representing the number of cells of the population;

`planktonic-cells` which is a natural number representing the number of cells of the population that are in planktonic state;

`sessile-cells` which is a natural number representing the number of cells of the population that are in sessile state;

`c-di-GMP-global` which is a natural number representing the global concentration of c-di-GMP for the entire population and is expressed in nanomoles (nM) with respect to the global volume of the cells;

`biofilm` which is a boolean stating whether the biofilm is formed or not.

We preferred to keep the multiset of `Bacterium` objects 'outside' the population data, rather than incorporating it as a field of the `Population` object. This choice aims at considering the 'global population' and the 'multiset of bacteria' as a sort of pair of 'interacting agents' whereby, in a prospective extension of our approach, global data on the population behaviour may actually effect the development of the multiset of agents. In fact, it is easier in biology to have availability of data on the behaviour of the population as a whole rather than on the behaviour of the single cells that make up the population.

Therefore, the system that describes the bacterial ecosystem consists of one object of class `Population` and a multiset of objects of class `Bacterium`. Figure 2 illustrates the initial creation of the bacterial population and the evolution of the

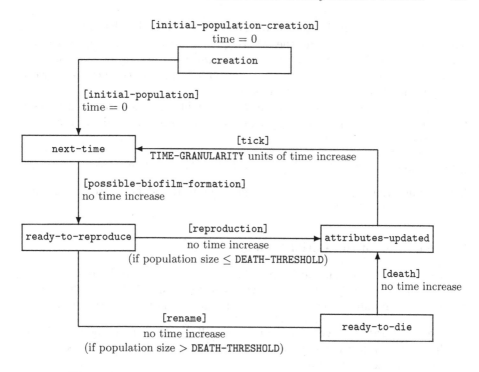

Fig. 2. State transitions in the model of the bacterial population.

population. Evolution consists of TIME-GRANULARITY unit cycles. During each cycle the one object of class Population goes through the different states that update the attributes of all objects (bacteria and population) and terminate the cycle with a TIME-GRANULARITY unit time increment.

With reference to Fig. 2, in Sect. 2.2, 2.3, 2.4, 2.5 and 2.6 we illustrate the rewrite rules that drive the population initial creation and its evolution. Section 2.7 illustrate how our model may be extended to include intervention preventing biofilm formation. Section 2.1 set the context for the next sections by briefly explaining the notion of system state and overviewing the syntax and semantics of rewrite rules.

2.1   Real-Time Maude Configuration and Rewrite Rules

The *global system state* is a term of pre-defined sort Configuration and is a *multiset* of objects. Multiset union is denoted by an associative and commutative juxtaposition operator, so that rewriting is *multiset rewriting*. Transitions between global system states are defined using *rewrite rules*.

Maude *labeled rewrite rules*

$$\text{rl } [l] : \{t\} \Rightarrow \{t'\} \quad \text{or} \quad \text{crl } [l] : \{t\} \Rightarrow \{t'\} \text{ if } cond$$

define transitions from the global state pattern t to the global state pattern t'. The transition is enabled, and the rule is applied, if the state pattern t matches the current global system state and, for *conditional rules* (crl), the condition *cond* is met. Complex conditions may be built using the conjuction operator $/\backslash$. Conditions may also be of the form $v := t''$ in order to assign a term t'', containing only variables occurring in t, to variable v, which can then be used to define the new term t'. These special conditions are evaluated to true.

Real-Time Maude *tick rewrite rules*

rl [l] : {t} => {t'} in time Δ or   crl [l] : {t} => {t'} in time Δ if *cond*

have the additional function of advancing time in the global state t by Δ time units.

2.2   Creation of the Initial Population

In order to start with an initial population of planktonic cells uniformly distributed in term of cell age, we consider a constant value INITIAL-POPULATION for the initial number of bacteria and use the following two rewrite rules:

initial-population-creation which cyclically assigns an age between 1 and the age at duplication (i.e., the duration of the cell life cycle) for the specific species to the newly created cell;

initial-population which stops the creation process by changing the population state from create to next-time, when the bacterial population reaches the value INITIAL-POPULATION, thus disabling the previous rule.

The first rule also initialises the concentration of c-di-GMP internal to the cell. This concentration depends on the age of the cell and on food availability.

2.3   Biofilm Formation

The transition of the object of class Population from state next-time to state ready-to-reproduce updates the information about the biofilm formation and the changes of state of the single cells (from planktonic to sessile and vice versa). We consider two threshold values for the concentration of c-di-GMP: C-DI-GMP-THRESHOLD-BIOFIM and C-DI-GMP-THRESHOLD-SESSILE.

The constant C-DI-GMP-THRESHOLD-BIOFIM represents the global concentration of c-di-GMP that triggers the transition of the bacterial colony to a biofilm, when the threshold is reached or exceeded, and the transition back to a dispersed colony, when the concentration drops below the threshold. The transition is recorded in the boolean attribute biofilm of the object of class Population.

The constant C-DI-GMP-THRESHOLD-SESSILE represents the internal concentration of c-di-GMP of a single cell that triggers the transition of the state of that cell to sessile, when the threshold is reached or exceeded, and the transition back to planktonic, when the concentration drops below the threshold.

The rewrite rule `possible-biofilm-formation` models the transition to biofilm and back:

```
crl [possible-biofilm-formation] :
  {BACTERIA
    < P : Population | state : next-time,
                      size : N,
                      planktonic-cells : NP,
                      sessile-cells : NS,
                      c-di-GMP-global : C,
                      biofilm : BOOL >}
=>
  {NEW-BACTERIA
    < P : Population |
              state : ready-to-reproduce,
              size : N,
              planktonic-cells : countCells(NEW-BACTERIA, planktonic),
              sessile-cells : countCells(NEW-BACTERIA, sessile),
              c-di-GMP-global : C,
              biofilm : (C >= C-DI-GMP-THRESHOLD-BIOFIM) >}
  if NEW-BACTERIA := changeState(BACTERIA) .
```

Note that this rewrite rule is always enabled in the state `next-time` in order to update the state of each single cell after the concentration of c-di-GMP internal to the cell has been updated during the last time increment. The operator `changeState` recursively changes the state of the entire multiset of bacteria by comparing the concentration of c-di-GMP internal to the cell with the threshold `C-DI-GMP-THRESHOLD-SESSILE`. The operator `countCells` recursively counts the number planktonic and sessile cells of the `NEW-BACTERIA` multiset, which is the bacterial colony after updating the states of the single cells.

2.4   Cell Reproduction

Cell reproduction may only occur when the bacterial population does not exceed a given `REPRODUCTION-THRESHOLD` threshold. The reproduction process is modeled by the operator `mitoses` which, for each cell that has reached the reproduction age, i.e., whose `toDuplication` attribute equals 0,

1. resets the attribute `toDuplication` of that cell to a given `LIFE-DURATION` value, which represents the duration of the life cycle of the cell;
2. creates a new cell identical to the previous one apart from a 0 value for the concentration of c-di-GMP internal to the cell;
3. uses the size of the population, passed as the second argument, to define the object identifiers of the new cell by recursively incrementing such argument.

We have chosen to leave the entire concentration of c-di-GMP within one of the two cells. This is consistent with recent literature, which has shown that asymmetric division results in a better colonization of the surface [8], with the formation of multiple microcolonies [14].

The rewrite rule `reproduction` models the cell reproduction process and its impact on the attributes of the `Population` object:

```
crl [reproduction] :
  {BACTERIA
   < P : Population | state : ready-to-reproduce,
                     size : N,
                     planktonic-cells : NP,
                     sessile-cells : NS,
                     c-di-GMP-global : C,
                     biofilm : BOOL >}
=>
  {NEW-BACTERIA
   < P : Population |
           state : attributes-updated,
           size : NEW-NP + NEW-NS,
           planktonic-cells : NEW-NP,
           sessile-cells : NEW-NS,
           c-di-GMP-global : NEW-C-DI-GMP,
           biofilm : (NEW-C-DI-GMP >= C-DI-GMP-THRESHOLD-BIOFIM) >}
  if N <= REPRODUCTION-THRESHOLD  /\
     NEW-BACTERIA := mitoses(BACTERIA, N)  /\
     NEW-NP := countCells(NEW-BACTERIA, planktonic)  /\
     NEW-NS := countCells(NEW-BACTERIA, sessile)  /\
     NEW-C-DI-GMP := count-c-di-GMP(NEW-BACTERIA) .
```

All attributes of the object of the class `Population` are updated to take into account the newly created cells. In particular, the global concentration of c-di-GMP is updated by using the operator `count-c-di-GMP`, which sums up the concentrations of c-di-GMP internal to all the single cells in multiset `NEW-BACTERIA` (after the reproduction has occurred).

2.5 Cell Death

When the bacterial population exceeds the given `REPRODUCTION-THRESHOLD` threshold, cell reproduction can non longer occur. Instead, cells start dying at a rate that has been estimated around 5% for each life cycle [2].

The rewrite rule `death` models such a form of death:

```
crl [death] :
  {BACTERIA
   < P : Population | state : ready-to-die,
                      size : N,
                      planktonic-cells : NP,
                      sessile-cells : NS,
                      c-di-GMP-global : C,
                      biofilm : BOOL >}
=>
  {NEW-BACTERIA
   < P : Population | state : attributes-updated,
```

```
                 size : NEW-NP + NEW-NS,
                 planktonic-cells : NEW-NP,
                 sessile-cells : NEW-NS,
                 c-di-GMP-global : NEW-C-DI-GMP,
                 biofilm : (C >= C-DI-GMP-THRESHOLD-BIOFIM) >}
   if M := ((N * DEATH-RATE * TIME-GRANULARITY) quo 100) quo LIFE-DURATION /\
      NEW-BACTERIA := starvation(BACTERIA, M, 0) /\
      NEW-NP := countCells(NEW-BACTERIA, planktonic) /\
      NEW-NS := countCells(NEW-BACTERIA, sessile) /\
      NEW-C-DI-GMP := count-c-di-GMP(NEW-BACTERIA) .
```

As shown in Fig. 2, before applying the rewrite rule **death**, we need to use the rewrite rule **rename** to rename all objects of the class **Bacteria**. This purely technical manipulation, which has no biological meaning, allows us to reuse the object names and prevents the number of system states to grow arbitrarily. Since, the balance between reproduction and death keeps the population below some size threshold, the behaviour of the model has a finite (though very large) number of states and can, in principle, be analysed using model checking with no time limitations. However, in practice, we normally introduce a time upper bound when using model checking to avoid the state explosion problem.

The rewrite rule **death** is enabled by the population state **ready-to-die** which, as shown in Fig. 2, is changed from **ready-to-reproduce** by the rewrite rule **rename**, when the attribute **size** of the **Population** object exceeds the threshold **REPRODUCTION-THRESHOLD**. The rewrite rule **death** uses the operator **starvation** to remove a **DEATH-RATE** per cent of the population over a duration corresponding to the cell life cycle (i.e., **LIFE-DURATION**).

Let **TIME-GRANULARITY** be the number of units time advances at each increment. The number M of cells to remove during one time unit is calculated by considering the number of cells N * DEATH-RATE quo 100 to be removed during an entire life cycle and dividing it by **LIFE-DURATION**. This value has to be multiplied by **TIME-GRANULARITY** to get the number of cells to be removed at each time increment. Note that the terms of the expression have been rearranged in the rewrite rule condition to avoid the inclusion of term N * DEATH-RATE quo 100 quo LIFE-DURATION, which may become 0 for small values of N even for a coarse time granularity (values of **TIME-GRANULARITY** greater than 1).

In addition to removing M cells from the multiset **BACTERIA** independently of their ages, the reduction of expression **starvation(BACTERIA, M, 0)** recursively increments its third argument by 1 and uses it to rename cells that do not have to be removed from the multiset. In this way, the resultant multiset of bacteria will be named with all natural numbers between 1 and the size of the bacterial population. Furthermore, the operator **starvation** resets the **toDuplication** attribute of each bacteria that is not removed to **LIFE-DURATION**. This ensures that the uniform distribution of the cell ages is preserved.

2.6 Time Increment

Both rewrite rules **reproduction** and **death** change the state of the object of class **Population** to **attributes-updated**. This is the final state for the current time interval and features the updated values for all attributes of the objects of the system configuration.

In the state `attributes-updated` time is incremented discretely as intervals of TIME-GRANULARITY units by the following tick rewrite rule:

```
rl [tick] :
  {BACTERIA
   < P : Population | state : attributes-updated >}
=>
  {idle(BACTERIA, TIME-GRANULARITY)
   < P : Population | state : next-time >}
  in time TIME-GRANULARITY .
```

The operator `idle` not only advances time for all cells but also calculates the internal concentration of c-di-GMP, depending on the age of the cell after the the increment, and changes the `Population` state to `next-time` to be ready for updating all the object attributes during the new time interval.

2.7   Intervention to Prevent Biofilm Formation

In this section we show how to model a simple form of intervention to prevent the formation of a biofilm on a specific surface: the replacement of the material infrastructure that comprises such a surface. To this purpose we consider a constant time TIME-BETWEEN-INTERVENTIONS, we extend the class `Population` by defining a subclass `Intervention` which has the additional following attribute:

`next-intervention` which is the possibly infinite time before the next intervention;

and we replace the `tick` rewrite rule introduced in Sect. 2.6 with the following `tick-without-intervention` tick rewrite rule:

```
crl [tick-without-intervention] :
  {BACTERIA
   < I : Intervention | next-intervention : T,
                        state : attributes-updated >}
=>
  {idle(BACTERIA, TIME-GRANULARITY)
   < I : Intervention | next-intervention : T monus 1,
                        state : next-time >}
  in time TIME-GRANULARITY
 if T > 0 .
```

When the `next-intervention` attribute of the `Intervention` object has become as low as 0, the following `tick-with-intervention` rewrite rule reset the system to the initial population:

```
rl [tick-with-intervention] :
  {BACTERIA
   < I : Intervention | next-intervention : 0,
                        state : attributes-updated >}
=>
   {< I : Intervention | next-intervention : TIME-BETWEEN-INTERVENTIONS,
                         state : creation,
                         size : 0,
                         planktonic-cells : 0,
                         sessile-cells : 0,
                         c-di-GMP-global : 0,
                         biofilm : false >}
  in time TIME-GRANULARITY .
```

Note that when TIME-BETWEEN-INTERVENTIONS is set to infinite value INF, rule tick-with-intervention can never be applied.

3   In Silico Experiments and Formal Analysis

Maude modules are executable and the Real-Time Maude toolset provides a variety of formal analysis methods.

The *timed rewriting* command

$$(\text{tfrew } [r] \text{ in } m : s_0 \text{ in time} <= t \text{ .})$$

simulates *one* of the system behaviours of module m by rewriting the initial state s_0 using up to r term rewrites and up to duration t.

The timed rewriting command provides us with an important tool to perform in silico experiments, by simulating experiments that would last for hours within a few seconds. Although only one of the possible system behaviour of a nondeterministic system is shown during simulation, this may provide important information on the biological system evolution.

The *timed search* command supports the analysis of all possible behaviours from a given initial state, relative to the chosen time sampling strategy. The command performs *reachability analysis* by searching for the states that match a search pattern and are reachable in a given time interval (if indicated). There are several variants for the syntax of the search command, such as:

$$(\text{tsearch } [n] \text{ in } m : s \text{ with no time limit .})$$
$$(\text{tsearch } [n] \text{ in } m : s \text{ in time} <= t \text{ .})$$
$$(\text{tsearch } [n] \text{ in } m : s \text{ in time} >= t \text{ .})$$

where s is the search pattern, n is the number of solutions searched for and t is the time at which to stop the search.

Section 3.1 introduces the case study that we use to illustrate our approach. Section 3.2 illustrates the use of timed rewriting to perform in silico experiments and Sect. 3.3 illustrates the use of timed search to perform formal analysis.

3.1   Pseudomonas Aeruginosa

Pseudomonas aeruginosa is a Gram-negative microorganism, an opportunistic pathogen, actually one of the most important pulmonary pathogens and the predominant cause of morbidity and mortality in cystic fibrosis. *P. aeruginosa* forms rapidly biofilms on plastic surfaces, agar medium, graphite, metals and other materials. The composition of its extracellular polymeric substance has been studied in details and high quality data are available on the c-di-GMP distribution in cells, division upon replication and concentration with time measured through fluorescence in recombinant laboratory strains.

The life cycle of *P. aeruginosa* has a duration of 120 min [31] and the concentration of c-di-GMP internal to a cell in relation to the cell age is given in Table 1 [1].

3.2   Simulation

In order to illustrate our approach we consider the simulation reported in Table 2. We have defined Real-Time Maude module P-AERUGINOSA, which models a simplified bacterial ecosystem with values of the parameters taken from the literature on *P. areruginosa* [1,25,31]. The model is defined without intervention. The results in Table 2 have been produced using the command

```
(tfrew [1000000] in P-AERUGINOSA : {init} in time <= t .)
```

with t representing the considered time in minutes (second column of Table 2).

The duration of the simulation is 12 h. We use an initial population of 120 cells in order to have a uniform distribution of the cells within the 120 min of cell life cycle. We adopt a 10 min time granularity to be able to observe cell death at each time increment, when the population size is above the REPRODUCTION-THRESHOLD threshold. In fact, due to the small population size we considered, using a finer granularity would result in a 0% death rate for each time increment. The small population size has been chosen due to the illustrative purpose of the simulation and to the need to have a computational response time of the order of seconds.

The chosen 10 min time granularity is a sufficient time step to model the biofilm formation phenomenon and is within the range adopted in previous studies. In general the time step is chosen depending on the bacterial species considered and on the phenomenon under investigation (e.g., biofilm initial attachment, biofilm detachment, viscoelastic modification of the matrix, etc.). It is commonly accepted that the time step for microbial phenomena is much higher than for hydrodynamic phenomena. The time step used in previous studies range from five minutes in *P. aeruginosa* biofilm growth [7] to one hour for oral biofilm formation [15] and hours in biofilm formation and bacteria decay [26].

The simulation in Table 2 shows a growth of the population size and of the global concentration of c-di-GMP due to cell reproduction, with a biofilm formation at time 2:50, when the c-di-GMP global concentration threshold is reached. The growth of both values then continues until time 3:00, when the population

Table 1. Concentration of c-di-GMP internal to a cell of *A. aeruginosa* [1].

Cell age	0–20	20–40	40–60	60–120
c-di-GMP (nM)	40	270	110	40

Table 2. In silico experiments performed with time granularity 10 for an initial population of 120 cells with 120 min time to reproduction, reproduction threshold of 350 cells, dear rate 5% and c-di-GMP concentration: 200 for cell transition to sessile and back to planktonic and 40,000 for biofilm transition and back to disperse community.

Time		Population size			Global	Biofilm	From death or
hr:min	min	total	planktonic	sessile	c-di-GMP	presence	reproduction
00:00	0	120	100	20	15 500	No	Initial population
00:10	10	130	110	20	15 500	No	Reproduction
00:30	30	150	130	20	16 300	No	Reproduction
01:00	60	180	140	40	23 400	No	Reproduction
02:00	120	240	200	40	30 600	No	Reproduction
02:30	150	300	260	40	32 600	No	Reproduction
02:40	160	320	260	60	38 000	No	Reproduction
02:50	170	340	260	80	43 400	Yes	Reproduction
03:00	180	360	280	80	46 800	Yes	Reproduction
03:10	190	359	279	80	51 490	Yes	Death
03:30	210	357	277	80	54 070	Yes	Death
04:00	240	354	316	38	45 840	Yes	Death
04:30	270	351	312	39	41 530	Yes	Death
04:40	280	350	290	60	44 920	Yes	Death
04:50	290	389	310	79	45 290	Yes	Reproduction
05:00	300	388	310	78	50 501	Yes	Death
06:00	360	382	346	36	48 680	Yes	Death
10:00	600	358	326	32	45 440	Yes	Death
11:00	660	352	280	72	45 650	Yes	Death
11:10	670	351	279	72	46 680	Yes	Death
11:20	680	350	239	111	56 940	Yes	Death
11:30	690	366	255	111	57 220	Yes	Reproduction
12:00	720	363	317	46	48 310	Yes	Death

threshold that stops reproduction (REPRODUCTION-THRESHOLD) is exceeded (population size 360 > 350 threshold). Cells start then to die until the population size drops again down to the threshold level at time 4:40. We have then an alternation of long time intervals of cell death and short time intervals of reproduction, with the biofilm persisting throughout. This behaviour mimics on a smaller scale real cell behaviour and is based on biological data for *P. aeruginosa* [1,25,31]. However, we can also consider a single cell as a representative of a cluster of cells that, globally, exhibits a homogeneous behaviour. This approach is commonly used and considered realistic [22,27].

3.3   Formal Analysis Using Model Checking

The search command can be used to *predict* the biofilm formation in an in silico experiments. With reference to the experiment considered in Sect. 3.2, we can use the search command

```
(tsearch [3] in P-AERUGINOSA init =>*
    {C:Configuration
     < P-aeruginosa : Population | state : attributes-updated,
                                   biofilm : true >}
 with no time limit .)
```

to find the solutions for times 170, 180 and 190 in Table 2. Note that we must include the state `attributes-updated` in the search pattern to make sure that the solution has all attributes updated for the specific time unit.

Moreover, the results of the experiment shown in Table 2 seem to suggest that the biofilm, once formed, will persist forever. Such a conjecture cannot be validated through an experiment, since we do not know for how long we need to continue the experiment to possibly observe the biofilm disappearing. However, using the search command

```
(tsearch [1] in P-AERUGINOSA init =>*
    {C:Configuration
     < P-aeruginosa : Population | state : attributes-updated,
                                   biofilm : false >}
 in time >= 170 .)
```

we find out that after 860 min (14 h and 20 min) the biofilm disappears and the dispersed population consists of 385 cells (357 planktonic and 28 sessile) with 38 670 as a global c-di-GMP concentration. This proves that the conjecture suggested by the experiment results was actually false.

We have also defined module `P-AERUGINOSA-INTERVENTION`, which extends module `P-AERUGINOSA` by modelling a replacement intervention to be repeated every 160 min, namely `TIME-BETWEEN-INTERVENTIONS` equals 160. Then the search command

```
(tsearch [1] in P-AERUGINOSA-INTERVENTION init =>*
    {C:Configuration
     < P-aeruginosa : Intervention | state : attributes-updated,
                                     biofilm : true >}
 in time <= 3000 .)
```

will return 'No Solution' thus predicting that no biofilm would be formed even if we could extend the duration of the experiment to 3 000 min (50 h).

4   Conclusion and Future Work

We have used Real-Time Maude to define an approach for the formal modelling and analysis of early biofilm formation. Our approach supports both simulation to mimic lab experiments and formal analysis by exploiting Real-Time Maude timed search command to predict

1. a specific outcome of an experiment;
2. the absence of a given outcome from all possible results of an experiments.

Prediction 2 is essential for planning effective interventions to prevent the formation of a biofilm. Although the kind intervention considered in this paper is a simple replacement, as part of our future work we plan to consider more sophisticated forms of intervention, such as the use of antibacterial and quenching.

Quenching refers to the capture/deactivation of c-di-GMP and other messengers or signalling molecules involved in the process of biofilm formation and maturation. Recent examples of c-di-GMP quenching agents include the aromatic compound coumarin [32], the fungal-produced antimicrobial terrein [13], the immunosuppressive drug azathioprine [5] and the antimetabolite drug sulfathiazole [4]. These and other c-di-GMP quenching compounds can be used to reduce biofilm formation without eliciting antimicrobial resistance in the target microorganisms.

We also plan to extend our model by including more accurate biological mechanisms and by improving the precision of the generated behaviour. For example, in terms of biological mechanisms, we have neglected the cell grows through time and normalised the c-di-GMP concentration with respect to the growing volume of the cell. Separating the two mechanisms, cell growth and c-di-GMP concentration, would result in a more accurate model. For the case study of *P. aeruginosa*, detailed microbial growth parameters are reported by Schleheck *et al.* [25]: duration of the log growth phase, stationary phase, and death phase. The precision of the generated behaviour could be improved by using the Population class to record further global aspects in order to support the mapping of a global behaviour observed in lab experiments to the behaviour of individual cells. For example, we could record the death toll over a period of time that equals the life cycle and make adjustments during the rewrite process to keep it within two given thresholds in accordance with the given birth rate. This would allow us to avoid the problem discussed in Sect. 2.5 and make the death rewrite rule work with higher precision and with no constraints on the size of the population and time granularity. Finally we plan to consider a time interval rather than an exact time for cell life-cycle duration and, at a later stage, introduce stochasticity into our model.

References

1. Abel, S., et al.: Bi-modal distribution of the second messenger c-di-GMP controls cell fate and asymmetry during the Caulobacter cell cycle. PLOS Genet. **9**(9), e1003744 (2013)
2. Ahmadi, M., Jorfi, S., Kujlu, R., Ghafari, S., Soltani, R.D.C., Haghighifard, N.J.: A novel salt-tolerant bacterial consortium for biodegradation of saline and recalcitrant petrochemical wastewater. J. Environ. Manag. **191**, 198–208 (2017). https://doi.org/10.1016/j.jenvman.2017.01.010
3. Alpkvist, E., Klapper, I.A.: Multidimensional multispecies continuum model for heterogeneous biofilm development. Bull. Math. Biol. **69**, 765–789 (2007). https://doi.org/10.1007/s11538-006-9168-7

4. Antoniani, D., Maciag, P.B.A., et al.: Monitoring of diguanylate cyclase activity and of cyclic-di-GMP biosynthesis by whole-cell assays suitable for high-throughput screening of biofilm inhibitors. Appl. Microbiol. Biotechnol. **85**, 1095–1104 (2010). https://doi.org/10.1007/s00253-009-2199-x
5. Antoniani, D., Rossi, E., Rinaldo, S., Bocci, P., Lolicato, M., Paiardini, A., et al.: The immunosuppressive drug azathioprine inhibits biosynthesis of the bacterial signal molecule cyclic-di-GMP by interfering with intracellular nucleotide pool availability. Appl. Microbiol. Biotechnol. **97**, 7325–7336 (2013). https://doi.org/10.1007/s00253-013-4875-0
6. Bartocci, E., Lió, P.: Computational modeling, formal analysis, and tools for systems biology. PLoS Comput. Biol. **12**(1), e1004591 (2016). https://doi.org/10.1371/journal.pcbi.1004591
7. Biggs, M.B., Papin, J.A.: Novel multiscale modeling tool applied to Pseudomonas aeruginosa biofilm formation. PLoS ONE **8**(10), e78011 (2013). https://doi.org/10.1371/journal.pone.0078011
8. Christen, M., Kulasekara, H.D., Christen, B., Kulasekara, B.R., Hoffman, L.R., Miller, S.I.: Asymmetrical distribution of the second messenger c-di-GMP upon bacterial cell division. Science **328**, 1295–1297 (2010)
9. Flemming, H.-C., Wingender, J., Szewzyk, U., Steinberg, P., Rice, S.A., Kjelleberg, S.: Biofilms: an emergent form of bacterial life. Nat. Rev. Microbiol. **14**, 563–575 (2016)
10. Flemming, H.-C., Wuertz, S.: Bacteria and archaea on earth and their abundance in biofilms. Nat. Rev. Microbiol. **17**, 247–260 (2019)
11. Francolini, I., Donelli, G.: Prevention and control of biofilm-based medical-device-related infections. FEMS Immun. Med. Microbiol. **59**(3), 227–238 (2010)
12. Jin, X., Marshall, J.S., Wargo, M.J.: Hybrid model of bacterial biofilm growth. Bull. Math. Biol. **82**(27), 1–32 (2020). https://doi.org/10.1007/s11538-020-00701-6
13. Kim, B., Park, J.S., Choi, H.Y., et al.: Terrein is an inhibitor of quorum sensing and c-di-GMP in Pseudomonas aeruginosa: a connection between quorum sensing and c-di-GMP. Sci. Rep. **8**(8617), 1–13 (2018). https://doi.org/10.1038/s41598-018-26974-5
14. Laventie, B.-J., et al.: A surface-induced asymmetric program promotes tissue colonization by Pseudomonas aeruginosa. Cell Host Microbe **25**(1), 140–152 (2019). https://doi.org/10.1016/j.chom.2018.11.008
15. Martin, B., Tamanai-Shacoori, Z., Bronsard, J., Ginguené, F., Meuric, V., et al.: A new mathematical model of bacterial interactions in two-species oral biofilms. PLoS ONE **12**(3), e0173153 (2017). https://doi.org/10.1371/journal.pone.0173153
16. Mattei, M.R., Frunzo, L., D'Acunto, B., et al.: Continuum and discrete approach in modeling biofilm development and structure: a review. J. Math. Biol. **76**, 945–1003 (2018). https://doi.org/10.1007/s00285-017-1165-y
17. McDougald, D., Rice, S.A., Barraud, N., Steinberg, P.D., Kjelleberg, S.: Should we stay or should we go: mechanisms and ecological consequences for biofilm dispersal. Nat. Rev. Microbiol. **10**, 39–50 (2012)
18. Meseguer, J.: Twenty years of rewriting logic. J. Logic Algebr. Program. **81**, 721–781 (2012)
19. Ölveczky, P.C.: Real-Time Maude and its applications. In: Escobar, S. (ed.) WRLA 2014. LNCS, vol. 8663, pp. 42–79. Springer, Cham (2014). https://doi.org/10.1007/978-3-319-12904-4_3
20. Ölveczky, P.C.: Designing Reliable Distributed Systems. UTCS. Springer, London (2017). https://doi.org/10.1007/978-1-4471-6687-0

21. Ölveczky, P.C., Meseguer, J.: Semantics and pragmatics of Real-Time-Maude. High.-Order Symbol. Comput. **20**(1–2), 161–196 (2007)

22. Paula, A.J., Hwang, G., Koo, H.: Dynamics of bacterial population growth in biofilms resemble spatial and structural aspects of urbanization. Nat. Commun. **11**(1354), 1–14 (2020). https://doi.org/10.1038/s41467-020-15165-4

23. Pearce, P., et al.: Flow-induced symmetry breaking in growing bacterial biofilm. Phys. Rev. Lett. **123**(25), 258101–258106 (2019). https://link.aps.org/doi/10.1103/PhysRevLett.123.258101

24. Păun, G.: P systems with active membranes: attacking NP-complete problems. Autom. Lang. Comb. **6**(1), 65–90 (2001)

25. Schleheck, D., et al.: Pseudomonas aeruginosa PAO1 preferentially grows as aggregates in liquid batch cultures and disperses upon starvation. PLoS ONE **4**(5), e5513 (2009)

26. Skoneczny, S.: Cellular automata-based modelling and simulation of biofilm structure on multi-core computers. Water Sci. Technol. **72**(11), 2071–2081 (2015)

27. Stewart, P., Franklin, M.: Physiological heterogeneity in biofilms. Nat. Rev. Microbiol. **6**, 199–210 (2008). https://doi.org/10.1038/nrmicro1838

28. Stickler, D.: Bacterial biofilms in patients with indwelling urinary catheters. Nat. Rev. Urol. **5**, 598–608 (2008)

29. Wang, H., Masters, S., Edwards, M., Falkinham, J., Pruden, A.: Effect of disinfectant, water age, and pipe materials on bacterial and eukaryotic community structure in drinking water biofilm. Environ. Sci. Technol. **48**(3), 1426–1435 (2014)

30. Whiteley, M., Bangera, M., Bumgarner, R., et al.: Gene expression in Pseudomonas aeruginosa biofilms. Nature **413**, 860–864 (2001). https://doi.org/10.1038/35101627

31. Yang, L., et al.: In situ growth rates and biofilm development of Pseudomonas aeruginosa populations in chronic lung infections. J. Bacteriol. **190**(8), 2767–2776 (2008)

32. Zhang, Y., et al.: Coumarin reduces virulence and biofilm formation in Pseudomonas aeruginosa by affecting quorum sensing, type III secretion and c-di-GMP levels. Front. Microbiol. **9**, 1952 (2018). https://www.frontiersin.org/article/10.3389/fmicb.2018.01952

Data Mining and Processing Related Approaches

Query Rewriting on Path Views Without Integrity Constraints

Julien Romero[1]([✉]) [iD], Nicoleta Preda[2], and Fabian Suchanek[1]

[1] LTCI, Télécom Paris, Institut Polytechnique de Paris, Paris, France
{julien.romero,fabian.suchanek}@telecom-paris.fr
[2] University of Versailles, Versailles, France
nicoleta.preda@uvsq.fr

Abstract. A view with a binding pattern is a parameterised query on a database. Such views are used, e.g., to model Web services. To answer a query on such views, one has to orchestrate the views together in execution plans. The goal is usually to find equivalent rewritings, which deliver precisely the same results as the query on all databases. However, such rewritings are usually possible only in the presence of integrity constraints – and not all databases have such constraints. In this paper, we describe a class of plans that give practical guarantees about their result even if there are no integrity constraints. We provide a characterisation of such plans and a complete and correct algorithm to enumerate them. Finally, we show that our method can find plans on real-world Web Services.

1 Introduction

A view with binding patterns is a parameterised query defined in terms of a global schema [6]. Such a query works like a function: it requires specific values as input and delivers the query results as output. For example, consider the database instance about employees at Fig. 1. The call to the function *getCompany*

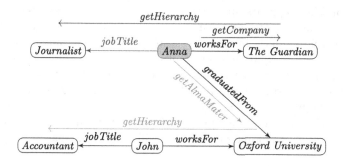

Fig. 1. An equivalent execution plan (blue) and a maximally contained rewriting (orange) executed on a database instance (black). (Color figure online)

© Springer Nature Switzerland AG 2021
J. Bowles et al. (Eds.): DataMod 2020, LNCS 12611, pp. 155–173, 2021.
https://doi.org/10.1007/978-3-030-70650-0_10

with an employee *Anna* as input, returns the company *The Guardian* as output. Abstractly, the function is represented as the rule: *getCompany(in, out)* ← *worksFor(in, out)*. The *worksFor* relation is of the global schema, which is orthogonal to the schema of the actual data. Unlike query interfaces like SPARQL endpoints, functions prevent arbitrary access to the database engines. In particular, one can model Web forms or REST Web Services as views with binding patterns. According to programmableweb.com, there are currently more than 22,000 such REST Web Services.

If we want to answer a query on a global database that can be accessed only through functions, we have to orchestrate the functions into an execution plan. In our example from Fig. 1, if we want to find the job title of Anna, we first have to find her company (by calling *getCompany*), and then her job title (by calling *getHierarchy* on her company, and filtering the results about Anna). Our problem is thus as follows: Given a user query (such as *jobTitle(Anna, x)*) and a set of functions (each being a parameterised conjunctive query), find an execution plan (i.e., a sequence of function calls) that delivers the answer to the query on a database that offers these functions. While the schema of the database is known to the user, she or he does not know whether the database contains the answer to the query at all.

Much of the literature concentrates on finding *equivalent rewritings*, i.e., execution plans that deliver the same result as the original query on all databases that offer this specific set of functions. Unfortunately, our example plan is not an equivalent rewriting: it will deliver no results on databases where (for whatever reasons) Anna has a job title but no employer. The plan is equivalent to the query only if an integrity constraint stipulates that every person with a job title must have an employer and the database instance is complete.

Such constraints are hard to come by in real life, because they may not hold (a person can have a job title but no employer; a person may have a birth date but no death date; some countries do not have a capital[1]; etc.). Even if they hold in real life, they may not hold in the database due to the incompleteness of the data. Hence, they are also challenging to mine automatically. In the absence of constraints, however, an atomic query has an equivalent rewriting only if there is a function that was defined precisely for that query.

This problem appears in particular in data integration settings, where databases are incomplete, and the equivalent rewritings usually fail to deliver results. Therefore, data integration systems often use *maximally contained rewritings* instead of equivalent rewritings. Intuitively speaking, maximally contained rewritings are execution plans that try to find all calls that could potentially lead to an answer. In our example, the plan *getAlmaMater, getHierarchy* is included in the maximally contained rewriting: It asks for the university where Anna graduated, and for their job positions. If Anna happens to work at the university where she graduated, this plan will answer the query.

---

[1] e.g., the Republic of Nauru.

This plan appears somehow less reasonable that our first plan because it works only for people who work at their alma mater. However, both plans are equal concerning their formal guarantees: none of them can guarantee to deliver the answers to the query. This is a conundrum: Unless we have information about the data distribution or more schema information, we have no formal means to give the first plan higher chances of success than the second plan – although the first plan is intuitively much better.

In this paper, we propose a solution to this conundrum: We can show that the first plan (*getCompany, getHierarchy*) is "smart", in a sense that we formally define. We can give guarantees about the results of smart plans in the absence of integrity constraints. We also give an algorithm that can enumerate all smart plans for a given **atomic query** and **path-shaped functions** (as in Fig. 1). We show that under a condition that we call the *Optional Edge Semantics* our algorithm is complete and correct, i.e., it will exhaustively enumerate all such smart plans. We apply our method to real Web services and show that smart plans work in practice and deliver more query results than competing approaches.

This paper is structured as follows: Sect. 2 discusses related work, Sect. 3 introduces preliminaries, and Sect. 4 gives a definition of smart plans. Section 5 provides a method to characterise smart plans, and Sect. 6 gives an algorithm that can generate smart plans. We provide extensive experiments on synthetic and real Web services to show the viability of our method in Sect. 7.

All the proofs and technical details are in the appendix of the accompanying technical report [13].

2 Related Work

Equivalent Rewritings. An equivalent rewriting of a query is an alternative formulation of the query that has the same results as the query on all databases. Equivalent rewritings have also been studied in the context of views with binding patterns [2,12]. However, they may not be sufficient to answer the query [6]. Equivalent rewritings rely on integrity constraints, which may not be available. These constraints are difficult to mine, as most real-life rules have exceptions. Also, equivalent rewritings may falsely return empty answers only because the database instance is incomplete with respect to the integrity constraints. We aim to come up with new relevant rewritings that still offer formal guarantees about their results.

Maximally Contained Rewriting. In data integration applications, where databases are incomplete, and equivalent rewritings are likely to fail, maximally contained rewritings have been proposed as an alternative. A maximally contained rewriting is a query expressed in a chosen language that retrieves the broadest possible set of answers [6]. By definition, the task does not distinguish between intuitively more reasonable rewritings and rewritings that stand little chance to return a result on real databases. For views with binding patterns, the problem has been studied for different rewriting languages and under different constraints [4,5,7]. Some works [8,9] propose to prioritise the execution of the calls in order to produce the first results fast. While the first work [8] does not give guarantees about the plan results, the second one [9] can give guarantees only for very few plans. Our work is much more general and includes all the plans generated by [9], as we will see.

Plan Execution. Several works study how to optimise given execution plans [14,15]. Our work, in contrast, aims at *finding* such execution plans.

Federated Databases. In federated databases [1,3], a data source supports any queries in a predefined language. In our setting, in contrast, the database can be queried only through *functions*, i.e., specific predefined queries with input parameters.

3   Preliminaries

We use the terminology of [12], and recall the definitions briefly.

Global Schema. We assume a set $\mathcal{C}$ of constants and a set $\mathcal{R}$ of binary relation names. A *fact* $r(a,b)$ is formed from a relation name $r \in \mathcal{R}$ and two constants $a, b \in \mathcal{C}$. A *database instance* I, or simply *instance*, is a set of facts.

Queries. An *atom* takes the form $r(\alpha, \beta)$, where $r \in \mathcal{R}$, and α and β are either constants or variables. It can be equivalently written as $r^-(\beta, \alpha)$. A *query* takes the form:

$$q(\alpha_1, ..., \alpha_m) \leftarrow B_1, ..., B_n$$

where $\alpha_1, ...\alpha_m$ are variables, each of which must appear in at least one of the body atoms $B_1, ...B_n$. We assume that queries are *connected*, i.e., each body atom must be transitively linked to every other body atom by shared variables.

An *embedding* for a query q on a database instance I is a substitution σ for the variables of the body atoms so that $\forall B \in \{B_1, ..., B_n\} : \sigma(B) \in I$. A *result* of a query is an embedding projected to the variables of the head atom. We write $q(\alpha_1, ..., \alpha_m)(I)$ for the results of the query on I. An *atomic query* is a query that takes the form $q(x) \leftarrow r(a, x)$, where a is a constant and x is a variable. A *path query* is a query of the form:

$$q(x_i) \leftarrow r_1(a, x_1), r_2(x_1, x_2), ..., r_n(x_{n-1}, x_n)$$

where a is a constant, x_i is the output variable, each x_j except x_i is either a variable or the constant a, and $1 \leq i \leq n$.

Functions. We model functions as views with binding patterns [10], namely:

$$f(\underline{x}, y_1, ..., y_m) \leftarrow B_1, ..., B_n$$

Here, f is the function name, x is the *input variable* (which we underline), $y_1, ..., y_m$ are the *output variables*, and any other variables of the body atoms are *existential variables*. In this paper, we are concerned with *path functions*, where the body atoms are ordered in a sequence $r_1(\underline{x}, x_1), r_2(x_1, x_2), ..., r_n(x_{n-1}, x_n)$. The first variable of the first atom is the input of the plan, the second variable of each atom is the first variable of its successor, and the output variables follow the order of the atoms.

Calling a function for a given value of the input variable means finding the result of the query given by the body of the function on a database instance.

Plans. A *plan* takes the form

$$\pi(x) = c_1, \ldots, c_n, \gamma_1 = \delta_1, \ldots, \gamma_m = \delta_m$$

Here, a is a constant and x is the output variable. Each c_i is a *function call* of the form $f(\underline{a}, \beta_1, \ldots, \beta_n)$, where f is a function name, the input α is either a constant or a variable occurring in some call in $c_1, \ldots, c_{i-1}$, and the outputs $\beta_1, \ldots, \beta_n$ are variables. Each $\gamma_j = \delta_j$ is called a *filter*, where γ_j is an output variable of any call, and δ_j is either a variable that appears in some call or a constant. If the plan has no filters, then we call it *unfiltered*. The *semantics* of the plan is the query

$$q(x) \leftarrow \phi(c_1), \ldots, \phi(c_n), \gamma_1 = \delta_1, \ldots, \gamma_m = \delta_m$$

Here, x is the output variable of the plan, and $\cdot = \cdot$ is an atom that holds in any database instance if and only if its two arguments are identical. Each $\phi(c_i)$ is the body of the query defining the function f of the call c_i, in which we have substituted the constants and variables given by c_i, and where we have used fresh existential variables across the different $\phi(c_i)$.

To *evaluate* a plan on an instance means running the query above. In practice, this boils down to calling the functions in the order given by the plan. Given an execution plan π_a and a database I, we call $\pi_a(I)$ the answers of the plan on I.

Example 3.1. *Consider our example in Fig. 1. There are 3 relation names in the database: worksFor, jobTitle, and graduatedFrom. The functions are:*

$$getCompany(\underline{x}, y) \leftarrow worksFor(\underline{x}, y)$$

$$getHierarchy(\underline{y}, x, z) \leftarrow worksFor^-(\underline{y}, x), jobTitle(x, z)$$

$$getAlmaMater(\underline{x}, y) \leftarrow graduatedFrom(\underline{x}, y)$$

The following is an execution plan:

$$\pi_1(z) = getCompany(\underline{Anna}, x), getHierarchy(\underline{x}, y, z), y = Anna$$

The first element is a function call to getCompany with the name of the person (Anna) as input, and the variable x as output. The variable x then serves as input in the second function call to getHierarchy. Figure 1 shows the plan with an example instance. This plan computes the query:

$$worksFor(Anna, x), worksFor^-(x, y), jobTitle(y, z), y = Anna$$

In our example instance, we have the embedding:

$$\sigma = \{x \rightarrow The\ Guardian, y \rightarrow Anna, z \rightarrow Journalist\}.$$

An execution plan π is *redundant* if it has no call using the constant a as input, or if it contains a call where none of the outputs is an output of the plan or an input to another call.

An *equivalent rewriting* of an atomic query $q(x) \leftarrow r(a, x)$ is an execution plan that has the same results as q on all database instances. For our query language, a *maximally contained rewriting* for the query q is a plan whose semantics contains the atom $r(a, x)$.

4   Defining Smart Plans

Given an atomic query, and given a set of path functions, we want to find a reasonable execution plan that answers the query.

Introductory Observations. Let us consider again the query $q(x) \leftarrow jobTitle(Anna, x)$ and the two plans in Fig. 1. The first plan seems to be smarter than the second one. The intuition becomes more formal if we look at the queries in their respective semantics. The first plan is the plan $\pi_1(z)$ given in Example 3.1. Its semantics is the query: $worksFor(Anna, x), worksFor^-(x, y), jobTitle(y, z), y = Anna$. If the first atom has a match in the database instance, then $y = Anna$ is indeed a match, and the plan delivers the answers of the query. If the first atom has no match in the database instance, then the plan returns no result, while the query may have one. To make the plan equivalent to the query on all database instances, we would need the following unary inclusion dependency: $jobTitle(x, y) \rightarrow \exists z : worksAt(x, z)$. In our setting, however, we cannot assume such an integrity constraint. Let us now consider the second plan:

$$\pi_2(z) = getAlmaMater(\underline{Anna}, x), getHierarchy(\underline{x}, y, z), y = Anna$$

Its semantics are: $graduatedFrom(Anna, x), worksFor^-(x, y), jobTitle(y, z), y = Anna$. To guarantee that $y = Anna$ is a match, we need one constraint at the schema level: the inclusion dependency $graduatedFrom(x, y) \rightarrow worksFor(x, y)$. However, this constraint does not hold in the real world, and it is stronger than a unary inclusion dependency (which has an existential variable in the tail). Besides, π_2, similarly to π_1, needs the unary inclusion dependency $jobTitle(x, y) \rightarrow \exists z : graduatedFrom(x, z)$ to be an equivalent rewriting.

Definition. In summary, the first plan, π_1, returns the query answers if all the calls return results. The second plan, π_2, may return query answers, but in most of the cases even if the calls are successful, their results are filtered out by the filter $y = Anna$. This brings us to the following definition of smart plans:

Definition 4.1 (Smart Plan). *Given an atomic query q and a set of functions, a plan π is* smart *if the following holds on all database instances I: If the filter-free version of π has a result on I, then π delivers exactly the answers to the query.*

We also introduce weakly smart plans:

Definition 4.2 (Weakly Smart Plan). *Given an atomic query q and a set of functions, a plan π is* weakly smart *if the following holds on all database instances I where q has at least one result: If the filter-free version of π has a result on I, then π delivers a super-set of the answers to the query.*

Weakly smart plans deliver a superset of the answers of the query, and thus do not actually help in query evaluation. Nevertheless, weakly smart plans can be useful: For example, if a data provider wants to hide private information, like the phone number of a given person, they do not want to leak it in any way, not even among other results. Thus, they will want to design their functions in such a way that no *weakly smart plan* exists for this specific query.

Every smart plan is also a weakly smart plan. Some queries will admit only weakly smart plans and no smart plans, mainly because the variable that one has to filter on is not an output variable.

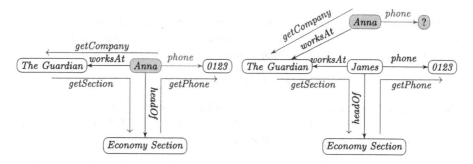

Fig. 2. A non-smart execution plan for the query *phone(Anna,x)*. Left: a database where the plan answers the query. Right: a database where the unfiltered plan has results, but the filtered plan does not answer the query.

Smart Plans Versus Equivalent Plans. Consider again the plans π_1 (smart) and π_2 (not-smart) above. Both plans assume the existence of a unary inclusion dependency. The difference is that in addition, π_2 relies on an additional role inclusion constraint. Is it thus sufficient to assume unary inclusion dependencies between all pairs of relations, and apply the algorithm in [12] to find equivalent rewritings? The answer is no: Fig. 2 shows a plan that is equivalent if the necessary unary inclusion dependencies hold. However, the plan is not smart. On the database instance shown on the right-hand side, the unfiltered plan returns a non-empty set of results that does not answer the query.

Problem. After having motivated and defined our notion of smart plans, we are now ready to state our problem: Given an atomic query, and a set of path functions, we want to enumerate all smart plans.

5   Characterizing Smart Plans

5.1   Web Service Functions

We now turn to generating smart plans. As previously stated, our approach can find smart plans only under a certain condition. This condition has to do with the way Web services work. Assume that for a given person, a function returns the employer and the address of the working place:

$$getCompanyInfo(\underline{x}, y, z) \leftarrow worksAt(\underline{x}, y), locatedIn(y, z)$$

Now assume that, for some person, the address of the employer is not in the database. In that case, the call will not fail. Rather, it will return only the employer y, and return a null-value for the address z. It is as if the atom $locatedIn(y, z)$ were optional. To model this phenomenon, we introduce the notion of *sub-functions*: Given a path function $f : r_1(\underline{x_0}, x_1), r_2(x_1, x_2), \dots r_n(x_{n-1}, x_n)$, the sub-function for an output variable x_i is the function $f_i(\underline{x_0}, \dots, x_i) \leftarrow r_1(\underline{x_0}, x_1), \dots r_i(x_{i-1}, x_i)$.

Example 5.1. *The sub-functions of the function getCompanyInfo are* $f_1(\underline{x}, y) \leftarrow worksAt(\underline{x}, y)$, *which is associated to* y, *and* $f_2(\underline{x}, y, z) \leftarrow worksAt(\underline{x}, y), locatedIn(y, z)$, *which is associated to* z.

We can now express the Optional Edge Semantics:

Definition 5.2 (Optional Edge Semantics). *We say that we are under the optional edge semantics if, for any path function f, a sub-function of f has exactly the same binding for its output variables as f.*

The optional edge semantics mirrors the way real Web services work. Its main difference to the standard semantics is that it is not possible to use a function to filter out query results. For example, it is not possible to use the function *get-CompanyInfo* to retrieve only those people who work at a company. The function will retrieve companies with addresses and companies without addresses, and we can find out the companies without addresses only by skimming through the results after the call. This contrasts with the standard semantics of parametrised queries (as used, e.g., in [8,9,12]), which do not return a result if any of their variables cannot be bound.

This has a very practical consequence: As we shall see, smart plans under the optional edge semantics have a very particular shape.

5.2   Preliminary Definitions

Our main intuition is that smart plans under the optional edge semantics walk forward until a turning point. From then on, they "walk back" to the input constant and query (see again Fig. 1). As a more complex example, consider the atomic query $q(x) \leftarrow r(a, x)$ and the database shown in Fig. 3. The plan f_1, f_2, f_3, f_4 is shown in blue. As we can see, the plan walks "forward" and then

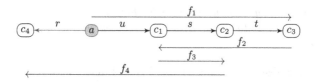

Fig. 3. A bounded plan

"backward" again. Intuitively, the "forward path" makes sure that certain facts exist in the database (if the facts do not exist, the plan delivers no answer, and is thus trivially smart). If these facts exist, then all functions on the "backward path" are guaranteed to deliver results. Thus, if a has an r-relation, the plan is guaranteed to deliver its object. Let us now make this intuition more formal.

We first observe (and prove in the technical report) that the semantics of any filter-free execution plan can be reduced to a path query. The path query of Fig. 3 is:

$$q(a, x) \leftarrow u(a, y_1), s(y_1, y_2), t(y_2, y_3), t^-(y_3, y_2), s^-(y_2, y_1),$$
$$s(y_1, y_2), s^-(y_2, y_1), u^-(y_1, y_0), r(y_0, x)$$

Now, any filter-free path query can be written unambiguously as the sequence of its relations – the *skeleton*. In the example, the skeleton is:

$$u.s.t.t^-.s^-.s.s^-.u^-.r$$

In particular, the skeleton of an atomic query $q(x) \leftarrow r(a, x)$ is just r. Given a skeleton $r_1.r_2...r_n$, we write $r_1...r_n(a)$ for the set of all answers of the query when a is given as input. For path functions, we write the name of the function as a shorthand for the skeleton of the semantics of the function. For example, in Fig. 3, we have $f_1(a) = \{c_3\}$, and $f_1 f_2 f_3 f_4(a) = \{c_4\}$. We now introduce two notions to formalise the "forward and backward" movement:

Definition 5.3 (Forward and Backward Step). *Given a sequence of relations $r_0...r_n$ and a position $0 \leq i \leq n$, a forward step consists of the relation r_i, together with the updated position $i + 1$. Given position $1 \leq i \leq n + 1$, a backward step consists of the relation r_{i-1}^-, together with the updated position $i - 1$.*

Definition 5.4 (Walk). *A walk to a position k $(0 \leq k \leq n)$ through a sequence of relations $r_0...r_n$ consists of a sequence of steps (forward or backward) in $r_0...r_n$, so that the first step starts at position $n + 1$, every step starts at the updated position of the previous step, and the last step leads to the updated position k.*

If we do not mention k, we consider that $k = 0$, i.e., we cross the sequence of relations entirely.

Example 5.5. *In Fig. 3, a possible walk through $r^- ust$ is $t^- s^- ss^- u^- r$. This walk goes from c_3 to c_2 to c_1, then to c_2, and back through c_1, c, c_4 (as indicated by the blue arrows).*

We can now formalise the notion of the forward and backward path:

Definition 5.6 (Bounded plan). *A bounded path for a set of relations $\mathcal{R}$ and a query $q(x) \leftarrow r(a, x)$ is a path query P, followed by a walk through $r^- P$. A bounded plan for a set of path functions $\mathcal{F}$ is a non-redundant execution plan whose semantics are a bounded path. We call P the forward path and the walk though $r^- P$ the backward path.*

Example 5.7. *In Fig. 3, $f_1 f_2 f_3 f_4$ is a bounded path, where the forward path is f_1, and the backward path $f_2 f_3 f_4$ is a walk through $r^- f_1$.*

5.3 Characterising Smart Plans

Our notion of bounded plans is based purely on the notion of skeletons, and does not make use of filters. This is not a problem, because smart plans depend on constraint-free plans. Furthermore, we show in the technical report that we can restrict ourselves to execution plans whose semantics is a path query. This allows for the following theorems (proven in the technical report):

Theorem 5.8 (Correctness). *Let $q(x) \leftarrow r(a, x)$ be an atomic query, F a set of path functions and F_{sub} the set of sub-functions of F. Let π_a be a non-redundant bounded execution plan over the F_{sub} such that its semantics is a path query. Then π_a is weakly smart.*

Theorem 5.9 (Completeness). *Let $q(x) \leftarrow r(a, x)$ be an atomic query, F a set of path functions and F_{sub} the set of sub-functions of F. Let π_a be a weakly smart plan over F_{sub} such that its semantics is a path query. Then π_a is bounded.*

We have thus found a way to recognise weakly smart plans without executing them. Extending this characterisation from weakly smart plans to fully smart plans consists mainly of adding a filter. The technical report gives more technical details.

6 Generating Smart Plans

We have shown that weakly smart plans are precisely the bounded plans. We will now turn to generating such plans. Let us first introduce the notion of minimal plans.

6.1   Minimal Smart Plans

In line with related work [12], we will not generate redundant plans. These contain more function calls, and cannot deliver more results than non-redundant plans. More precisely, we will focus on *minimal plans*:

Definition 6.1 (Minimal Smart Plan). *Let $\pi_a(x)$ be a non-redundant execution plan organised in a sequence $c_0, c_1, \ldots, c_k$ of calls, such that the input of c_0 is the constant a, every other call c_i takes as input an output variable of the previous call c_{i-1}, and the output of the plan is in the call c_k. π_a is a minimal (weakly) smart plan if it is a (weakly) smart plan and there exists no other (weakly) smart plan $\pi'_a(x)$ composed of a sub-sequence $c_{i_1}, \ldots, c_{i_n}$ (with $0 \le i_1 < \ldots < i_n \le k$).*

Example 6.2. *Let us consider the two functions $f_1(x, y) = r(x, y)$ and $f_2(y, z) = r^-(y, t).r(t, z)$. For the query $q(x) \leftarrow r(a, x)$, the plan $\pi_a(x) = f_1(a, y), f_2(y, x)$ is obviously weakly smart. It is also non-redundant. However, it is not minimal. This is because $\pi'_a(x) = f_1(a, x)$ is also weakly smart, and is composed of a sub-sequence of calls of π_a.*

In general, it is not useful to consider non-minimal plans because they are just longer but cannot yield more results. On the contrary, a non-minimal plan can have fewer results than its minimal version, because the additional calls can filter out results. The notion of minimality would make sense also in the case of equivalent rewritings. However, in that case, the notion would impact just the number of function calls and not the results of the plan, since equivalent rewritings deliver the same results by definition. In the case of smart plans, as we will see, the notion of minimality allows us to consider only a finite number of execution plans and thus to have an algorithm that terminates.

6.2   Bounding and Generating the Weakly Smart Plans

We can enumerate all minimal weakly smart plans because their number is limited. We show in the technical report the following theorem:

Theorem 6.3 (Bound on Plans). *Given a set of relations $\mathcal{R}$, a query $q(x) \leftarrow r(a, x)$, $r \in \mathcal{R}$, and a set of path function definitions $\mathcal{F}$, there can be no more than $M!$ minimal smart plans, where $M = |\mathcal{F}|^{2k}$ and k is the maximal number of atoms in a function. Besides, there exists an algorithm to enumerate all minimal smart plans.*

This bound is very pessimistic: In practice, the plans are very constrained and thus, the complete exploration is quite fast, as we will show in Sect. 7.

The intuition of the theorem is as follows: Let us consider a bounded path with a forward and a backward path. For each position i, we consider a state that represents the functions crossing the position i (we also consider function starting and ending there). We notice that, as the plan is minimal, there cannot be two functions starting at position i (otherwise the calls between these functions would be useless). This fact limits the size of the state to $2k$ functions (where k is the maximal size of a function, the 2 is due to the existence of both a forward and backward path). Finally, we notice that a state cannot appear at two different positions; otherwise, the plan would not be minimal (all function calls between the repetition are useless). Thus, the algorithm we propose explores the space of states in a finite time, and yields all minimal smart plans. At each step of the search, we explore the adjacent nodes that are consistent with the current state. In practice, these transitions are very constrained, and so the complexity is rarely exponential (as we will see in the experiments).

6.3   Generating the Weakly Smart Plans

Theorem 6.3 allows us to devise an algorithm that enumerates all minimal weakly smart plans. For simplicity, let us first assume that no function definition contains a loop, i.e., no function contains two consecutive relations of the form rr^-. This means that a function cannot be both on a forward and backward direction. We will later see how to remove this assumption. Algorithm 1 takes as input a query q and a set of function definitions $\mathcal{F}$. It first checks whether the query can be answered trivially by a single function (Line 1). If that is the case, the plan is printed (Line 2). Then, the algorithm sets out to find more complex plans. To avoid exploring states twice, it keeps a history of the explored states in a stack H (Line 3). The algorithm finds all non-trivial functions f that could be used to answer q. These are the functions whose short notation ends in q (Line 4). For each of these functions, the algorithm considers all possible functions f' that could start the plan (Line 5). For this, f' has to be *consistent* with f, i.e., the functions have to share the same relations. The pair of f and f' constitute the first state of the plan. Our algorithm then starts a depth-first search from that first state (Line 6). For this purpose, it calls the function *search* with the current state, the state history, and the set of functions. In the current state, a marker (a star) designates the forward path function.

Algorithm 1. FindMinimalWeakSmartPlans

Data: Query $q(a) \leftarrow r(a, x)$, set of path function definitions and all their sub-functions $\mathcal{F}$

Result: Prints minimal weakly smart plans

1 **if** $\exists f = r \in \mathcal{F}$ **then**
2     $\quad\lfloor$ print(f)

3 $H \leftarrow Stack()$
4 **foreach** $f = r_1...r_n.r \in \mathcal{F}$ **do**
5     $\quad$ **foreach** $f' \in \mathcal{F}$ *consistent with* $r_n^-...r_1^-$ **do**
6         $\qquad\lfloor$ search$(\{\langle f, n, backward\rangle, \langle f', 1, forward\rangle^*\}, H, \mathcal{F})$

Algorithm 2 executes a depth-first search on the space of states. It first checks whether the current state has already been explored (Line 1). If that is the case, the method just returns. Otherwise, the algorithm creates the new state S' (Line 3). For this purpose, it considers all positioned functions in the forward direction (Lines 5–7). If any of these functions ends, the end counter is increased (Line 6). Otherwise, we advance the positioned function by one position. The $(*)$ means that if the positioned function happens to be the designated forward path function, then the advanced positioned function has to be marked as such, too. We then apply the procedure to the backwards-pointing functions (Lines 8–11).

Once that is done, there are several cases: If all functions ended, we have a plan (Line 12). In that case, we can stop exploring because no minimal plan can include an existing plan. Next, the algorithm considers the case where one function ended, and one function started (Line 13). If the function that ended were the designated forward path function, then we would have to add one more forward function. However, then the plan would contain two functions that start at the current state. Since this is not permitted, we just do not do anything (Line 14), and the execution jumps to Line 29. If the function that ended was some other function, then the ending and the starting function can form part of a valid plan. No other function can start or end at the current state, and hence we just move to the next state (Line 15). Next, the algorithm considers the case where one function starts and no function ends (Line 16). In that case, it has to add another backward function. It tries out all functions (Line 17–19) and checks whether adding the function to the current state is consistent (as in Algorithm 1). If that is the case, the algorithm calls itself recursively with the new state (Line 19). Lines 20–23 do the same for a function that ended. Here again, the $(*)$ means that if f was the designated forward path function, then the new function has to be marked as such. Finally, the algorithm considers the case where no function ended, and no function started (Line 24). In that case, we can just move on to the next state (Line 25). We can also add a pair of a starting function and an ending function. Lines 26–28 try out all possible combinations of a starting function and an ending function and call the method recursively. If none of the previous cases applies, then $end > 1$ and $start > 1$. This means that the current plan cannot be minimal. In that case, the method pops the current state from the stack (Line 29) and returns.

Theorem 6.4 (Algorithm). *Algorithm 1 is correct and complete, terminates on all inputs, and runs in time $\mathcal{O}(M!)$, where $M = |\mathcal{F}|^{2k}$ and k is the maximal number of atoms in a function.*

The worst-case runtime of $\mathcal{O}(M!)$ is unlikely to appear in practice. Indeed, the number of possible functions that we can append to the current state in Lines 19, 23, 28 is severely reduced by the constraint that they must coincide on their relations with the functions that are already in the state. In practice, very few functions have this property. Furthermore, we can significantly improve the bound if we are interested in finding only a single weakly smart plan:

Algorithm 2. Search

Data: A state S with a designated forward path function, a set of states $\mathcal{H}$, a
set of path functions $\mathcal{F}$

Result: Prints minimal weakly smart plans

1   if $S \in H$ then return

2   $H.push(S)$

3   $S' \leftarrow \emptyset$

4   $end \leftarrow 0$

5   foreach $\langle r_1...r_n, i, forward \rangle \in S$ do

6   if $i + 1 > n$ then $end + +$

7   else $S' \leftarrow S' \cup \{\langle r_1...r_n, i + 1, forward \rangle^{(*)}\}$

8   $start \leftarrow 0$

9   foreach $\langle r_1...r_n, i, backward \rangle \in S$ do

10   if $i = 1$ then $start + +$

11   else $S' \leftarrow S' \cup \{\langle r_1...r_n, i - 1, backward \rangle\}$

12   if $S' = \emptyset$ then $print(H)$

13   else if $start = 1 \wedge end = 1$ then

14   if the designated function ended then pass

15   else $search(S', H, \mathcal{F})$

16   else if $start = 1 \wedge end = 0$ then

17   foreach $f \in \mathcal{F}$ do

18      $S'' \leftarrow S' \cup \{\langle f, |f|, backward \rangle\}$

19   if S'' is consistent then $search(S'', H, \mathcal{F})$

20   else if $start = 0 \wedge end = 1$ then

21   foreach $f \in \mathcal{F}$ do

22      $S'' \leftarrow S' \cup \{\langle f, 1, forward \rangle^{(*)}\}$

23   if S'' is consistent then $search(S'', H, \mathcal{F})$

24   else if $start = 0 \wedge end = 0$ then

25    $search(S', H, \mathcal{F})$

26   foreach $f, f' \in \mathcal{F}$ do

27      $S'' \leftarrow S' \cup \{\langle f, 1, forward \rangle, \langle f', |f'|, backward \rangle\}$

28   if S'' is consistent then $search(S'', H, \mathcal{F})$

29   $H.pop()$

Theorem 6.5. *Given an atomic query and a set of path function definitions*
$\mathcal{F}$, *we can find a single weakly smart plan in* $\mathcal{O}(|\mathcal{F}|^{2k})$, *where k is the maximal*
number of atoms in a function.

Functions with Loops. If there is a function that contains a loop of the form
$r.r^-$, then Algorithm 2 has to be adapted as follows: First, when neither functions
are starting nor ending (Lines 24–28), we can also add a function that contains a
loop. Let $f = r_1...r_i r_i^- ...r_n$ be such a function. Then the first part $r_1...r_i$ becomes

the backward path, and the second part $r_i^-...r_n$ becomes the forward path in Line 27.

When a function ends (Lines 20–23), we could also add a function with a loop. Let $f = r_1...r_i r_i^- r_n$ be such a function. The first part $r_1...r_i$ will create a forward state $\langle r_1...r_i, 1, forward \rangle$. The second part, $r_i^-...r_n$ will create the backward state $\langle r_i^-...r_n, |r_1...r_i|, backward \rangle$. The consistency check has to be adapted accordingly. The case when a function starts (Lines 16–19) is handled analogously. Theorems 6.4 and 6.5 remain valid, because the overall number of states is still bounded as before.

7 Experiments

We have implemented the Susie Algorithm [9] (more details in the technical report), the equivalent rewriting approach [12] (using Pyformlang [11]), as well as our method (Sect. 6.2) in Python. The code is available on Github[2]. We conduct two series of experiments – one on synthetic data, and one on real Web services. All our experiments are run on a laptop with Linux, 1 CPU with four cores at 2.5 GHz, and 16 GB RAM.

7.1 Synthetic Functions

In our first set of experiments, we use the methodology introduced by [12] to simulate random functions. We consider a set of artificial relations $\mathcal{R} = \{r_1, ..., r_n\}$, and randomly generated path functions up to length 3, where all variables are existential except the last one. Then we try to find a smart plan for each query of the form $q(x) \leftarrow r(a, x), r \in \mathcal{R}$.

In our first experiment, we limit the number of functions to 30 and vary the number n of relations. All the algorithms run in less than 2 s in each setting for each query. Figure 4a shows which percentage of the queries the algorithms answer. As expected, when increasing the number of relations, the percentage of answered queries decreases, as it becomes harder to combine functions. The difference between the curve for weakly smart plans and the curve for smart plans shows that it was not always possible to filter the results to get exactly the answer of the query. Weakly smart plans can answer more queries but at the expense of delivering only a super-set of the query answers. In general, we observe that our approach can always answer strictly more queries than Susie and the equivalent rewriting approach.

In our next experiment, we fix the number of relations to 10 and vary the number of functions. Figure 4b shows the results. As we increase the number of functions, we increase the number of possible function combinations. Therefore, the percentage of answered queries increases for all approaches. As before, our algorithm outperforms the other methods by a wide margin. The reason is that Susie cannot find all smart plans (see the technical report for more details).

---

[2] https://github.com/Aunsiels/smart_plans.

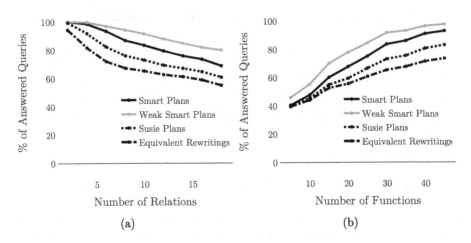

Fig. 4. Percentage of answered queries

Equivalent rewritings, on the other hand, can find only those plans that are equivalent to the query on all databases – which are very few in the absence of constraints.

7.2   Real-World Web Services

In our second series of experiments, we apply the methods to real-world Web services. We use the functions provided by [9, 12]. These are the functions of the Web services of Abe Books, ISBNDB, LibraryThing, MusicBrainz, and MovieDB. Besides, as these Web services do not contain many existential variables, we added the set of functions based on information extraction techniques (IE) from [9].

Table 2 shows the number of functions and the number of relations for each Web service. Table 1 gives examples of functions. Some of them are recursive. For example, MusicBrainz allows querying for the albums that are related to a given album. All functions are given in the same schema. Hence, in an additional setting, we consider the union of all functions from all Web services.

Note that our goal is not to call the functions. Instead, our goal is to determine whether a smart plan exists – before any functions have to be called.

For each Web service, we considered all queries of the form $q(x) \leftarrow r(a, x)$ and $q(x) \leftarrow r^-(a, x)$, where r is a relation used in the function definitions of that Web service. We ran the Susie algorithm, the equivalent rewriting algorithm, and our algorithm for each of these queries. The run-time is always less than 2 s for each query. Table 2 shows the ratio of queries for which we could find smart plans. We first observe that our approach can always answer at least as many queries as the other approaches can answer. Furthermore, there are cases where our approach can answer strictly more queries than Susie.

Table 1. Examples of real functions (3 of MusicBrainz, 1 of ISBNdb, 1 of Library-Thing).

$$getDeathDate(\underline{x}, y, z) \leftarrow hasId^-(x, y) \wedge diedOnDate(y, z)$$
$$getSinger(\underline{x}, y, z, t) \leftarrow hasRelease^-(x, y) \wedge released^-(y, z) \wedge hasId(z, t)$$
$$getLanguage(\underline{x}, y, z, t) \leftarrow hasId(x, y) \wedge released(y, z) \wedge language(z, t)$$
$$getTitles(\underline{x}, y, z, t) \leftarrow hasId^-(x, y) \wedge wrote^-(y, z) \wedge title(z, t)$$
$$getPublicationDate(\underline{x}, y, z) \leftarrow hasIsbn^-(x, y) \wedge publishedOnDate(y, z)$$

Table 2. Percentage of queries with smart plans (numbers in parenthesis represent the results with IE).

Web service	Functions	Relations	Susie	Eq. Rewritings	Smart plans
MusicBrainz (+IE)	23	42	48% (32%)	48% (32%)	48% (35%)
LastFM (+IE)	17	30	50% (30%)	50% (30%)	50% (32%)
LibraryThing (+IE)	19	32	44% (27%)	44% (27%)	44% (35%)
Abe Books (+IE)	9	8	75% (14%)	63% (11%)	75% (14%)
ISBNdb (+IE)	14	20	65% (23%)	50% (18%)	65% (23%)
Movie DB (+IE)	12	18	56% (19%)	56% (19%)	56% (19%)
UNION with IE	74	82	52%	50%	54%

The Advantage of our Algorithm is Not that it Beats Susie by Some Percentage Points on Some Web Services. Instead, the Crucial Advantage of our Algorithm is the Guarantee that the Results Are Complete. If our algorithm does not find a plan for a given query, it means that there cannot exist a smart plan for that query. Thus, even if Susie and our algorithm can answer the same number of queries on AbeBooks, only our algorithm can guarantee that the other queries cannot be answered at all. Thus, only our algorithm gives a complete description of the possible queries of a Web service.

Table 3. Example Plans (2 of MusicBrainz, 1 of ABEBooks).

Query	Plan
hasTrackNumber	getReleaseInfoByTitle, getReleaseInfoById
hasIdCollaborator	getArtistInfoByName, getCollaboratorIdbyId, getCollaboratorsById
publishedByTitle	getBookInfoByTitle, getBookInfoById

Rather short execution plans can answer some queries. Table 3 shows a few examples. However, a substantial percentage of queries cannot be answered at all. In MusicBrainz, for example, it is not possible to answer $produced(a, x)$ (i.e., to know which albums a producer produced), $hasChild^-(a,x)$ (to know the parents of a person), and $marriedOnDate^-(a, x)$ (to know who got married on a given day). These observations show that the Web services maintain control over the data, and do not allow exhaustive requests.

8 Conclusion

In this paper, we have introduced the concept of smart execution plans for Web service functions. These are plans that are guaranteed to deliver the answers to the query if they deliver results at all. We have formalised the notion of smart plans, and we have given a correct and complete algorithm to compute smart plans. Our experiments have demonstrated that our approach can be applied to real-world Web services. All experimental data, as well as all code, is available at the URL given in Sect. 7. We hope that our work can help Web service providers to design their functions, and users to query the services more efficiently.

References

1. Aebeloe, C., Montoya, G., Hose, K.: A decentralized architecture for sharing and querying semantic data. In: Hitzler, P., et al. (eds.) ESWC 2019. LNCS, vol. 11503, pp. 3–18. Springer, Cham (2019). https://doi.org/10.1007/978-3-030-21348-0_1
2. Benedikt, M., Leblay, J., ten Cate, B., Tsamoura, E.: Generating Plans from Proofs: The Interpolation-Based Approach to Query Reformulation. Synthesis Lectures on Data Management. Morgan & Claypool, San Rafael (2016)
3. Buron, M., Goasdoué, F., Manolescu, I., Mugnier, M.L.: Obi-Wan: ontology-based RDF integration of heterogeneous data. Proc. VLDB Endow. **13**(12), 2933–2936 (2020). https://doi.org/10.14778/3415478.3415512
4. Calì, A., Martinenghi, D.: Querying data under access limitations. In: ICDE (2008)
5. Duschka, O.M., Genesereth, M.R.: Answering recursive queries using views. In: PODS (1997)
6. Halevy, A.Y.: Answering queries using views: a survey. VLDB J. **10**, 270–294 (2001). https://doi.org/10.1007/s007780100054
7. Nash, A., Ludäscher, B.: Processing unions of conjunctive queries with negation under limited access patterns. In: Bertino, E., et al. (eds.) EDBT 2004. LNCS, vol. 2992, pp. 422–440. Springer, Heidelberg (2004). https://doi.org/10.1007/978-3-540-24741-8_25
8. Preda, N., Kasneci, G., Suchanek, F.M., Neumann, T., Yuan, W., Weikum, G.: Active knowledge: dynamically enriching RDF knowledge bases by web services. In: SIGMOD (2010)
9. Preda, N., Suchanek, F.M., Yuan, W., Weikum, G.: SUSIE: search using services and information extraction. In: ICDE (2013)
10. Rajaraman, A., Sagiv, Y., Ullman, J.D.: Answering queries using templates with binding patterns. In: PODS (1995)
11. Romero, J.: Pyformlang: an educational library for formal language manipulation. In: SIGCSE. Springer International Publishing (2021)
12. Romero, J., Preda, N., Amarilli, A., Suchanek, F.: Equivalent rewritings on path views with binding patterns. In: Harth, A., et al. (eds.) ESWC 2020. LNCS, vol. 12123, pp. 446–462. Springer, Cham (2020). https://doi.org/10.1007/978-3-030-49461-2_26. Extended version with proofs. https://arxiv.org/abs/2003.07316
13. Romero, J., Preda, N., Suchanek, F.: Query rewriting on path views without integrity constraints. In: Datamod (2020). Extended version with proofs. https://arxiv.org/abs/2010.03527

14. Srivastava, U., Munagala, K., Widom, J., Motwani, R.: Query optimization over web services. In: VLDB (2006)
15. Thakkar, S., Ambite, J.L., Knoblock, C.A.: Composing, optimizing, and executing plans for bioinformatics web services. VLDB J. **14**, 330–353 (2005). https://doi.org/10.1007/s00778-005-0158-4

Evaluating Trace Encoding Methods in Process Mining

Sylvio Barbon Junior[1], Paolo Ceravolo[2], Ernesto Damiani[3],
and Gabriel Marques Tavares[2(✉)]

[1] Londrina State University (UEL), Londrina, Brazil
barbon@uel.br
[2] Università degli Studi di Milano (UNIMI), Milan, Italy
{paolo.ceravolo,gabriel.tavares}@unimi.it
[3] Khalifa University (KUST), Abu Dhabi, UAE
ernesto.damiani@kustar.ac.ae

Abstract. Encoding methods affect the performance of process mining tasks but little work in the literature focused on quantifying their impact. In this paper, we compare 10 different encoding methods from three different families (trace replay and alignment, graph embeddings, and word embeddings) using measures to evaluate the overlaps in the feature space, the accuracy obtained, and the computational resources (time) consumed with a classification task. Across hundreds of event logs representing four variations of five scenarios and five anomalies, it was possible to identify the edge2vec method as the most accurate and effective in reducing class overlapping in the feature space.

Keywords: Trace encoding · Word embeddings · Graph embeddings · Classification · Process Mining

1 Introduction

Process Mining (PM) is aimed at extracting knowledge from business process event logs. Trace encoding, i.e. encoding the sequence of events in a case, is then a crucial stage for any PM task [8]. Event logs incorporate multiple information such as activity sequences, time spans, dependency between activities or attribute values, replaceability between activities or resources, concurrent or iterative behavior, and others [3,11,12,19] that can be hardly summarized in a single representation. Encoding transforms this information into a feature space enabling data processing. For this reason, the choice of the encoding method can drive the successful implementation of PM tasks. A bad encoding creates ambiguity, sparsity and complex separation boundaries [17,20]. A good encoding

This study was financed in part by Coordination for the National Council for Scientific and Technological Development (CNPq) of Brazil - Grant of Project 420562/2018-4 and Fundação Araucária (Paraná, Brazil). It was also partly supported by the program "Piano di sostegno alla ricerca 2019" funded by Università degli Studi di Milano.

J. Bowles et al. (Eds.): DataMod 2020, LNCS 12611, pp. 174–189, 2021.
https://doi.org/10.1007/978-3-030-70650-0_11

boosts performances by correctly and effectively discriminating traces and the impact on computational costs.

The machine learning community has deeply discussed the relationship between data encoding and the complexity of classification tasks. For example, Ho and Basu, in [17], studied several properties, such as class ambiguity, data sparsity, non-discriminative features, and the intrinsic complexity of class separation boundaries. Lorena et al. [20], grouped some of these properties to support measures of complexity of the classification problems. The Maximum Fisher's Discriminant Ratio (F1) and the Volume of Overlapping Region (F2) were suggested to measure how effectively the feature vectors can separate classes. F1 uses the largest discriminating ratio among all the dimensions provided by the encoding method, indicating if the problem classes can be separable using this high-discriminant feature. F2 is related to the overlapping intervals between the problem classes [10]. The Average Number of Principal Component Analysis (PCA) dimensions compared to the original dimensions (T4) can be used for evaluating dimensionality [20].

Despite trace encoding is widely discussed in the PM community [3,11,12,19], to the best of our knowledge, we lack a study on the quality achieved by the different methods proposed in the literature. In this work, we compared 10 different encoding methods (alignment, trace replay, edge2vec, node2vec, fasttext, tfidf, count2vec, word2vec, one-hot, and hash2vec) representative of both traditional PM methods, such a trace replay and alignment, and methods producing highly informative but low-dimensional vectors such as graph embeddings and word embeddings. These methods are compared against a classification problem as it directly relates to well-known PM tasks such as trace clustering and anomaly detection. More specifically, the Random Forest algorithm was employed to measure accuracy and time for binary classification of event logs. The F1, F2, and T4 measures were used to assess the quality of the compared encoding methods. The classes to be identified were common PM anomalies (early, insert, late, rework, and skip) with four different shares across five different scenarios, analyzing a total of 100 event logs.

Our results bring important insights into the optimal representation of traces in PM. More specifically, the paper starts by presenting the relevance of trace encoding in the PM literature (Sect. 2). Then, we expand on the encoding methods evaluated (Sect. 3). Section 4 presents the event logs and experiments, along with an application scenario in the classification domain. The results are presented and discussed in Sect. 5. Final remarks and conclusions are presented in Sect. 6.

2   Related Work

As process data may be analyzed according to multiple perspectives, there exists a considerable amount of encoding techniques that could be applied to event logs. Traditional PM goals, such as discovering a process model, require some level of abstractions to represent information, which can be achieved by encodings. In process discovery techniques, relations from the log are extracted and transformed into other forms of representations, such as directly-follows mappings [27]. Leontjeva et al. [19] presented a complex sequence encoder based on indexes and hidden Markov models encoding. A last state encoding method was proposed by Polato et al. [24] for time and activity prediction in processes. Inspired by natural language processing research, Koninck et al. [11] applied word2vec and doc2vec for representational learning in business processes. The authors adapted these encodings to work on several business process layers, activities, traces, logs, and models. Also using word embeddings to learn representations, Hake et al. [16] combined word2vec and recurrent neural networks to label nodes in business process models.

Recently, graph embedding techniques have been proposed to encode information structured as graphs [15]. These techniques are suitable in PM environments as graphs can represent business process models, where nodes and edges are activities and directly-follows relations. A graph representation of the business process can be compared to graph representations of the traces similarly to traditional PM conformance checking methods. Furthermore, graph embeddings open new possibilities for PM analysis, such as capturing graph structures and finding similarities across different process models.

Nolle et al. [22] used autoencoders for the assessment of anomalies. Autoencoder is a class of neural networks trained to copy its input to an output that preserves the input's probability density function [14]. For that, it learns the input-output mapping ignoring the noise. The authors' method consists of first transforming the event log using the one-hot encoding technique. Then, the autoencoder is trained with back-propagation using the event log both as input and output label. However, the vector size increases linearly with the number of activities, meaning that complex processes are encoded in huge dimensions. Also, autoencoders involve relevant computational costs that limit their application.

3   Encoding Methods

To limit the scope of our work, we decided to investigate the control-flow perspective, that is, the selected encoding methods are pertinent to the analysis of the sequence of executed activities. Moreover, autoencoders were not considered due to their extremely high computational costs, making applications in business processes difficult. The selected methods can be organized into three main groups: trace replay and alignment, word embeddings, and graph embeddings. Table 1 details the encoding methods we studied with their features, types, and ranges.

3.1   Trace Replay and Alignment

Most PM quality measures are based on conformance checking methods, which aim at comparing a process execution to a process model [25]. The measures produced by conformance checking techniques can be interpreted as features.

Table 1. Encoding characteristics, produced features and their possible values

Encoding	Family	Feature	Type	Range
trace replay	PM-based	trace is fit	Boolean	{True, False}
		fitness	Numeric	$[0, 1]$
		consumed tokens	Integer	$[0, \infty[$
		remaining tokens	Integer	$[0, \infty[$
		produced tokens	Integer	$[0, \infty[$
alignment	PM-based	cost	Integer	$[0, \infty[$
		visited states	Integer	$[0, \infty[$
		queued states	Integer	$[0, \infty[$
		traversed arcs	Integer	$[0, \infty[$
		fitness	Numeric	$[0, 1]$
word2vec	Text-based	n-dimensions*	Numeric	$]-\infty, \infty[$
fasttext	Text-based	n-dimensions*	Numeric	$]-\infty, \infty[$
count2vec	Text-based	n-dimensions**	Integer	$[0, \infty[$
one-hot	Text-based	n-dimensions**	Integer	$\{0, 1\}$
tfidf	Text-based	n-dimensions**	Numeric	$[0, 1]$
hash2vec	Text-based	n-dimensions*	Numeric	$[-1, 1]$
node2vec	Graph-based	n-dimensions*	Numeric	$]-\infty, \infty[$
edge2vec	Graph-based	n-dimensions*	Numeric	$]-\infty, \infty[$

* encoding vector size is determined by a parameter
** encoding vector size is determined by the vocabulary size

More specifically, we exploited two conformance checking algorithms to encode traces: trace replay and trace alignment.

Trace Replay. These techniques replay traces into a model trying to consume the executed activities according to the constraints imposed by the model. By counting the missing and remaining activities, a measure of the conformance is produced [6].

Trace Alignment. These techniques also perform a comparison between a model and a trace but directly relate a trace to the valid execution sequences, i.e. allowed by the model [6]. Ultimately, an alignment can be seen as a sequence of moves that can be synchronous if originated from both the model and the trace, model-dependent if originated from the model only, or log-dependent if originated from the trace only. It follows that more than one alignment is possible when comparing a trace to a model. Thus, the technique aims at finding an optimal alignment, minimizing the number of model- and log-moves, which are measured by a cost function.

3.2   Word Embeddings

Word embeddings are grounded in information retrieval and natural language processing. Neural network algorithms are exploited to create highly informative but low-dimensional vectors modeling the context in which words of a corpus are inserted. We applied the following text-based encodings: word2vec, fasttext, count2vec, one-hot, tfidf and hash2vec.

Word2vec. The word embeddings come from the weights of a two-layer neural network created to reconstruct the linguistic context of words in a corpus [21]. This way, words appearing in similar contexts generate more similar encodings than words present in different contexts. In the process domain, a trace can be described by its sequence of activities, which can be treated as words in a corpus. From this perspective, a trace is a sentence and a log is a text, i.e., a sequence of sentences. Consequently, the trace encoding is the aggregation of its activities encodings, which is obtained by their mean.

Fasttext. Fasttext represents each word as a bag of n-gram characters, trying to capture the morphemes of a corpus. The final vector representation of a word is, then, retrieved by the sum of its n-gram character representations [2]. Given this construction, the method performs well in the representation of rare words and can generate encodings for words that do not appear in the training data.

Count2vec. The count vectorizer is a simple way of encoding words by accounting for their frequencies in a text document. This tokenization process outputs a matrix of word counts. The length of the features is determined by the number of unique words in the document. For this method, the event log is interpreted as a document and the activity frequency regulates the resulting feature vector for each trace.

One-Hot. The one-hot encoding technique encodes categorical values in a binary representation. For that, it first maps words into integers and, then, transforms the generated integer values to a binary value. Like count2vec, the number of dimensions linearly increases with the vocabulary size, with the tendency of generating sparse features.

Tdidf. Term frequency-inverse document frequency (tdidf) is a traditional information retrieval metric aimed at capturing the importance of a word in a document given a collection of documents. The term frequency weights a term occurrence proportionally to its frequency in a document. The inverse document frequency quantifies the importance of a term as the inverse function of its occurrence across a collection of documents.

Hash2vec. Tdidf creates a dictionary of words, which increases linearly to the vocabulary size, often generating large and sparse representations. To overcome this issue, the hash2vec maps a feature into an index (word) using a hash function. Then, word frequencies are computed based on previously mapped indices. The technique allows a vector of a predetermined size, on the other hand, if a small vector size is used, hash collisions, where different words are represented by the same index, can take place [28].

3.3   Graph Embeddings

Graph embeddings emerged from the necessity of modeling more complex relations, such as entity links and long-term relations. Graphs are suitable for this task due to their data representation format, enabling exploration of nodes and edges. We applied two versions of node2vec: one encodes the nodes, while the other encodes the edges.

Node2vec. Built on top of word2vec, node2vec aims at encoding graph data while preserving neighborhoods and structures. The low-dimensional node representations are based on second-order random walks that propose a trade-off between breadth and width searches, exploring neighbors and neighborhoods. The flexibility of node exploration allows for a richer representation of diverse neighborhoods.

Edge2vec. Edge2vec captures the links (edges) that connect nodes. For our evaluation, this behavior is interesting as process models can be represented as graphs. This way, by grouping the edges representations, we can generate another encoding using the same method.

4   Materials and Methods

This section presents the event logs, the experimental setup, and the quality metrics used in our experimental analysis. Generated event logs and code for experiments are publicly available[1], following open-science principles.

4.1   Event Logs

Our experimental design implies relying on labeled data providing the ground truth for the evaluation of the compared methods. We then generated synthetic event logs following standard practices in PM research and injecting anomalies to the generated traces. This way we achieved two goals. Traces are labeled as anomalous or normal, making our data set suitable for supervised learning. Heterogeneous behaviors are introduced in the event logs, making our data set more realistic.

First, five different process models were generated using the PLG2 tool [5]. PLG2 performs a random generation of process models capable of representing several business process behaviors such as sequential, parallel, and iterative control flows. For that, the tool combines traditional control-flow patterns [26], e.g., sequence, parallel split and synchronization. The patterns are progressively combined, given a predetermined set of rules, to simulate real-world scenarios. The five generated process models define five different base scenarios differing because of the number of activities and gateways [9]. The next step was to simulate the process model to generate the log. For that, we applied the *Perform a simple*

---

[1] https://github.com/gbrltv/business_process_encoding.

simulation of a (stochastic) Petri net ProM plug-in[2]. The number of simulated cases was set to 1000, and the arrival rate of new cases was set to 30 min. The other hyperparameters were unchanged. As a post-processing step, we injected anomalies by perturbing regular traces. Injecting anomalies into event logs is a common practice in the literature [1]. For that, we applied the anomalies proposed by Nolle et al. [23]: 1. skip: a sequence of 3 or less necessary events is skipped;2. insert: 3 or less random activities are inserted in the case;3. rework: a sequence of 3 or less necessary events is executed twice;4. early: a sequence of 2 or fewer events executed too early, which is then skipped later in the case;5. late: a sequence of 2 or fewer events executed too late.

The anomalies were applied in normal traces, replacing their occurrence. Moreover, to analyze to which extent anomalies affect the encodings, we injected different percentages of anomalies for each scenario: 5%, 10%, 15%, and 20%. Given five scenarios (our base models), five anomalies, and four anomaly percentages, a total of 100 event logs were generated. To facilitate the interpretation of the logs, we added two additional attributes: label and description. Case labels represent if a case belongs to a normal execution or one of the anomalous types. Furthermore, the description is a natural language sentence describing the anomaly and its impact on the case. Descriptive statistics about the generated event logs are listed in Table 2. The different scenarios are of increasing complexity, scenario 3 contains the longest traces and, consequently, logs composed of more events.

Table 2. Event log statistics demonstrating different levels of complexity. 20 event logs with 1k cases were generated for each scenario

Log name	#gateways	#events	trace size	#activities
scenario 1	8	10k–11k	9–13	22
scenario 2	12	26k	26–30	41
scenario 3	22	43k–44k	42–50	64
scenario 4	30	11k–13k	3–30	83
scenario 5	34	18k–19k	4–37	103

4.2   Trace Encoding

Since trace replay and alignment require a process model, we generated a model using the Inductive Miner Directly Follows algorithm [18]. Process model and encodings were extracted using the PM4Py library[3]. For word embeddings, we used the Gensim[4] library to compute word2vec and fasttext and the Scikit-learn

---

[2] http://www.promtools.org/doku.php.
[3] https://pm4py.fit.fraunhofer.de/.
[4] https://radimrehurek.com/gensim/.

library[5] compute the remaining encodings. For the graph embeddings, a graph model is expected as input. Thus, we generated a directly-follows graph using the event log to capture node and edge frequency. The encodings were extracted with the node2vec[6] library. For all encoding methods, the recommended standard hyperparameters were used.

4.3   Feature Vector Measures and Classification Algorithm

In our experiments, we computed F1, F2 and T4 measures using the ECoL (*Extended Complexity Library*) R package, available at Github[7] and CRAN[8], using standard hyperparameters. Although multiple PM tasks could exploit trace encoding, we drove our evaluation using a binary classification task for anomaly detection. This is a basic supervised approach that can be easily evaluated and whose connections to other tasks are well known. We used the Random Forest classification algorithm [4] following the Scikit-learn implementation with standard parameters. The Random Forest was chosen due to its high predictive performance and wide use in related papers. The traditional holdout method was used to divide the data into train and test sets, with an 80%/20% proportion. Each classification was performed 30 times to compute a mean accuracy value, eliminating possible eccentric performances. Moreover, the meantime consumption for the performed executions was computed.

5   Results and Discussion

This section presents the results obtained in evaluating the impact of the studied encoding methods from several complementary perspectives.

5.1   Accuracy Performance

One of the main goals when choosing an encoding method is to support high predictive performance. Figure 1 presents the accuracy results (along with their standard deviation) aggregated over the event logs of all the scenarios presented in Table 2. *Trace replay* and *alignment* methods obtained very similar results, an average accuracy of 91.93% and 92.62%, respectively. The word embedding family obtained average accuracy varying from 88.72% (*one-hot*) to 94.16% (*tfidf*), with the latter being the best performing text-based encoding. The best performances were achieved with methods of the graph embedding family. *Node2vec* reached an average accuracy of 94.18% while *edge2vec* obtained 96.08%, the best overall performance.

Trace replay and *alignment* methods rely on the comparison of an event log to a model. Since the model is induced from the event log, anomalies may

---

[5] https://scikit-learn.org/stable/.
[6] https://github.com/eliorc/node2vec.
[7] https://github.com/lpfgarcia/ECoL.
[8] https://cran.r-project.org/package=ECoL.

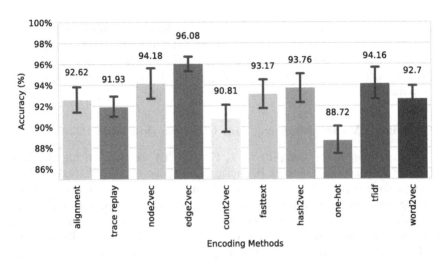

Fig. 1. Average accuracy obtained using all encoding methods across binary problems related to anomaly detection (early, insert, late, rework and skip) affected by four different levels of compromised samples (5%, 10%, 15% and 20%).

have been modeled as normal transitions. Ideally, a model could be constructed from a filtered event log, without anomalies. However, in reality, often event data is not labeled, and manually detecting anomalies is a resource-consuming task. Nonetheless, these methods produce the most interpretable features, easily understandable by process stakeholders. This characteristic has gained more attention in data mining research, as black-box models may not offer sufficient basis for their choices. Overall, the trade-off between performance and interpretability plays an important role when applying trace encodings.

Word embeddings present a wider range of performances. *One-hot* encoding and *count2vec* appear with the worst results. Both methods are grounded in word frequencies and fail to encode global information, such as accounting differences between traces in the same log. Besides, the ordering of the traces is lost by these methods. This way, counting frequencies demonstrate to be a shallow method that does not meet business process modeling requirements. *Word2vec* and *fasttext*, which are more recent advancements in text processing, capture activities context by considering their neighborhood. These methods allow for a better overall trace description and, consequently, higher accuracy values. Moreover, *fasttext* performs slightly better than *word2vec*, probably a result of its consideration of n-grams when encoding a word. *Hash2vec* and *tfidf* are the best performing methods within this family. Both methods propose a frequency analysis that also covers inter-trace behavior, i.e., global event log characteristics. Even though these encodings do not consider the ordering, their performance surpasses methods that capture context information. This implies that trace context, i.e., activities neighborhood, from a text analysis perspective, is not so determinant as a descriptor when compared to weighted frequencies. A possible explanation for the inferior performance obtained by *word2vec* and *fasttext* is that these methods require a rich corpus for training their models. According to Table 2, the richest log, in the number of unique activities, only contains 103 words. This highly limits the capacity of capturing context information. In most cases, the set of activities in a business process is considerably smaller than the vocabulary of a document collection. This way, in the business process domain, modern word embedding techniques are not necessarily the best. Finally, the length of the event log also plays a role in this performance since a higher number of traces may increase the encoding quality of context-based methods.

The graph embedding family was the best performing for the classification task. *Node2vec* and *edge2vec* are built on top of word2vec, thus, the goal is also to capture context information. Further, the graph structure is capable of representing many complex behaviors. Therefore, their performance overcomes all other families. Within graph embeddings, *edge2vec* displays an accuracy considerably higher than *node2vec*. This happens because *node2vec* is limited to encode node (activity) behavior only. On the other hand, *edge2vec* encodes the connections within activities and long-term relations are captured.

5.2   Time Usage

Time costs of an encoding method can directly influence its selection since costly methods are prohibitive to real-life event logs with huge volume of data. In our experiments, we considered the time consumed during the classification task. Figure 2 presents the time variation among all methods. *Trace replay* and *alignment* obtained similar results, with trace replay (0.258 s) being the fastest and most stable method. Graph embeddings were the most time-costly, with an average of 0.349 s. The *edge2vec* method, which uses edge information, was the slowest, spending an average of 0.391 s. Text-encoding family reveals to be faster, except for the *word2vec* method that required an average of 0.341 s and resulted the most unstable, obtaining the highest standard deviation (0.07 s).

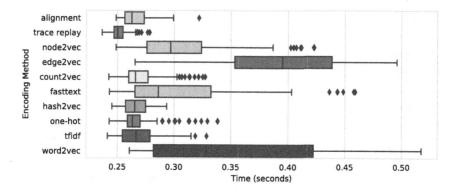

Fig. 2. Average time required in the classification task for each trace encoding across all scenarios.

It is important to note that concerning the time dispensed to perform the encoding procedure, our results confirmed what is well known in the literature. However, due to space limits, we do not report these results in detail in this paper. *Trace replay* and *alignment* are time costly, mainly alignment [13], followed by graph embeddings [15]. The high cost of alignment is related to the multi-step approximation required to find an optimal alignment. Moreover, the alignment procedure has a computational complexity that grows exponentially to the number of states and transitions, becoming impractical in most scenarios. On the other hand, when dealing with graph embeddings representation, *node2vec* generates random walks, which require several iterations (time perspective). Methods from the word embedding family, such as *one-hot* and *fasttext* are less costly and can be employed in tasks focused on light-weight processing, such as online PM [7].

5.3   Encoding Representativeness

The capacity to represent knowledge towards providing low ambiguity between classes and reduce the inherent complexity to the problem guides a high-quality encoding method. Moreover, this capacity is made by constructing a short and highly informative feature vector. In our experiments, we measured the Maximum Fisher's Discriminant Ratio (F1), the Volume of Overlapping Region (F2), and the Ratio of the PCA dimensions to the original dimensions (T4).

Using F1, we can assess how informative the encoding methods are to separate the classes of the analyzed problems. Figure 3 presents a scatter plot of the F1 values for all the encoding methods in the studied scenarios with the average value indicated by the cross. The values that represent good quality are the lower ones. From the F1 perspective, it is possible to observe *trace replay*, *node2vec*, *edge2vec* and *fasttext*, as the methods with low overlapping of a single feature in particular cases.

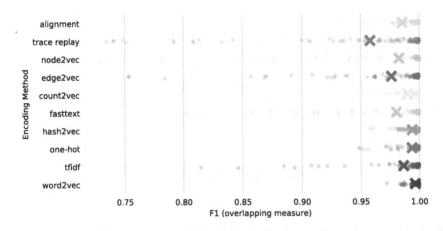

Fig. 3. Maximum Fisher's Discriminant Ratio (F1) values, for the studied scenarios. F1 measures the overlap in classes of the best-disjunct feature.

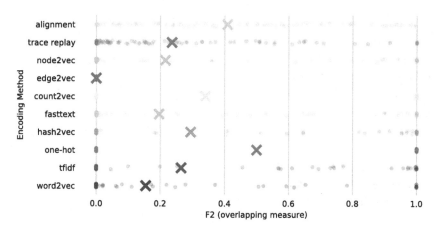

Fig. 4. Volume of Overlapping Region (F2) of the feature values distributions within the problem classes. Low F2 values implies low overlapping.

Encoding quality comparison can be performed by observing the overlapping of the feature values distribution produced by each encoding method. This evaluation is supported by F2, where higher values refer to higher overlap between the classes. As Fig. 4 shows, *edge2vec* achieved the lowest metric value, i.e., the most disjoint representation. On the other hand, *alignment* and *one-hot* encodings generated the most overlapping distributions.

Scenarios with high F1 and F2 values can lead to difficulties in choosing a proper classification algorithm and even demanding hyperparameter tuning to achieve accurate results in classification tasks. Conversely, low F1 and F2 values imply a broader set of algorithms and hyperparametrizations that can discriminate the classes of the problem.

Some encoding methods depend on hyperparameters to determine their feature vector dimension. Using default values, we compared the relevance of dimensions settled by each encoding method to describe most of the data variability through T4. T4 takes advantage of the PCA projection of principal components to identify the number of features capable of representing more than 95% of data variability. The higher the T4 value, the more the encoded features are needed to describe data variability, representing a concise problem description. Lower values represent a waste of features to explain data variability (Fig. 5).

Table 3 shows the T4 values of all encoding methods obtained in the different scenarios. Graph embeddings obtained the lowest T4 values. *Node2vec* obtained 0.02, delivering feature vectors capable of describing the data variability with few samples. On the other hand, *trace replay* and *alignment* presented vectors of dimension closer to the original samples. Several word embedding methods build feature vectors with adaptive sizes to better represent the problem. Among them, *tfidf* was able to obtain competitive results, reaching an average T4 of 0.21. In some scenarios, *tfidf* was superior to both *trace replay* and *alignment*.

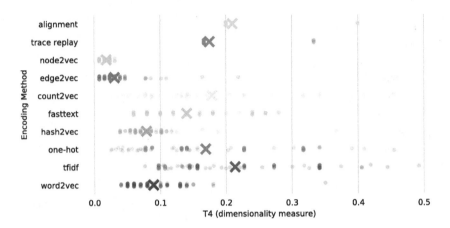

Fig. 5. Ratio of the PCA dimension to the original dimension (T4) of all encoding methods. High T4 means more original features are relevant.

Table 3. Encoding methods dimensionality and T4 values (mean and standard deviation)

Encoding method	T4	Dimensions
trace replay	0.18 (±0.04)	5
alignment	0.21 (±0.04)	5
word2vec	0.09 (±0.04)	100
fasttext	0.14 (±0.07)	50
count2vec	0.18 (±0.10)	22–103*
one-hot	0.17 (±0.10)	22–103*
tfidf	0.21 (±0.10)	22–103*
hash2vec	0.08 (±0.04)	128
node2vec	0.02 (±0.01)	128
edge2vec	0.03 (±0.03)	128

* encoding vector size is determined by the vocabulary size

Complex scenarios, such as Scenarios 4 and 5, required higher dimensionality in the feature space. When dealing with simple scenarios, e.g., Scenario 1, a small number of features is required for all encoding methods. Thus, the demand for dimensions, i.e., larger feature vectors, is strictly related to complex problems.

5.4   Encoding Ranking

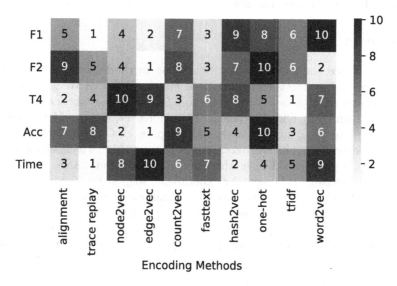

Fig. 6. Ranking of each metric across all encoding methods. The rank ranges from 1 to 10, where the best-ranked position is 1 and the worst-ranked is 10.

Figure 6 presents a heatmap created by ranking each encoding method across mean values of accuracy (Acc), time, F1, F2, and T4. For a concisely and resource-friendly encoding method considering just the classification task, we can take advantage of the *trace replay* and *alignment* methods. Regarding F1 and F2 metrics, the graph embeddings present high performance, mostly with *edge2vec* being the best and second-best in F1 and F2, respectively. This performance demonstrates a great encoding capability proposed in this method. Moreover, *fasttext* regularly ranks well in these two metrics, showing high informative and quality encodings. *Word2vec* has the second-best F2 (low overlap between features) while, at the same time, has the worst F1. This means that the encoding does not produce a unique, highly descriptive feature, and it depends on the conjunction of its created features to encode behavior. *Trace replay* being the best F1 demonstrates its capability of proposing quality encodings.

We need to emphasize that word and graph embedding families can reduce time considerably by performing a feature selection procedure. Also, *count2vec*, *tfidf* and *one-hot* can dynamically adapt the feature vector and *word2vec*, *fasttext*, *hash2vec*, *node2vec* and *edge2vec* have their feature vector size according to user definition. This means parameters for controlling the trade-off between computational time and accuracy are made available by most techniques. Additionally, the complexity of the encoding process needs to be considered. Encoding generation is more time and resource-consuming than the classification task. This way, methods such as *alignment*, which are known to be slow [13], have their applicability hindered in most real situations. At the same time, medium performance methods, such as *fasttext* and *hash2vec*, demand less computational resources. This way, a trade-off between all the presented perspectives must be considered when choosing an encoding for business processes.

6   Conclusion

In this work, we compared ten trace encoding methods across 100 event logs depicting several scenarios with different levels of complexity. We assessed encodings in classification tasks towards collecting feature vector metrics such as overlapping (F1 and F2) and dimension (T4). Moreover, we considered accuracy and time outcomes to support a general comparison. Overall, the experiments show that encoding significantly contributes to the results of a classification algorithm. Also, a good encoding method can improve a wide range of algorithms without need of tuning. In fact, our experiments suggest that an improper trace encoding can bring additional complexity, obtaining a suboptimal classification performance. In future work, we expect to expand the encoding families, e.g., deep learning encoding approaches. Finally, it is important to study anomalies with more attention and spot their effect on the metrics and performance of different PM tasks.

References

1. Bezerra, F., Wainer, J.: Algorithms for anomaly detection of traces in logs of process aware information systems. Inf. Syst. **38**(1), 33–44 (2013)
2. Bojanowski, P., Grave, E., Joulin, A., Mikolov, T.: Enriching word vectors with subword information. Trans. Assoc. Comput. Linguist. **5**, 135–146 (2017)
3. Bose, R.J.C., Van der Aalst, W.M.: Context aware trace clustering: towards improving process mining results. In: Proceedings of the 2009 SIAM International Conference on Data Mining, pp. 401–412 (2009)
4. Breiman, L.: Random forests. Mach. Learn. **45**(1), 5–32 (2001). https://doi.org/10.1023/A:1010933404324
5. Burattin, A.: PLG2: multiperspective processes randomization and simulation for online and offline settings (2015)
6. Carmona, J., van Dongen, B.F., Solti, A., Weidlich, M.: Conformance Checking - Relating Processes and Models. Springer, Heidelberg (2018). https://doi.org/10.1007/978-3-319-99414-7
7. Ceravolo, P., Tavares, G.M., Junior, S.B., Damiani, E.: Evaluation goals for online process mining: a concept drift perspective. IEEE Trans. Serv. Comput. 1 (2020). https://ieeexplore.ieee.org/abstract/document/9124702
8. Ceravolo, P., Damiani, E., Torabi, M., Barbon, S.: Toward a new generation of log pre-processing methods for process mining. In: Carmona, J., Engels, G., Kumar, A. (eds.) BPM 2017. LNBIP, vol. 297, pp. 55–70. Springer, Cham (2017). https://doi.org/10.1007/978-3-319-65015-9_4
9. Chinosi, M., Trombetta, A.: BPMN: an introduction to the standard. Comput. Stand. Interfaces **34**(1), 124–134 (2012)
10. Cummins, L., Bridge, D.: On dataset complexity for case base maintenance. In: Ram, A., Wiratunga, N. (eds.) ICCBR 2011. LNCS (LNAI), vol. 6880, pp. 47–61. Springer, Heidelberg (2011). https://doi.org/10.1007/978-3-642-23291-6_6

11. De Koninck, P., vanden Broucke, S., De Weerdt, J.: act2vec, trace2vec, log2vec, and model2vec: representation learning for business processes. In: Weske, M., Montali, M., Weber, I., vom Brocke, J. (eds.) BPM 2018. LNCS, vol. 11080, pp. 305–321. Springer, Cham (2018). https://doi.org/10.1007/978-3-319-98648-7_18
12. Delias, P., Doumpos, M., Grigoroudis, E., Matsatsinis, N.: A non-compensatory approach for trace clustering. Int. Trans. Oper. Res. **26**(5), 1828–1846 (2019)
13. Fani Sani, M., van Zelst, S.J., van der Aalst, W.M.P.: Conformance checking approximation using subset selection and edit distance. In: Dustdar, S., Yu, E., Salinesi, C., Rieu, D., Pant, V. (eds.) CAiSE 2020. LNCS, vol. 12127, pp. 234–251. Springer, Cham (2020). https://doi.org/10.1007/978-3-030-49435-3_15
14. Goodfellow, I., Bengio, Y., Courville, A.: Deep Learning. MIT Press, Cambridge (2016)
15. Goyal, P., Ferrara, E.: Graph embedding techniques, applications, and performance: a survey. Knowl.-Based Syst. **151**, 78–94 (2018)
16. Hake, P., Zapp, M., Fettke, P., Loos, P.: Supporting business process modeling using RNNs for label classification. In: Frasincar, F., Ittoo, A., Nguyen, L.M., Métais, E. (eds.) NLDB 2017. LNCS, vol. 10260, pp. 283–286. Springer, Cham (2017). https://doi.org/10.1007/978-3-319-59569-6_35
17. Ho, T.K., Basu, M.: Complexity measures of supervised classification problems. IEEE Trans. Pattern Anal. Mach. Intell. **24**, 289–300 (2002)
18. Leemans, S.J.J., Fahland, D., van der Aalst, W.M.P.: Scalable process discovery with guarantees. In: Gaaloul, K., Schmidt, R., Nurcan, S., Guerreiro, S., Ma, Q. (eds.) CAISE 2015. LNBIP, vol. 214, pp. 85–101. Springer, Cham (2015). https://doi.org/10.1007/978-3-319-19237-6_6
19. Leontjeva, A., Conforti, R., Di Francescomarino, C., Dumas, M., Maggi, F.M.: Complex symbolic sequence encodings for predictive monitoring of business processes. In: Motahari-Nezhad, H.R., Recker, J., Weidlich, M. (eds.) BPM 2015. LNCS, vol. 9253, pp. 297–313. Springer, Cham (2015). https://doi.org/10.1007/978-3-319-23063-4_21
20. Lorena, A.C., Garcia, L.P.F., Lehmann, J., Souto, M.C.P., Ho, T.K.: How complex is your classification problem? A survey on measuring classification complexity. ACM Comput. Surv. **52**(5), 1–34 (2019)
21. Mikolov, T., Chen, K., Corrado, G.S., Dean, J.: Efficient estimation of word representations in vector space. CoRR abs/1301.3781 (2013)
22. Nolle, T., Luettgen, S., Seeliger, A., Mühlhäuser, M.: Analyzing business process anomalies using autoencoders. Mach. Learn. **107**(11), 1875–1893 (2018). https://doi.org/10.1007/s10994-018-5702-8
23. Nolle, T., Luettgen, S., Seeliger, A., Mühlhäuser, M.: BINet: multi-perspective business process anomaly classification. Inf. Syst. 101458 (2019). https://www.sciencedirect.com/journal/information-systems/special-issue/10419P9FG88
24. Polato, M., Sperduti, A., Burattin, A., de Leoni, M.D.: Time and activity sequence prediction of business process instances. Computing **100**(9), 1005–1031 (2018). https://doi.org/10.1007/s00607-018-0593-x
25. Rozinat, A., van der Aalst, W.: Conformance checking of processes based on monitoring real behavior. Inf. Syst. **33**(1), 64–95 (2008)
26. Russell, N., ter Hofstede, A., van der Aalst, W., Mulyar, N.: Workflow control-flow patterns: a revised view. BPM reports (2006)
27. van der Aalst, W., Weijters, T., Maruster, L.: Workflow mining: discovering process models from event logs. IEEE Trans. Knowl. Data Eng. **16**(9), 1128–1142 (2004)
28. Weinberger, K., Dasgupta, A., Langford, J., Smola, A., Attenberg, J.: Feature hashing for large scale multitask learning. In: Proceedings of the 26th Annual International Conference on Machine Learning, ICML 2009, pp. 1113–1120. Association for Computing Machinery (2009)

Semantic Annotations in Clinical Guidelines

Fahrurrozi Rahman[✉] and Juliana Bowles

School of Computer Science, University of St Andrews,
St Andrews KY16 9SX, UK
{f27,jkfb}@st-andrews.ac.uk

Abstract. Clinical guidelines are evidence-based recommendations developed to assist practitioners in their decisions on appropriate care for patients with specific clinical circumstances. They provide succinct instructions such as what drugs should be given or taken for a particular condition, how long such treatment should be given, what tests should be conducted, or other situational clinical circumstances for certain diseases. However, as they are described in natural language, they are prone to problems such as variability and ambiguity. In this paper, we propose an approach to automatically infer the main components in clinical guideline sentences. Knowing the key concepts in the sentences, we can then feed them to model checkers to validate their correctness. We adapt semantic role labelling approach to mark the key entities in our problem domain. We also implement the technique used for Named-Entity Recognition (NER) task and compare the results. The aim of our work is to build a reasoning framework that combines the information gained from real patient data and clinical practice, with clinical guidelines to give more suitable personalised recommendations for treating patients.

Keywords: Therapy algorithms · Formal verification · Natural language processing · Machine learning · Text tagging

1 Introduction

Recent studies have shown that over the next 20 years there will be an increased expansion of morbidity, and particularly complex multimorbidity which occurs when individuals have several concurrent chronic conditions [12]. One of the challenges of treating patients with multimorbidity is that clinical guidelines are generally focused on single disease. It is hence difficult to understand treatment options, and their consequences in the long term, when patients have to follow a considerable number of single disease oriented treatments simultaneously.

Furthermore, there are also several challenges inherent in clinical guidelines: they are written mostly in natural language and hence prone to ambiguity; the way they are presented may be very different from one guideline to another; clinical practice varies and may at times deviate from clinical guidelines, and

J. Bowles et al. (Eds.): DataMod 2020, LNCS 12611, pp. 190–205, 2021.
https://doi.org/10.1007/978-3-030-70650-0_12

we need to take into account this variability. When there are multiple treatment options available, we want to know how likely these options are followed in practice.

We have built a framework to formalise the written text of a therapy algorithm for lowering blood glucose for people with type 2 diabetes (T2D) in our previous work [19]. The generated model is a network of timed automata, where each transition represents the medication taken by the patient and the state is the patient's condition after getting such treatment and over time. The model also takes into account how the value of HbA1c, i.e., the glycated haemoglobin that is commonly measured to determine the average blood sugar levels for patients with diabetes, may deteriorate over time, and force further intensifications in the treatment. The advantage of a formalisation is that it enables us to detect gaps or omissions in the textual algorithm, which can then be used to further clarify treatment steps.

Although this approach is promising, it depends entirely on their own curated controlled natural language (CNL) to design and hand-tune complex rules to extract information from the therapy algorithm written in a natural language string. This approach becomes problematic when recommendations are expressed in very different ways as either the CNL needs to be refined or the recommendation sentences need to be adjusted to the CNL, which in most cases it involves both. Expanding the breadth and complexity of the CNL also demands a lot of human development work, linguistic knowledge as well as a deep understanding in the specific domain. This rigid and unscalable approach is not suitable for the long term goal: to process any clinical guidelines automatically.

In this paper, we propose a different approach to address this issue of capturing the main concepts in clinical guideline sentences using semantic role labeling and named-entity recognition. This approach will limit the human effort needed to design the grammar for a CNL. The result can then be used for further linguistic analysis in clinical guideline domain. It can also be utilised to check the correctness of the guideline by transforming the main concepts in the guideline into formal representations such as UPPAAL [2], PRISM [13], or Z3 [16].

The remainder of this paper is structured as follows. In Sect. 2 we discuss related work that serve as the foundation of this paper. Section 3 describes the framework of the system that we want to build. Section 4 explains the semantic annotations covering the ontology concepts, the relationships between each concept and named-entity recognition. The learning process, including the syntactic and the semantic analysis as well as the features used and the learning models are discussed in Sect. 5. The outcome of the experiments using several learning models is discussed in Sect. 6. Finally, in Section 7, we draw some conclusions on our research.

2   Related Work

Considerable research in modelling and formalising clinical guidelines has been done over the past years. Pérez et al. [18] built a framework to enable authoring and verification of clinical guidelines. They use UML statecharts to represent the guidelines and provide a pattern-based approach to define commonly occurring types of requirements in guidelines to ease the non-expert to write formal specifications. The statecharts are transformed into process meta language (PROMELA) and the specifications are translated into linear temporal logic (LTL). The verification of the guideline model and its specification is then performed using the SPIN model checker [10].

Bäumler et al. [1] also apply formal modelling and verification to improve the quality of medical guidelines. To model the guidelines, they must be written in Asbru language [21], a predefined language for guideline-application tasks. With the properties formulated in the Action Computational Tree Logic (ACTL) language, the model is then verified using the Cadence SMV model checker [14].

Another implementation of model checking to verify clinical guidelines is done by Giordano et al. [7]. They use the GLARE language [22], a domain-independent prototypical system for acquiring, representing and executing clinical guidelines. With an XML intermediary layer which then is translated to PROMELA, the model and its specification written in LTL are verified using the SPIN model checker.

In software engineering, Carvalho et al. [4] have created a framework to formally generate test cases from the written software requirements into several formalisms using natural language processing (NLP) techniques. Written in a controlled natural language, the requirements are transformed into data flow reactive system (DFRS), where inputs and outputs are modelled as signals, with timers to capture the time-based behaviour.

Another work by Diamantopoulos et al. [5] shows a system that automatically maps software requirements into formal representations to detect problems hidden in the written texts at the early stage of development process. The system is built upon ontology class hierarchies to represent the semantic roles in the requirement texts. The hierarchies are built by training a semantic role labelling system from software requirements project classes in Europe. The inference process is done after the ontology is represented in the web ontology language (OWL).

In this research, we modify our previous work [19] following the approach used by Diamantopoulos et al. [5] and NER. Concretely, we will adapt the work in [5] and NER to annotate the key concepts in guideline sentences domain so it becomes less labour intensive, more scalable, and more general purpose.

3   The Framework

Figure 1 shows the whole framework in our research. We simplify our previous work by adding the syntactic and semantic analysis module. Instead of manually crafting a CNL, we use machine learning to achieve the goal.

Firstly, we provide the guideline sentences that we want to map into some formal representations. Some guidelines would have an implicit orders on how therapy should be given while others are orderless. Next, our syntactic and semantic

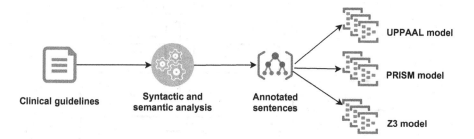

Fig. 1. The mapping of clinical guidelines framework

analysis module will mark the key concepts in the sentences. The learning process for this module is further explained in Sect. 5.

The result of this process will be annotated sentences as illustrated in Fig. 2, i.e., some words in the sentences are given semantic markers. Knowing these semantic markers means that we can move on to transforming the guideline into any further modelling approach we have in mind, for example, a formal representation. We believe it would be beneficial to help the transformation process from guidelines to UPPAAL models as done in [19].

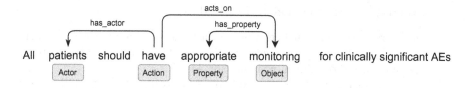

Fig. 2. Example of an annotated sentence

4   Semantic Annotations

4.1   A Hierarchy of Concepts

In order to build a learning model to mark the roles of a word or a phrase in a sentence, we first need to define the classes of roles that we allow in our domain. Following [5], we made several ontology concepts to represent the static aspects of the guidelines. The design focuses on the concept of an actor doing some action(s) on some object(s) with some properties. Figure 3 shows our current ontology class hierarchy for our domain.

The ontology hiearchy in Fig. 3 states that every class is a `Concept`. They are furthermore diversified into `ThingType` and `OperationType`. `OperationType` refers to the operations performed by an actor to another entity, whereas `ThingType` refers to any entity that can be an actor of an action, an object

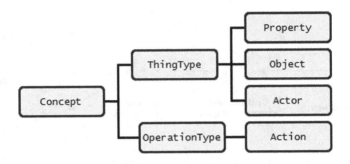

Fig. 3. Ontology class hierarchy

that is acted upon, or a property that can further explain an action, an actor, or an object.

The class `OperationType` covers all operations performed in the sentence, either transitive or not. Its subclass is:

- `Action` denotes an operation performed on some `Object` by an `Actor` (if exists). Different from [5], we also consider the ownership type as an `Action`. E.g. "All patients should *have* appropriate monitoring for clinically significant AEs."

A `ThingType` can furthermore be classified as:

- `Actor` refers to the explicit performer of an `Action`. In many cases, the actor is invisible from the guideline sentences. E.g. "All *patients* should have appropriate monitoring for clinically significant AEs."
- `Object` denotes the entity that an `Action` is performed on. E.g. "All patients should have appropriate *monitoring* for clinically significant AEs."
- `Property` describes all modifiers of an `Action`, an `Actor`, or an `Object`. E.g. "All patients should have *appropriate* monitoring for clinically significant AEs."

Although our ontology classes can still be further diversified into lower subclasses as in [5], we find that they are not needed and too complex for our problem at the moment.

4.2 Relationship Between Classes

When designing the concept classes, we also need to introduce the relationship between them. This relationship defines the allowed interactions between one concept to another, and possibly from different level of concept. Table 1 shows the set of relationship between classes and concept in general.

   `acts_on` defines that an `Action` is performed on either an `Object` or a `Property`. The inverse relation is `receives_action` that connects an `Object` or a `Property` to an `Action`. From here, we can say that *monitoring* `receives_action` from *have*.

The performer of an `Action` is defined by the `has_actor` relation to an `Actor`. Likewise, the `Actor` of an `Action` is defined by the `is_actor_of` relation. E.g. *have* `has_actor` *patients*.

The last two relations can cover the whole `ThingType` concept as their participants. This is because a `Property` can be used to modify an `Actor`, an `Object`, or a `Property` itself. Hence, we set the rule that any `ThingType` can have the `has_property` to a `Property` or a `Property` is connected to any `ThingType` by the `is_property_of` relation. E.g. *monitoring* `has_property` *appropriate*.

Table 1. Relationship between classes

Concept class	Relationship	Concept class
Action	acts_on	Object, Property
Object, Property	receives_action	Action
Action	has_actor	Actor
Actor	is_actor_of	Action
ThingType	has_property	Property
Property	is_property_of	ThingType

As each pair of the relations is an inverse of themselves, we will only use three of them in our end system, namely: `acts_on`, `has_actor`, and `has_property`.

4.3   Named-Entity Recognition

We also investigate a different approach to mark the important part of the sentence using named-entity recognition (NER) technique. NER is a task in NLP to detect the entity in the text that can be referred to with a proper name such as a person, a location, an organisation, or even things that are not proper entities such as dates, times, or prices [11].

In NER, the entities are usually marked using IOB format. The beginning of an entity type is marked with B-prefix tag, and I-prefix tag marks every token inside an entity type. An O tag is used for tokens that do not belong to any entity. Figure 4 shows a sentence marked with IOB format.

Fig. 4. A sentence marked with IOB format

We use the same ontology concepts for NER in IOB format. We consider four entities, i.e., `Action`, `Actor`, `Object`, and `Property` (as shown in Fig. 3).

As there are two tags for each entity, i.e. the B-tag and the I-tag, our label set size becomes 9 (from $2n + 1$ where n is the number of entities) namely B-action, I-action, B-actor, I-actor, B-object, I-object, B-property, I-property, and O. In reality, we only use 7 tags, namely B-action, B-actor, B-object, I-object, B-property, I-property, and O as we do not have instances for either I-action or I-actor.

5   Learning

5.1   Syntactic Analysis of Guideline Sentences

In this section, we will use the following common terminology. Part-of-speech (POS) is a category of words that have similar grammatical properties. Noun (e.g., noun NN or plural noun NNS), verb (VB), adjective (JJ), determiner (DT), adverb (RB), and punctuation (PUNCT) are some common POS in English language. The complete POS tags set that we use and their description can be found on Penn Treebank POS Tags[1].

A lemma is a word that can be inflected into several forms. E.g. *eat* as a verb is the lemma for *eat, eats, eating, ate,* and *eaten.*

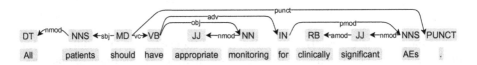

Fig. 5. An example of dependency tree

In order to build the features for the learning model which will be explained further in the next section, we need to perform syntactic analysis tasks on the sentences. These tasks are encapsulated as a pipeline which consists of several steps, namely:

- tokenisation that splits every component in the sentence into a single token. In *All patients should have appropriate monitoring for clinically significant AEs.*, there will be ten tokens: *All, patients, should, have, appropriate, monitoring, for, clinically, significant, AEs,* and *..*
- POS tagging that marks up the words corresponding to a particular part of speech. Following the previous example, the POS tags are as follow: *All/DT, patients/NNS, should/MD, have/VB, appropriate/JJ, monitoring/NN, for/IN, clinically/RB, significant/JJ, AEs/NNS, ./PUNCT.*
- lemmatisation which groups the same uninflected base form of each word into the same cluster. Using the previous example, the lemmas are as follow: *All/all, patients/patient, should/should, have/have, appropriate/appropriate, monitoring/monitor, for/for, clinically/clinically, significant/significant, AEs/aes, ./..*

---

[1] https://www.ling.upenn.edu/courses/Fall_2003/ling001/penn_treebank_pos.html.

– dependency parsing which parses the sentence based on the dependency relation of the words, i.e. every word is connected to each other by a direct link. Figure 5 shows the dependency parse tree for the sentence *All patients should have appropriate monitoring for clinically significant AEs.*. The dependency relationship marks the link between two words. For example, the link connecting *monitoring* to *appropriate* is marked by the relation *nmod*, or ⟨*nmod*⟩ → ⟨*monitoring, appropriate*⟩, which means that *appropriate* is a noun modifier for *monitoring*.

We follow the approach used in [5] to utilise the Mate Tools[2] [3] to perform the steps in the syntactic analysis. This tool has achieved state of the art performance on the shared task for syntactic analysis [8] so we can incorporate it in our system.

5.2   Semantic Analysis of Guideline Sentences

Similar to the syntactic analysis, we adapt the approach done in [5] into our semantic analysis. This step is analogous to the semantic role labelling pipeline in [3], namely the *predicate identification, predicate disambiguation, argument identification*, and *argument classification*. In relation to our problem domain, each of these steps in the pipeline deals with one particular task as follows:

1. identifying words that are either `Action` or `Object`, which corresponds to the *predicate identification*. The reasoning behind choosing these two concepts is because they govern the relationship to other ontology concepts in the hierarchy. For example, by knowing if a word is an `Action` or an `Object`, we can further find the rest of the concepts through the relationships `acts_on`, `has_actor`, and `has_property`.
2. classifying words identified in step 1 to their correct concept, similar to the *predicate disambiguation*. For every verb and noun that can be either an `Action` or an `Object`, this step classifies them into the actual ontology concept, e.g. *have*/`Action`, *monitoring*/`Object`.
3. identifying words that are related to the instances in step 1, which corresponds to the *argument identification*. The instances that we are looking for in this step are the `Actor` of an `Action` and the `Property` related to any `TypeThing` concept. For example, this step will recognise *patients* as an `Actor` and *appropriate* as a `Property`.
4. classifying the relationship holds between a pair of instances from step 1 and step 3, which corresponds to the *argument classification*. The input of this step is a pair of words and its corresponding pair of concepts such as ⟨*patients, have*⟩ → ⟨`Actor`, `Action`⟩ and ⟨*have, monitoring*⟩ → ⟨`Action`, `Object`⟩.

---

[2] http://code.google.com/p/mate-tools/.

Table 2. Feature sets and their usage

	Action and Object		Related concepts	
	Identification	Classification	Identification	Classification
word form	•	•	•	•
word lemmata	•	—	—	—
word POS	•	—	•	•
dependency relation	•	—	•	•
parent POS	•	•	—	—
child words	•	—	—	—
child POS	•	—	—	—
dependency words	—	—	•	•
position	—	—	•	•
word embedding	•	•	•	•

5.3   Features

In order to do the semantic analysis, we build one learning model for every step in the pipeline. This means we need to have a set of features for every learning model as it is more likely that one set of features for a task will not perform as well as when it is used for a different task. We based our feature sets on the intersection between the approach used by [5] and [6] for semantic role labeling task.

Most of the basic features have been implemented by Mate Tools as explained in Sect. 5.1. Furthermore, our additional features can be derived from the ones that have been provided. These features are as follow:

1. *affected word form*, which is the original word in the sentence
2. *affected word lemmata* taken from the lemmatisation step in syntactic analysis
3. *affected word part-of-speech* taken from the part-of-speech tagging in syntactic analysis
4. *relation to parent*, which is taken from the relation of dependency parsing in syntactic analysis
5. *parent part-of-speech*. The parent word can be derived from the dependency parsing in syntactic analysis
6. *child words*, the same with *affected word form* but for all children of current word. This is derived from the dependency parsing in syntactic analysis
7. *child part-of-speech*, the same with *parent part-of-speech* but for all children of current word
8. *dependency between words*, i.e. the words in dependency relations between the action and its object, the action and its actor, or the property and its action/actor/object.
9. *position of affected words*, e.g. *before* or *after* the predicate

10. *word vector representation*, which is the word embedding or the numerical representation for every word

Vectorising categorical features into numerical will inevitably generate a very sparse feature matrix. To compensate this phenomenon, we add the last feature 10 which is a dense feature matrix in nature. This feature is also used to add more generalisation to other features, for instance the POS features, which are specifically important for the semantic analysis task. Slightly different from the approach used in [5], we utilise the GloVe 6 billion tokens[3] [17] and the fastText 16 billion tokens[4] [15] as our word vector representation.

Table 2 shows the features and their usage in each semantic analysis steps.

5.4   Learning Algorithm

To get the best learning model for our semantic analysis steps, we run our dataset against several classifiers. To achieve this, we annotate our guideline sentences following the ontology concepts needed for each particular step. For example, in the first and second step, we only annotated words in the sentences as either `Action` or `Object`. Then we give the label for those words as either 1 (for potential `Action` or `Object`) or 0 (for others). For the second step, the classifier will learn to distinguish the words recognised in step 1 as either 1 (for `Action`) or 0 (for `Object`).

After comparing several classifiers, we choose perceptron [20] as our learning algorithm as it shows the best result compared to the rests, e.g. decision tree, and random forests. We use the free perceptron library from scikit-learn. In perceptron, during the training step, for every input $\mathbf{x}_j$ and the expected output y_j in the training set, the algorithm will calculate the output $\hat{y}_j(t)$ using the weight matrix $\mathbf{w}(t)$ and activation (also called *step*) function f as in Eq. (1). In every iteration, the weight matrix is updated following Eq. (2) where w_i is the weight for feature i, $x_{j,i}$ is the ith feature value of jth training data, and η is the learning rate.

$$\hat{y}_j(t) = f[\mathbf{w}(t) \cdot \mathbf{x}_j] \tag{1}$$

$$w_i(t+1) = w_i(t) + \eta \cdot (\hat{y}_j - y_j(t))x_{j,i} \tag{2}$$

The learning process will stop until it reaches a converging point, i.e. the value of $|\hat{y}_j - y_j| \leq \epsilon$ where ϵ is a very small threshold value. Otherwise, it will stop until it passes the maximum number of learning iteration.

5.5   Long Short-Term Memory for NER

For our NER approach, we built a neural network learning model using long short-term memory (LSTM) [9]. LSTM is an architecture in recurrent neural

---

[3] https://nlp.stanford.edu/projects/glove/.
[4] https://fasttext.cc/docs/en/english-vectors.html.

network (RNN). RNNs are commonly used to analyse sequence and time series data. However, unlike RNNs, LSTMs can also capture long-term dependencies in the data. This is due to an LSTM unit/cell is made up of an input gate, output gate, and forget gate that make an LSTM cell can learn an important input, keep it as long as it is deemed important, and extract it when it is required.

Figure 6 illustrates our NER model using LSTM for the first 4 words in the sentence "*All patients should have appropriate monitoring for clinically significant AEs.*" Although Fig. 6 shows that the input is represented by word embeddings and part-of-speech features, we also ran many experiments using the combination of all possible feature sets in Table 2. We also conducted experiments to see the effect of using different embedding dimensions.

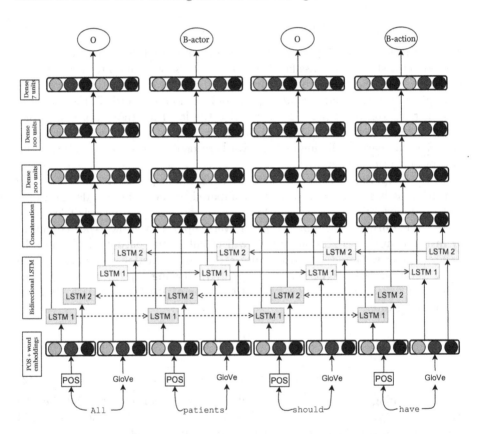

Fig. 6. Named-entity recognition using LSTM

For every word token and its part-of-speech in the sentence, we use bidirectional LSTM with 128 units to recognise the pattern in both forward and backward directions. The outputs of the LSTM layers are merged in the next layer. We added two subsequent dense layers with 200 and 100 units respectively. These additional layers added the depth of our model to learn better from the inputs. Finally, the output layer contains 7 units for each label in our data domain as described in Sect. 4.3.

6   Evaluation

6.1   Dataset Analysis

Our dataset has a total of 379 sentences, 216 of them are taken from The National Institute for Health and Care Excellence (NICE)[5], 98 are from The Scottish Intercollegiate Guidelines Network (SIGN)[6], and 65 are from Annals of the Rheumatic Diseases (ARD)[7]. These sentences are gathered from guidelines for various diseases to capture the nature of the sentences in a clinical guideline setting. Overall there are 7967 tokens and 1414 types, i.e. one sentence would have 21 words in average. The shortest sentence has 9 words in it whereas the longest has 66.

The annotation of the dataset was performed by a single annotator to mark the ontology of concepts on words following the hierarchy in Fig. 3. Some difficulties became evident when dealing with an `Actor` or an `Object` as well as a `Property`. For example, the annotator sometimes mixed up tagging a word as an `Actor` in a passive sentence where it should be an `Object`, and vice versa. Determining if there is a `Property` in a phrase can also be challenging. For example, in the phrase *adjuvant therapy*, the annotator initially marked both words as `Objects`. On a further examination, it was then revised so that now *adjuvant* is the `Property` of the `Object` *therapy*. We believe that it also becomes more difficult if we want to have a more fine-grained concepts in our annotations. Although all considerations have been taken into account, we may not be surprised if there are still several inconsistencies and/or ambiguities in our final dataset.

Table 3. Counts of instances of concepts and relations

Concept	Instances	Relations	Instances
Action	630		
Actor	261	has_actor	128
Object	691	acts_on	676
Property	825	has_property	823
Total	**2407**	**Total**	**1627**

Table 3 shows the counts of instances of concepts and relations. It should be noted that there are many actions without explicit actors in our dataset.

---

[5] https://www.nice.org.uk/.

[6] https://www.sign.ac.uk/.

[7] https://ard.bmj.com/.

Furthermore, some actors do not involve in any action, i.e. they just have some properties to modify them. As for our NER approach, the counts of named-entity instances can be seen in Table 4.

Table 4. Counts of named-entity instances

IOB tag	Instances
O	3785
B-action	472
B-actor	281
B-object	1507
I-object	769
B-property	928
I-property	225
Total	**7967**

6.2 Experiments

After finalising our dataset, we ran several machine learning classifier algorithms to evaluate the performance of our semantic annotations approach as we briefly mentioned in Sect. 5.4. We use the common evaluation metrics precision and recall. Precision is defined as the percentage of predicted instances that are correct whereas recall is defined as the percentage of correct instances that are predicted by the model. It is also often that we combine precision and recall into a single metric called F_1-score, particularly to simplify the comparison between several classifiers. The F_1-score is computed as the harmonic mean of precision and recall (Table 5).

Table 5. Evaluation F_1-score values for several classifiers

Classifier	Precision	Recall	F_1-score
Decision tree	0.745	0.512	0.603
Random forest	**0.792**	0.488	0.604
Perceptron	0.603	**0.678**	**0.638**
GloVe 300 + POS	0.854	0.881	**0.867**
GloVe 200 + POS & lemma	0.855	0.879	0.867
GloVe 300 + POS & parent	0.846	**0.888**	0.866
Wiki 300 + POS & dependency	0.853	0.876	0.864
Wiki 300 + POS & parent & dependency	**0.856**	0.872	0.864

Table 6. Evaluation F_1-score values for several relation classification

Classifier	F_1-score
300d 300/200/100/100	**0.885**
100d 100/100/100	0.881
100d 100/100/100	0.877

Table 6 shows the performance of several classifiers for our semantic annotation approach. For each classifier, we perform evaluation using tenfold cross-validation setting, i.e. in every fold, there will be ten equal portions of data where one portion out of ten will be used as testing. We can see variations of trend for each performance metric. Random forests has the best performance (79%) for correctly predicting the concepts and relations in the sentences, i.e. 4 out of 5 annotations are correct. Meanwhile, perceptron is the best for predicting all correct concepts and relations (67%), roughly 7 out of 10 correct annotations can be predicted. Using the F_1-score, the best one is achieved by perceptron (64%) with mean 0.97 and ± 0.007 standard deviation.

Table 6 also shows some experiments of NER using LSTM for our domain. Here, we only show 5 experiments although in reality we ran many more to get the best result. We tried using every possible combinations of features in Table 2. We also investigated the effect of using pre-trained word embeddings with varying dimension size. We found the best F_1-score of 87% using the combination of POS feature and GloVe embeddings of size 300.

As we adapted the approach done by [5], it would be interesting to see how our performance would be if we run it against their dataset. It will also answer the question on how much the domain used to build the model affects its performance when used in a different one. This was outside the scope of the present paper, but will be explored in future work.

7   Conclusion

In this paper, we presented our work to annotate semantic information in guideline sentences. We began by collecting guideline sentences from the English, Scottish, and European guideline corpora. These sentences serve as the preliminary dataset for applying linguistic analysis in the domain. Although we only have 379 sentences in our dataset, we have done around 4000 annotations for the concepts we are interested in.

Following the approach in [5], we annotated the dataset using a hierarchy of concepts. We adapted their ontology concepts using only concepts that we found useful for our problem at present. We also conducted a named-entity recognition task using the same ontology concepts to compare the results. Furthermore, the more fine-grained concepts we want to apply, the more challenging it becomes. As our current development only has one annotator for the whole dataset, to increase the accuracy of our annotation we should consider adding one or more annotators in the future.

The main aim for this work is to help people retrieve the key information in clinical guidelines. As shown in [19], we built a system to do formal verification of a therapy algorithm for type 2 diabetes. As guidelines are expressed in natural language, they are prone to ambiguity, incompleteness, and inconsistency. We expect that our work will help further the development of clearer and better clinical guidelines.

In future work, our aim is to build a framework that integrates the whole process defined in [19]. It means that we will also add functionalities to produce some formal models from the annotated guideline sentences. We need to further assess the performance of our approach when compared to different datasets. Finally, we also plan to build a user interface to help the annotation process and to visualise the annotation result.

References

1. Bäumler, S., Balser, M., Dunets, A., Reif, W., Schmitt, J.: Verification of medical guidelines by model checking – a case study. In: Valmari, A. (ed.) SPIN 2006. LNCS, vol. 3925, pp. 219–233. Springer, Heidelberg (2006). https://doi.org/10.1007/11691617_13

2. Behrmann, G., David, A., Larsen, K.G.: A tutorial on UPPAAL. In: Bernardo, M., Corradini, F. (eds.) SFM-RT 2004. LNCS, vol. 3185, pp. 200–236. Springer, Heidelberg (2004). https://doi.org/10.1007/978-3-540-30080-9_7

3. Björkelund, A., Hafdell, L., Nugues, P.: Multilingual semantic role labeling. In: Proceedings of the Thirteenth Conference on Computational Natural Language Learning (CoNLL 2009): Shared Task, pp. 43–48. Association for Computational Linguistics, Boulder (June 2009). https://www.aclweb.org/anthology/W09-1206

4. Carvalho, G., Carvalho, A., Rocha, E., Cavalcanti, A., Sampaio, A.: A formal model for natural-language timed requirements of reactive systems. In: Merz, S., Pang, J. (eds.) ICFEM 2014. LNCS, vol. 8829, pp. 43–58. Springer, Cham (2014). https://doi.org/10.1007/978-3-319-11737-9_4

5. Diamantopoulos, T., Roth, M., Symeonidis, A., Klein, E.: Software requirements as an application domain for natural language processing. Lang. Resour. Eval. 51(2), 495–524 (2017). https://doi.org/10.1007/s10579-017-9381-z

6. Gildea, D., Jurafsky, D.: Automatic labeling of semantic roles. Comput. Linguist. 28(3), 245–288 (2002). https://doi.org/10.1162/089120102760275983

7. Giordano, L., Terenziani, P., Bottrighi, A., Montani, S., Donzella, L.: Model checking for clinical guidelines: an agent-based approach. In: AMIA Annual Symposium, pp. 289–93 (2006)

8. Hajic, J., et al.: The CoNLL-2009 shared task: syntactic and semantic dependencies in multiple languages. In: Proceedings of the Thirteenth Conference on Computational Natural Language Learning (CoNLL 2009): Shared Task, pp. 1–18 (2009)

9. Hochreiter, S., Schmidhuber, J.: Long short-term memory. Neural Comput. 9, 1735–1780 (1997). https://doi.org/10.1162/neco.1997.9.8.1735

10. Holzmann, G.J.: The Spin Model Checker: Primer and Reference Manual. Addison-Wesley, Boston (2003)

11. Jurafsky, D., Martin, J.H.: Speech and Language Processing : An Introduction to Natural Language Processing, Computational Linguistics, and Speech Recognition. Pearson Prentice Hall, Upper Saddle River (2009)

12. Kingston, A., Robinson, L., Booth, H., Knapp, M., Jagger, C.: Projections of multi-morbidity in the older population in England to 2035: estimates from the population ageing and care simulation (PACSim) model. Age Ageing **47**, 374–380 (2018)

13. Kwiatkowska, M., Norman, G., Parker, D.: PRISM 4.0: verification of probabilistic real-time systems. In: Gopalakrishnan, G., Qadeer, S. (eds.) CAV 2011. LNCS, vol. 6806, pp. 585–591. Springer, Heidelberg (2011). https://doi.org/10.1007/978-3-642-22110-1_47

14. McMillan, K.L., Qadeer, S., Saxe, J.B.: Induction in compositional model checking. In: Emerson, E.A., Sistla, A.P. (eds.) CAV 2000. LNCS, vol. 1855, pp. 312–327. Springer, Heidelberg (2000). https://doi.org/10.1007/10722167_25

15. Mikolov, T., Grave, E., Bojanowski, P., Puhrsch, C., Joulin, A.: Advances in pre-training distributed word representations. In: Proceedings of the International Conference on Language Resources and Evaluation (LREC 2018) (2018)

16. de Moura, L., Bjørner, N.: Z3: an efficient SMT solver. In: Ramakrishnan, C.R., Rehof, J. (eds.) TACAS 2008. LNCS, vol. 4963, pp. 337–340. Springer, Heidelberg (2008). https://doi.org/10.1007/978-3-540-78800-3_24

17. Pennington, J., Socher, R., Manning, C.D.: Glove: global vectors for word representation. In: Empirical Methods in Natural Language Processing (EMNLP), pp. 1532–1543 (2014). http://www.aclweb.org/anthology/D14-1162

18. Pérez, B., Porres, I.: Authoring and verification of clinical guidelines: a model driven approach. J. Biomed. Inform. **43**(4), 520–536 (2010). https://doi.org/10.1016/j.jbi.2010.02.009

19. Rahman, F., Bowles, J.K.F.: Formal verification of CNL health recommendations. In: Polikarpova, N., Schneider, S. (eds.) IFM 2017. LNCS, vol. 10510, pp. 357–371. Springer, Cham (2017). https://doi.org/10.1007/978-3-319-66845-1_24

20. Rosenblatt, F.: The perceptron—a perceiving and recognizing automaton. Tech. rep. 85–460-1, Cornell Aeronautical Laboratory (1957)

21. Shahar, Y., Miksch, S., Johnson, P.: The Asgaard project: a task-specific framework for the application and critiquing of time-oriented clinical guidelines. Artif. Intell. Med. **14**(1), 29–51 (1998). https://doi.org/10.1016/S0933-3657(98)00015-3

22. Terenziani, P., Molino, G., Torchio, M.: A modular approach for representing and executing clinical guidelines. Artif. Intell. Med. **23**(3), 249–276 (2001). https://doi.org/10.1016/S0933-3657(01)00087-2

Deriving Performance Measures of Workflow in Radiation Therapy from Real-Time Data

Reshma Munbodh[1,2](✉) [iD], Kara L. Leonard[1,2,3], and Eric E. Klein[1,2]

[1] Department of Radiation Oncology,
Alpert Medical School of Brown University, Providence, RI, USA
reshma_munbodh@brown.edu
[2] Department of Radiation Oncology,
Rhode Island Hospital, Providence, RI, USA
[3] Department of Radiation Oncology, Tufts Medical Center,
Tufts University School of Medicine, Boston, MA, USA

Abstract. Radiation treatment planning is a complex process with multiple, dependent steps involving an interdisciplinary patient care team. We have previously implemented an interactive, web-based dashboard, which requires a standardised radiation treatment planning workflow and provides real-time monitoring and visualization of the workflow. We present this framework and the results of performance measures characterising the standardised workflow in an effort to optimize clinical efficiency and patient safety. Quantitative representations of longitudinal progression of carepath activities were computed from staff-reported timestamps queried from the EMR. Performance measures evaluated included staff compliance in completing assigned tasks, timeliness in task completion, and the time to complete different tasks. The framework developed allows for informed, data-driven decisions regarding clinical workflow management and the impact of changes on existing workflow as we seek to optimize clinical efficiency and safety, and incorporate new interventions into clinical practice.

Keywords: Workflow tracking · Performance evaluation · Cancer

1 Introduction

Approximately 50% of patients diagnosed with cancer receive radiation therapy. Radiation therapy is a complex process involving multiple, dependent stages whereby an interdisciplinary care team collaborates to create and deliver a personalised radiation treatment plan. Patient safety and clinical efficiency are important during this process [2].

The radiation therapy workflow, illustrated in Fig. 1, consists of acquiring a CT scan of the patient from which a highly conformal, three-dimensional, radiation treatment plan is created to deliver a physician-prescribed dose to the

© Springer Nature Switzerland AG 2021
J. Bowles et al. (Eds.): DataMod 2020, LNCS 12611, pp. 206–216, 2021.
https://doi.org/10.1007/978-3-030-70650-0_13

tumour while also sparing surrounding healthy tissue. After creation and quality assurance of the radiation plan and prior to treatment, a simulation of the treatment is performed to verify safe delivery of the plan to the patient. Treatment delivery is usually performed under image guidance. Following treatment, the images acquired and delivered dose are reviewed in the electronic medical record (EMR) system to verify that the prescription was fulfilled.

The focus of this study is on the radiation treatment planning (RTP) stage, which is perhaps the most complex process, in the radiation therapy workflow. It is also the stage where radiation treatment errors are most likely to originate [4]. Effective communication among staff [1], adequate staffing levels and the ability to optimise the distribution of work among resources along with process automation [6] are key to ensuring patient safety, clinical efficiency and timely treatment starts. However, a lack of standardisation in clinical practice, inherent limitations in the EMR to display consolidated information that effectively communicates progress in the creation of patients' treatment plans to the care team [7], the need for specialised skills to extract information from the EMR, and a consequent lack of quantitative performance measures of workflow in radiation oncology are all challenges towards achieving these goals.

Electronic whiteboards [10] and carepath management systems [5] have been shown to improve communication and task management in radiation oncology. In an effort to improve communication and the tracking of resource utilisation, we have previously implemented an interactive, web-based dashboard to track clinical workflow [9]. The dashboard integrates with the departmental EMR, and provides real-time monitoring and visualization of the RTP workflow. It consists of several tabs unified by date, physician name, treatment type and treatment location, and monitors utilisation of the linear accelerators, patient appointment status as well as the status of tasks associated with the creation of a patient's treatment plan for several patients simultaneously. As well as providing a consolidated overview of progress in the creation of a patient's radiation treatment plan, the dashboard implements a standardized, integrated framework to analyze data acquired in real-time for quantitative clinical workflow evaluation.

In this study, we derive important quantitative performance measures, which describe the RTP workflow, from these data in an effort to understand how different activities unfold over time. We also estimate the efficiency of clinical practices and processes. The performance measures are calculated from data automatically queried from the EMR, and which provide the status, start and completion times of various tasks completed by the patient's care team during treatment planning. The measures obtained will contribute towards the implementation of informed, data-driven decisions on clinical workflow management

Fig. 1. Radiation therapy clinical workflow. The five stages in the radiation therapy clinical workflow. In this article, we focus on the radiation treatment planning stage

and the development of process models for resource allocation with the long-term aim of improving radiation treatment safety and efficacy.

2   Methods

In this section, we describe a standardised model of the radiation treatment planning workflow, the implementation of a process to acquire data that tracks workflow in real-time, and the performance measures computed from these real-time data.

2.1   Standardised Model of the RTP Workflow

Process maps and flowcharts were created to model the RTP workflow. These described:

- Tasks representing standardised carepath activities associated with creation of a patient's radiation treatment plan from the time of CT simulation to treatment
- Task timeline and sequence
- Task ownership
- Staff interaction.

We considered patients treated with either of two treatment modalities, namely, three-dimensional (3D) conformal radiation therapy and intensity modulated radiation therapy (IMRT).

A simplified process map of the RTP workflow is shown in Fig. 2.

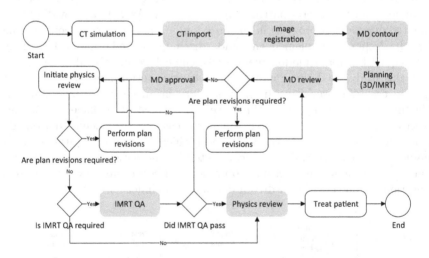

Fig. 2. RTP workflow. Standardised carepath activities associated with the creation of a patient-specific radiation treatment plan are shown. Tracked activities are in grey.

Radiation treatment planning starts with the acquisition of a CT scan of the patient during a process known as CT simulation. After CT simulation, the CT is imported into the treatment planning system (TPS) by a dosimetrist who then registers the CT to other images of the patient, if present. Afterwards, a physician contours the tumour and organs at risk and positions the radiation beams on the CT. The dosimetrist subsequently calculates a personalised radiation treatment plan using the CT, contoured anatomical structures and radiation beams. The plan is designed to deliver a physician-prescribed dose to the tumor while minimising irradiation of the organs at risk. After the plan has been calculated, it undergoes quality assurance in the form peer review by physicians and medical physicists. Peer review consists of a physician review, physician approval, IMRT QA, if applicable, and finally, a physics chart review by a medical physicist before the calculated radiation treatment plan is finally being approved for treatment. The planned treatment is then delivered to the patient. Tracked carepath activities during the RTP workflow are shaded in grey.

A description of the tasks created in the EMR to track the carepath activities, the staff responsible for completing the tasks, that is, the owners of the tasks, and the ideal timeline, τ, associated with completion of the tasks are listed in Table 1. An ideal timeline of 6 days from CT simulation to completion of the physics chart review was formulated. The number of days is counted post CT-acquisition, with zero being at the end of the day on which the CT was acquired. The tasks in Table 1 are listed in the sequence of completion during the RTP process. The granularity of the ideal timeline is limited at one day by the EMR. This led to sequential tasks having parallel timelines in the EMR.

Table 1. RTP tasks. The table lists, in sequential order, carepath activity tasks, task owner and ideal timeline, τ, for completing the task in terms of number of days following the CT simulation.

i	Task	Owner	τ (days)	Description
1	CT Import	Dosimetrist	0	CT import into TPS
2	Image Reg	Dosimetrist	0	Registration of CT to other images
3	MD Contour	Physician	1	Contouring of anatomy on CT and radiation beam placement
4	Planning	Dosimetrist	3	Calculation of 3D or IMRT treatment plan
5	MD Review	Physician	5	Review of calculated plan
6	MD Approval	Physician	5	Approval of calculated plan
7	IMRT QA	Medical physicist	5	Patient specific quality assurance
8	Physics Review	Medical physicist	6	Final review and approval of radiation plan for treatment

2.2 Real-Time Tracking and Display of RTP Workflow

The status of tasks comprised in a patient's treatment plan was recorded in the EMR by the task owner, and displayed in real-time on a web-based dashboard.

2.3 Performance Measures of RTP Workflow

The standardised RTP workflow was designed to provide measures to characterise and evaluate clinical practice. Task status information and timestamps were automatically queried from the EMR using SQL and used to compute a number of measures describing workflow performance. Of note to us, were: 1) Staff compliance in recording task completion, 2) Time to completion of various tasks, 3) On-time performance relative to the ideal timeline, 4) Elapsed time between different tasks.

A description of relevant variables, constants and performance parameters is provided below.

Variables

T_i	Task i
M_j	Treatment modality j
$t_{i,k}^j$	Time to complete T_i since date of CT for patient k and M_j
$\mathbb{1}(t_{i,k}^j) = \begin{cases} 1 \text{ if } t_{i,k}^j \neq 0 \\ 0 \text{ otherwise} \end{cases}$	Indicator function on $t_{i,k}^j$
$\mathbb{1}(\delta_{i,k}^j) = \begin{cases} 1 \text{ if } \delta_{i,k}^j \leq 0 \\ 0 \text{ otherwise} \end{cases}$	Indicator function on delay for T_i, M_j and patient k

Constants

N	Total number of patients studied
N_i^j	Number of patients for whom T_i was completed for M_j
τ_i	Ideal time to completion in days for T_i

Performance measures

$\beta_i^j = \frac{100}{N_i^j} \sum_k \mathbb{1}(t_{i,k}^j)$	Percentage number of patients with T_i completed for M_j
$\mu_i^j = \frac{1}{N_i^j} \sum_k t_{i,k}^j$	Mean completion time for T_i and M_j
$\sigma_i^j = \sqrt{\frac{1}{N_i^j - 1} \sum_k (t_{i,k}^j - \mu_i^j)^2}$	Standard deviation of completion time for T_i and M_j
$\delta_{i,k}^j = t_{i,k}^j - \tau_i$	Delay in completing T_i for M_j and patient k
$\psi_i^j = \mu_i^j - \tau_i$	Mean delay in completing T_i for M_j
$\eta_i^j = \frac{100}{N_i^j} \sum_k \mathbb{1}(\delta_{i,k}^j)$	Percentage on-time completion for T_i and M_j

3 Results

Staff were educated about the standardised RTP workflow and trained in the use of tasks in the EMR to record carepath activity status.

3.1   Real-Time Tracking and Display of Workflow

Workflow progression according to treatment date, physician, type of treatment and treatment location were displayed in real-time on web-based dashboard as shown in Fig. 3. For every patient, task status and timeline were conveyed by means of color-coded due dates. Overall progress in the creation of a patient's treatment plan was conveyed through a progress bar.

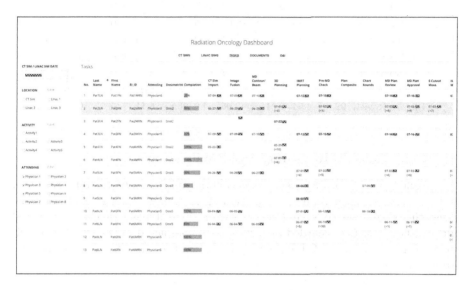

Fig. 3. Real-time tracking of radiation treatment planning workflow. A departmental web-based dashboard tracks carepath activities in the creation of a radiation treatment plan and the status of associated tasks, queried from the EMR, in real-time. (Color figure online)

3.2   Performance Measures

Data for $N = 85$ new patient treatments and 476 care path tasks that were completed in the EMR within 10 days of the CT simulation date were analyzed. As described previously, two treatment modalities, $M = \{3D, IMRT\}$, were considered with a breakdown of 54 and 31 patients, respectively. A summary of the calculated performance measures for the different tasks for 3D and IMRT treatments is given in Table 2. These results are described in more detail in the following sections.

Table 2. RTP performance measures. The performance measures associated with the different tasks tracked for patients treated with 3D or IMRT radiation therapy are shown below.

i	Task	3D					IMRT				
		β_i^1 (%)	μ_i^1 (days)	σ_i^1 (days)	ψ_i^1 (days)	η_i^1 (%)	β_i^2 (%)	μ_i^2 (days)	σ_i^2 (days)	ψ_i^2 (days)	η_i^2 (%)
1	CT Import	100	−0.42	0.18	−0.42	96.3	100	−0.32	0.40	−0.32	87.1
2	Image Reg	79.6	0.33	0.94	0.33	44.2	90.3	0.51	0.68	0.0.51	25.0
3	MD Contour	100	0.35	0.97	−0.65	87.0	100	1.41	0.91	0.41	32.3
4	Planning	87.0	3.47	2.11	0.47	34.0	67.7	5.98	1.45	2.98	23.8
5	MD Review	44.4	3.18	2.06	−1.82	87.5	22.6	5.25	1.54	0.25	42.9
6	MD Approval	42.6	3.23	2.09	−1.77	87.0	22.6	5.25	1.54	0.25	42.9
7	IMRT QA						83.9	6.06	2.11	1.06	46.2
8	Physics Review	92.6	3.94	2.31	−2.06	94.0	96.8	6.11	1.63	0.11	53.3

3.3   Compliance in Recording Task Completion

Compliance, β, in recording task completion ranged from 22% to 100% as shown in Table 2. Note that here, non-completion of the task does not indicate that the carepath activity was not completed, but rather that it was either not completed within 10 days or not recorded as having been completed in the EMR. Compliance was greatest for the CT Import task and least for the MD Review and MD Approval tasks.

3.4   Elapsed Time to Task Completion

Quantitative, longitudinal progression of the RTP workflow for 3D treatments is shown in Fig. 4 and for IMRT treatments in Fig. 5. The bubbles displayed are color-coded by staff role. The centre of the bubbles in the figures represents the average number of days, μ, to completion of a task post CT simulation. The diameter of the bubbles is proportional to the percentage times, η, the tasks were completed on time relative to the ideal timeline. The dotted line represents the ideal timeline for task completion.

The graphs permit evaluation of where bottlenecks are introduced in the clinic and help identify areas of improvement. The mean time (and standard deviation) from CT import to completion of the physics review for 3D and IMRT treatments, respectively, were 3.9 (2.3) and 6.1 (1.6) days. 3D task completion times were better than ideal, indicating that the timeline associated with the 3D RTP workflow is amenable to further refinement. For IMRT treatments, delays were introduced in the image registration and MD contour stages. The average time to completion of the physics review task, which was the last task in the RTP process, was close to the ideal completion time of 6 days.

3.5   On-Time Performance Relative to Ideal Timeline

Average on-time performance relative to the ideal timeline was 75/7% (44.2%–96.3%) for 3D plans and 44.2% (25–87.1%) for IMRT plans, with the lowest timeliness being for planning activities. Further analysis of the individual task completion times showed that the planning task was completed out-of-sequence by the dosimetrists. That is, tasks associated with planning activities were completed prior to the physics review rather than prior to the MD review as modelled in the standardised RTP workflow in Fig. 2, thus resulting in low on-time performance for this task.

3.6   Elapsed Time Between Tasks

The average time elapsed between completion of the different tasks is listed in Table 3. This provides an estimate of the average time required to perform each task. The times to complete the planning, MD review and MD approval tasks were calculated relative to completion of the MD contour task. The times to complete the IMRT QA and the Physics review tasks were calculated with respect to MD approval. As can be seen, individual IMRT tasks require more time to complete than 3D tasks, reflecting the increased complexity associated with IMRT plans.

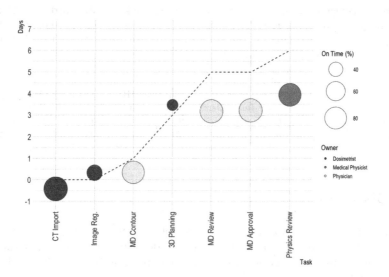

Fig. 4. 3D treatment planning workflow timeline. The average number of days to completion for the different tasks in the 3D planning workflow is shown by staff role. The diameter of the bubble is proportional to on time compliance relative to the ideal timeline (dotted line). (Color figure online)

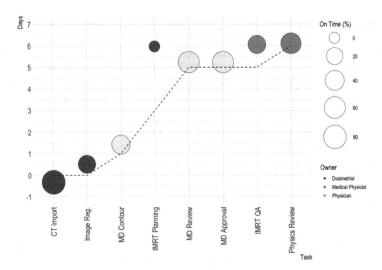

Fig. 5. IMRT treatment planning workflow timeline. The average number of days to task completion in the IMRT planning workflow colour-coded by staff role is shown. The diameter of the bubble is proportional to on-time compliance relative to the ideal timeline (dotted line). (Color figure online)

Table 3. Average time to complete a given task for 3D and IMRT treatments. The negative value for CT import is to end-of-day on the day that the CT is acquired being considered as the start time. [†]Calculated relative to MD Contour. [‡]Calculated relative to MD Approval.

Modality	Task							
	CT Import	Image Reg.	MD Contour	Planning[†]	MD Review[†]	MD Approval[†]	IMRT QA[‡]	Physics Review[‡]
Ideal time (days)	−0.5	−0.5	1	2	4	4	1	1
3D actual time (days)	−0.42	0.75	0.76	3.1	2.8	2.85		0.47
IMRT actual time (days)	−0.32	0.83	0.90	4.56	3.83	3.83	0.81	0.86

4   Discussion

We have presented performance measures of the radiation treatment planning workflow for cancer patients. The measures describe the completion time and compliance rates in the completion of key carepath activities in a standardised RTP workflow.

Formulating, implementing and adoption of a standardised workflow in radiation oncology that can be tracked by the EMR and displayed in real-time on the departmental dashboard was challenging due to the complexity of the RTP process, the large number and interdisciplinary nature of the staff involved in the creation of a patient's treatment plan, and inherent limitations of the EMR.

Ensuring effective communication amongst the stakeholders was key towards achieving a working solution.

Implementing an RTP process in the clinic that is event-driven and where progression to the next stage of planning is triggered by task completion relies on the timely completion of the tasks in the EMR by the owners of the task. It also relies on the tasks being completed in the correct sequence. This study has provided insight into how activities unfold in a busy clinical practice during the treatment planning process. It has helped us identify strengths in our clinical practice, for instance, on average the physics review is completed, and therefore patient treatment starts, within the ideal timeline. It has also helped identify limitations, for instance in the compliance of task completion for certain activities, the sequence of activity completion, and delays.

As patient loads increase and we move towards process automation in radiation oncology, optimal allocation of resources and an understanding of where bottlenecks and failure modes arise [3,8,11], the relationship between workload and staffing levels, as well as the impact of potential changes in workflow are crucial. The performance measures presented here are important for clinical practice improvement and process modelling particularly with respect to optimising allocation of resources and ensuring adequate staffing levels in a busy clinical setting. In future work, we will develop more advanced models of the radiation therapy workflow towards improving clinical practice and patient safety.

References

1. Chao, S.T., et al.: Workflow enhancement (we) improves safety in radiation oncology: putting the we and team together. Int. J. Radiat. Oncol.*Biol.*Phys. **89**(4), 765–772 (2014). https://doi.org/10.1016/j.ijrobp.2014.01.024
2. Chera, B.S., et al.: Quantification of the impact of multifaceted initiatives intended to improve operational efficiency and the safety culture: a case study from an academic medical center radiation oncology department. Pract. Radiat. Oncol. **4**(2), e101–e108 (2014). https://doi.org/10.1016/j.prro.2013.05.007
3. Ford, E.C., et al.: Evaluation of safety in a radiation oncology setting using failure mode and effects analysis. Int. J. Radiat. Oncol.*Biol.*Phys. **74**(3), 852–858 (2009). https://doi.org/10.1016/j.ijrobp.2008.10.038
4. Gopan, O., Zeng, J., Novak, A., Nyflot, M., Ford, E.: The effectiveness of pre-treatment physics plan review for detecting errors in radiation therapy. Med Phys. **43**(9), 5181 (2016). https://doi.org/10.1118/1.4961010. Place: United States
5. Kovalchuk, N., Russo, G.A., Shin, J.Y., Kachnic, L.A.: Optimizing efficiency and safety in a radiation oncology department through the use of aria 11 visual care path. Pract. Radiat. Oncol. **5**(5), 295–303 (2015). https://doi.org/10.1016/j.prro.2015.05.001. Safety Issue
6. Liu, S., et al.: Optimizing efficiency and safety in external beam radiotherapy using automated plan check (APC) tool and six sigma methodology. J. Appl. Clin. Med. Phys. **20**(8), 56–64 (2019). https://doi.org/10.1002/acm2.12678
7. Marks, L.B., et al.: The challenge of maximizing safety in radiation oncology. Pract. Radiat. Oncol. **1**(1), 2–14 (2011). https://doi.org/10.1016/j.prro.2010.10.001

8. Mugford, M., Banfield, P., O'Hanlon, M.: Effects of feedback of information on clinical practice: a review. BMJ **303**(6799), 398–402 (1991). https://doi.org/10.1136/bmj.303.6799.398

9. Munbodh, R., Roth, T.M., Leonard, K.L., Brindle, J., Klein, E.E.: Real-time analysis and display of quantitative measures to track and improve clinical workflow. Med. Phys. **46**(6), e197 (2019)

10. Wolfgang, J.A., Hong, T.S.: Radiation oncology whiteboard: data and workflow manager for enhanced communication and task management. J. Clin. Oncol. **30**(34_suppl), 304 (2012). https://doi.org/10.1200/jco.2012.30.34_suppl.304. pMID: 28146901

11. Wright, J.L., et al.: Real-time management of incident learning reports in a radiation oncology department. Pract. Radiat. Oncol. **8**(5), e337–e345 (2018). https://doi.org/10.1016/j.prro.2018.04.016

Handshape Classification in a Reverse Dictionary of Sign Languages for the Deaf

Alikhan Abutalipov[1], Aigerim Janaliyeva[1], Medet Mukushev[2] iD,
Antonio Cerone[1] iD, and Anara Sandygulova[2]([✉]) iD

[1] Department of Computer Science,
Nazarbayev University, Nur-Sultan, Kazakhstan
{alikhan.abutalipov,aigerim.janaliyeva,antonio.cerone}@nu.edu.kz
[2] Department of Robotics and Mechatronics,
Nazarbayev University, Nur-Sultan, Kazakhstan
{mmukushev,anara.sandygulova}@nu.edu.kz

Abstract. This paper showcases the work that aims at building a user-friendly mobile application of a reverse dictionary to translate sign languages to spoken languages. The concept behind the reverse dictionary is the ability to perform a video-based search by demonstrating a handshape in front of a mobile phone's camera. The user would be able to use this feature in two ways. Firstly, the user would be able to search for a word by showing a handshape for the application to provide a list of signs that contain that handshape. Secondly, the user could fingerspell the word letter by letter in front of the camera for the application to return the sign that corresponds to that word. The user can then look through the suggested videos and see their written translations. To offer other functionalities, the application also has Search by Category and Search by Word options. Currently, the reverse dictionary supports translations from Russian Sign Language (RSL) to Russian language.

Keywords: Reverse dictionary · Sign language dictionary · Fingerspelling recognition · Video-based search interface · Human-computer interaction · iOS application · Russian Sign Language (RSL)

1 Introduction

Deaf communities around the world use sign languages for everyday communication. Each country or region has its own sign language. Contrary to popular belief, Russian Sign Language (RSL) does not share structure or grammar with the Russian language. In addition, people native to RSL do not necessarily know how to read and write Russian and have to learn it as a foreign language.

Most online sign language (SL) dictionaries are alphabet-based which are convenient for people who are fluent in spoken languages. When searching for a sign, they need to know the written translation of it and search by its first

J. Bowles et al. (Eds.): DataMod 2020, LNCS 12611, pp. 217–226, 2021.
https://doi.org/10.1007/978-3-030-70650-0_14

letter. However, such functionality is useful for people who want to learn SL and cannot provide a reverse option - searching for meaning of unfamiliar signs.

There exists only a few reserve dictionaries where searching by sign is performed by one of its components, such as handshapes. Nonetheless, this is still not user-friendly as each handshape is described in a written form. Usually these descriptions are compiled by professional SL linguists, which makes it hard for a non-expert user to understand the description. Sometimes the pictorial representations of the handshapes are provided too, but then the creation of such dictionaries for every sign is time-consuming.

Therefore, this work aims to build an automatic reverse dictionary where a search is performed in the most natural way - searching by demonstration. Since each sign in a sign language consists of one or several handshapes, searching by handshape demonstration would yield the most intuitive method for people native to sign languages.

2   Related Work

2.1   Sign Language Dictionaries

Computer-based sign language dictionaries could be divided into two categories: search by textual description of the sign and demonstration of the sign.

Search by demonstration systems became popular with the introduction of Microsoft Kinect, which supports skeletal joints tracking [6]. Another approach is the use of systems that accept video demonstration of the sign as an input to find the list of similar signs [4,20]. However, such systems may have poor performance when tested on different users and users are required to perfectly demonstrate the sign in order to find its match.

Feature-based sign language dictionaries overcome the problems of computer-based sign language dictionaries by focusing only on features or components describing a sign. Bragg *et al.* [3] proposed a feature-based dictionary system that enables users to lookup unknown signs by selecting from features such as handshape, orientation, or location. Increase in the computational power of smartphones opens new opportunities for the development of sign language dictionaries. Some functional prototypes were built both for text-to-sign [8] or handshape-to-sign systems [14]. Alonzo *et al.* [1] highlight the difficulty of searching for an unfamiliar sign in dictionaries. Furthermore, they showed that the placement of the searched sign in the list (its position) and the similarity of the shown items affect user's opinion regarding the quality of the search results. In general, researchers agree that there are few resources available that are robust enough to overcome all existing limitations [2].

2.2   Sign Language Fingerspelling Recognition

Automatic sign language recognition has been an active field of research in the past couple of decades and fingerspelling recognition is one part of sign language recognition. Fingerspelling is used to express words that have no specific sign in the vocabulary of sign languages. Many approaches were used to solve this task such as hand crafted features, Convolutional Neural Networks, and depth features. The field largely benefits from the advances in computer vision.

The Australian Sign Language fingerspelling recognizer uses a combination of features extracted from skin detection which are later used to extract geometric features. For classification it applies Hidden Markov Models (HMM) to get the output probabilities for the given sequence of features. At word level this model achieves 88.61% recognition accuracy [7]. For the American Sign Language (ASL) a semi-Markov conditional model approach was developed. It achieves an 11.6% letter error rate compared to the HMM baseline with 16.3% [9].

Microsoft Kinect depth cameras showed good results when applied to finger-spelling recognition. Pugeault and Bowden [16] proposed a real-time ASL finger-spelling recognition system based on Microsoft Kinect. Their approach focuses on detecting user's hands and extracting handshape features and is based on Gabor filtering of the intensity and depth images. The classification part was performed with multi-class random forest and achieved 75% accuracy. Dong *et al.* [5] proposed a model for recognizing 24 static ASL alphabet signs with 90% accuracy. Their model first extracted hand segments based on depth contrast features which were then used to localize hand joint positions. For the classification part, a Random Forest algorithm was applied. Another interesting approach based on classification tree and machine learning was developed for the Japanese Sign Language. It supports the classification of 41 characters without movement with 86% accuracy [11]. Point cloud descriptors recorded with Microsoft Kinect were used to recognize static letters of the Polish Sign Language. The classification part was performed using HMM and achieved an accuracy of 78.8% [21].

Some specific hardware is required for the systems mentioned above which are not convenient for the end users. In contrast, vision-based approaches can be implemented using only web-cameras or mobile phone cameras. Shi et al. [17] introduced the largest dataset for ASL fingerspelling recognition used to detect fingerspelling "in the wild" in realistic conditions. Most of the previous works performed experiments on more controlled data with a limited number of participants. The proposed system has two parts: hand detector and sequence recognizer. The best letter accuracy was achieved with a CTC-based recognizer and was around 42%. Another approach for detecting fingerspelling in realistic conditions used end-to-end model with an iterative attention mechanism. In contrast to previous work, this approach is not using explicit hand detection or segmentation. The best accuracy was 61.2% on ChicagoFSWild dataset [18].

3 System Design and Architecture

Our system is based on a database where each sign video has a list of hand-shapes corresponding to that sign. We used a publicly available dictionary of RSL from the Spread the Sign dictionary[1]. Thus, every frame of the sign video

---
[1] www.spreadthesign.com.

was cropped to contain only the hand region using the "Hand-CNN" pre-trained hand detection model [13]. Then we utilized the "Deep Hand" pre-trained hand-shape recognition model [10] to classify handshapes in each sign video. Once the database was ready, we built a system consisting of two main components, an iOS mobile application and a server that runs the "Hand-CNN" and "Deep Hand" models. When a user takes a photo of a handshape, the application sends the image over HTTP as a request to the server, which in turn classifies the handshape in the photo and return the result to the application via an HTTP request. The application then shows the user the signs that contain the user's handshape by searching the database. When a user takes a photo of another handshape, the just-described process repeats itself, but this time the application shows the signs that contain both handshapes. The more handshapes are shown, the narrower the search is. Overall architecture of the application is presented in Fig. 1.

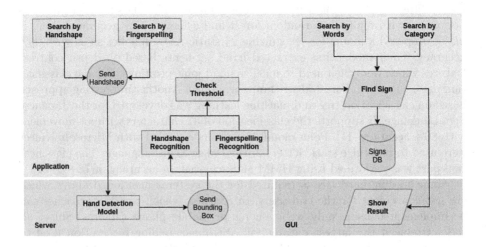

Fig. 1. System components

3.1 Datasets

In order to adapt the handshape classification to support RSL and fingerspelling in RSL, we utilized a manually labeled dataset of RSL handshapes [12] as well as a previously collected Cyrillic fingerspelling dataset [19] to perform transfer learning of the "Deep Hand" model to make two models for RSL handshape recognition and Cyrillic fingerspelling. In the end, the number of classes was 29 for 33 letters in the Russian alphabet as some cases were combined due to being different only in the movement. This is the case for the signs for the letters И, Й, Ш, Щ.

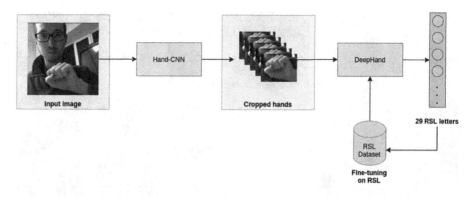

Fig. 2. Training process

3.2 Implementation Details

For the transfer learning, we decreased the overall learning rate from 0.0005 to 0.0002 while increasing the learning rate of the final layer by 2 and used the RSL datasets [12,19] to re-train the pre-trained "Deep Hand" model's weights. The results were: Top-1 results refer to the output deemed most probable by a model, while Top-5 results refer to the 5 most probable outputs of models. The reason for transfer learning was two-folds: first, the "Deep Hand" model already showed rather good results on their dataset: 85% for Top-1 results and 94.8% for Top-5 results [10] (see Table 1). It was beneficial to use the model's "knowledge". Secondly, the size of our datasets used for transfer learning was much smaller than the dataset used to train "Deep Hand" in [10]: 3201 images for 36 classes of the Handshapes model and 1587 images for the Fingerspelling model versus over 1 million handshape images in [10]. The training process is shown in Fig. 2.

Table 1. Transfer-learned models' accuracy

Model	Number of classes	Top-1 accuracy [%]	Top-5 accuracy [%]
Deep Hand [10]	45	85	94.8
Fingerspelling	29	88	97
Handshapes	35	74	94.6

4 System Functionality

The application is a reverse dictionary that supports Russian and Russian Sign Language. It has the following components: "Search by Words", "Search by Categories", "Search by Fingerspelling" and "Search by Handshapes", which are described below in more details. Its screenshots of various views are presented in Fig. 3 and 4.

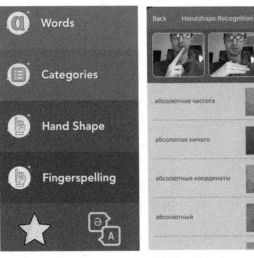

(a) Home view   (b) Search by Handshapes   (c) Search by Fingerspelling

Fig. 3. Application views

4.1   Search by Handshapes

The main functionality of the application is the ability to search for signs by the handshapes that are used to form them. The "Handshape" option from the home view launches the camera view for the user to take a photo of their hand. After taking a photo the "Search by Handshape" view is shown, where a top one-third part of the view shows the photos of the handshapes that the user uses to search for a sign. The rest of the view shows the list of signs that contain the user-provided handshapes. The signs are shown as videos in the loop. We assume that because deaf people are proficient in recognizing signs, they will not be confused by simultaneously playing videos of different signs.

The taking photo is on the top part of the view. If the application successfully classifies the handshape, the border around the photo of the handshape turns green. However, if the handshape is not classified or the application cannot reach the server, the image disappears. The user can also add other handshapes. To do so, the user taps on the "camera" button in the top right corner of the view, which presents the camera view, where the user can take a photo of another handshape. Moreover, the user can delete a handshape from the search by long pressing on the photo of the handshape and tapping on the "delete" button that will be shown as the result. The list of signs updates every time a new handshape is added or an existing one is deleted to reflect the most current state of the search. Finally, the user can tap on a sign, which will result in the "Sign" view to be shown.

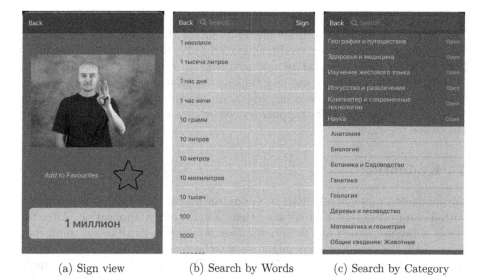

(a) Sign view   (b) Search by Words   (c) Search by Category

Fig. 4. Application views

4.2 Search by Fingerspelling

Another important feature of the application is "Search by Fingerspelling". Similarly to the "Search by Handshapes" it sends the handshape image shown during fingerspelling to the server, which returns back the bounding boxes that bound the hands in the image. The application classifies the image using the locally run "Fingerspelling" model. Here, however, the distinction between these two features is evident. The application does not search for signs immediately, but rather sends another image of handshape to the server and waits for the bounding boxes coordinates. It does so for a few dozen images, after which it checks whether there is a particular sign that corresponds to a minimum 80% percent of classified images of handshapes. If so, the application builds a word by adding the letter that is represented by the handshape that reached the 80% threshold. If the threshold is not met, the application discards the oldest frame, sends the latest frame to the server again and tests for the threshold again. After the word is built, the application sends a query to the database, fetches signs that relate to the built word and shows the result to the user.

4.3 Other Search Methods

In the "Search by Words" the user sees the list of all words and phrases that the application has in its vocabulary. Users can use the search bar at the top of the view to search for the word or phrase that they want the sign translation for. After the user taps on a specific word or phrase, the video of the signs that correspond to the selected word or phrase is shown in a loop. In addition to that, the word or phrase is shown at the bottom of the screen. Moreover, the user can tap on the star image to mark or unmark the sign as favorite. All favorite signs can be accessed quickly by clicking on the "Favorites" option in the home view. This method of searching will be mostly useful for the people who are learning the sign language. However, deaf people might also find this method useful, as it would allow them to translate unknown Russian words that they encounter.

In the home view, when the user taps on the "Category" option, "Search by Category" has multiple categories, which are presented in a way similar to the "Search by Words" view. By tapping a word or phrase in this list, the list of sign videos are presented.

5   Evaluation

We conducted a user study with two non-deaf people and conducted interviews with 6 non-deaf people after showing them a video of the application. After the result of the user study and interviews we come up with three broad comments. First of all, the non-deaf users might want to have additional capabilities in the app to help them in the learning of the Kazakh/Russian sign language. The application might have a list of handshapes that are used in the Kazakh/Russian sign language and in fingerspelling. Further, the app might have educational parts, where the user could learn by practicing fingerspelling and sign words/phrases. Second, the "Search by Categories" was deemed the least useful feature of the app by both groups. Thirdly, the app might need to include a tutorial of how to use the app. The tutorial might consist of a video that demonstrates and explains all the features when the app is first launched.

There were some other useful points from the user study. One participant said that looking for a word in "Search by Categories" was not very easy. In response, we included the A-Z index list shown in Fig. 4. Users can slide their fingers along the index list, and the app would "snap" or move to the words that begin with a particular letter in the index list. In addition, during the user study, searching by handshapes took a long time for both participants, in the range from 1 min to almost 2 min. The fingerspelling model gave reasonable results, for example, when the users were instructed to fingerspell the word "ЗАЯЦ", although the timing was not great, about 2 min for both participants. When the participants were instructed to fingerspell the word "НОЗДРЯ" the model could not recognize the handshape for the letter "Р" for both users.

6   Conclusion and Future Work

In this work we presented the prototype of an automatic reverse dictionary based on the video-based handshape configuration search. Handshape is the basic component of a sign. Thus, searching by demonstration provides the most natural way for the users. We also presented how transfer learning could be applied to sign language recognition. As most of the sign languages are considered as low-resource languages, such approach could be beneficial when annotated data is limited.

Future work will include training a hand detection model compatible with Core ML. This will allow us to run all models on the device and will allow the users to use the application without the need to be connected to the internet. Moreover, a user study with deaf people should be conducted and the feedback should be incorporated in the future version of the application. We plan to conduct a two-step usability study. Firstly, we plan to conduct a pilot study with approximately five hearing users and later conduct a usability study with approximately five deaf users. According to Nielsen and Landauer [15] five users should be enough to find most of the usability issues during the testing.

Acknowledgment. This work was supported by the Nazarbayev University Faculty Development Competitive Research Grant Program 2019–2021 "Kazakh Sign Language Automatic Recognition System (K-SLARS)". Award number is 110119FD4545.

References

1. Alonzo, O., Glasser, A., Huenerfauth, M.: Effect of automatic sign recognition performance on the usability of video-based search interfaces for sign language dictionaries. In: The 21st International ACM SIGACCESS Conference on Computers and Accessibility, pp. 56–67 (2019)
2. Bragg, D., et al.: Sign language recognition, generation, and translation: an interdisciplinary perspective. In The 21st International ACM SIGACCESS Conference on Computers and Accessibility, pp. 16–31 (2019)
3. Bragg, D., Rector, K., Ladner, R.E.: A user-powered American Sign Language dictionary. In: Proceedings of the 18th ACM Conference on Computer Supported Cooperative Work & Social Computing, pp. 1837–1848 (2015)
4. Cooper, H., Pugeault, N., Bowden, R.: Reading the signs: a video based sign dictionary. In: 2011 IEEE International Conference on Computer Vision Workshops (ICCV Workshops), pp. 914–919. IEEE (2011)
5. Dong, C., Leu, M.C., Yin, Z.: American sign language alphabet recognition using Microsoft Kinect. In: Proceedings of the IEEE Conference on Computer Vision and Pattern Recognition Workshops, pp. 44–52 (2015)
6. Elliott, R., Cooper, H., Ong, E.-J., Glauert, J., Bowden, R., Lefebvre-Albaret, F.: Search-by-example in multilingual sign language databases. In: Proceedings of the Sign Language Translation and Avatar Technologies Workshops (2011)
7. Goh, P., Holden, E.-J.: Dynamic fingerspelling recognition using geometric and motion features. In: 2006 International Conference on Image Processing, pp. 2741–2744. IEEE (2006)
8. Jones, M.D., Hamilton, H., Petmecky, J.: Mobile phone access to a sign language dictionary. In: Proceedings of the 17th International ACM SIGACCESS Conference on Computers & Accessibility, pp. 331–332 (2015)
9. Kim, T., Shakhnarovich, G., Livescu, K.: Fingerspelling recognition with semi-Markov conditional random fields. In: Proceedings of the IEEE International Conference on Computer Vision, pp. 1521–1528 (2013)
10. Koller, O., Ney, H., Bowden, R.: Deep hand: how to train a CNN on 1 million hand images when your data is continuous and weakly labelled. In: Proceedings of the IEEE Conference on Computer Vision and Pattern Recognition, pp. 3793–3802 (2016)
11. Mukai, N., Harada, N., Chang, Y.: Japanese fingerspelling recognition based on classification tree and machine learning. In: 2017 NICOGRAPH International (NICOInt), pp. 19–24. IEEE (2017)

12. Mukushev, M., Imashev, A., Kimmelman, V., Sandygulova, A.: Automatic classification of handshapes in Russian Sign Language. In: Proceedings of the LREC2020 9th Workshop on the Representation and Processing of Sign Languages: Sign Language Resources in the Service of the Language Community, Technological Challenges and Application Perspectives, Marseille, France, pp. 165–170. European Language Resources Association (ELRA), May 2020
13. Narasimhaswamy, S., Wei, Z., Wang, Y., Zhang, J., Hoai, M.: Contextual attention for hand detection in the wild (2019)
14. Nelson, A., Price, K., Multari, R.: ASL reverse dictionary-ASL translation using deep learning. SMU Data Sci. Rev. **2**(1), 21 (2019)
15. Nielsen, J., Landauer, T.K.: A mathematical model of the finding of usability problems. In: Proceedings of the INTERACT 1993 and CHI 1993 Conference on Human Factors in Computing Systems, CHI 1993, New York, NY, USA, pp. 206–213. Association for Computing Machinery (1993)
16. Pugeault, N., Bowden, R.: Spelling it out: real-time ASL fingerspelling recognition. In: 2011 IEEE International Conference on Computer Vision Workshops (ICCV Workshops), pp. 1114–1119. IEEE (2011)
17. Shi, B., et al.: American sign language fingerspelling recognition in the wild. In: 2018 IEEE Spoken Language Technology Workshop (SLT), pp. 145–152. IEEE (2018)
18. Shi, B., Rio, A.M.D., Keane, J., Brentari, D., Shakhnarovich, G., Livescu, K.: Fingerspelling recognition in the wild with iterative visual attention. In: Proceedings of the IEEE International Conference on Computer Vision, pp. 5400–5409 (2019)
19. Tazhigaliyeva, N., et al.: Cyrillic manual alphabet recognition in RGB and RGB-D data for sign language interpreting robotic system (SLIRS). In: 2017 IEEE International Conference on Robotics and Automation (ICRA), pp. 4531–4536. IEEE (2017)
20. Wang, H., Stefan, A., Moradi, S., Athitsos, V., Neidle, C., Kamangar, F.: A system for large vocabulary sign search. In: Kutulakos, K.N. (ed.) ECCV 2010. LNCS, vol. 6553, pp. 342–353. Springer, Heidelberg (2012). https://doi.org/10.1007/978-3-642-35749-7_27
21. Warchoł, D., Kapuściński, T., Wysocki, M.: Recognition of fingerspelling sequences in polish sign language using point clouds obtained from depth images. Sensors **19**(5), 1078 (2019)

Author Index

Printed in the United States
By Bookmasters